Investing in Commodities

Second Edition

by Amine Bouchentouf

for
dummies®
A Wiley Brand

Investing in Commodities For Dummies®, Second Edition

Published by: **John Wiley & Sons, Inc.**, 111 River Street, Hoboken, NJ 07030-5774, www.wiley.com

Copyright © 2023 by John Wiley & Sons, Inc., Hoboken, New Jersey

Published simultaneously in Canada

For general information on our other products and services, please contact our Customer Care Department within the U.S. at 877-762-2974, outside the U.S. at 317-572-3993, or fax 317-572-4002. For technical support, please visit https://hub.wiley.com/community/support/dummies.

Wiley publishes in a variety of print and electronic formats and by print-on-demand. Some material included with standard print versions of this book may not be included in e-books or in print-on-demand. If this book refers to media such as a CD or DVD that is not included in the version you purchased, you may download this material at http://booksupport.wiley.com. For more information about Wiley products, visit www.wiley.com.

Library of Congress Control Number: 2023941255

ISBN 978-1-394-20104-4 (pbk); ISBN 978-1-394-20105-1 (ebk); ISBN 978-1-394-20106-8 (ebk)

SKY10057699_101723

Contents at a Glance

Introduction 1

Part 1: Getting Started with Commodities 5
CHAPTER 1: Investors, Start Your Engines! The Basics of Commodities 7
CHAPTER 2: The Pros and Cons of Commodities 19

Part 2: In Power: Making Money in Energy 39
CHAPTER 3: It's a Crude World: Investing in Crude Oil 41
CHAPTER 4: What a Gas! Investing in Natural Gas 57
CHAPTER 5: Investing in Renewable and Alternative Energy 69
CHAPTER 6: Investing in Energy Companies 89

Part 3: Investing in Metals and Agricultural Products 105
CHAPTER 7: All That Glitters: Investing in Gold, Silver, and Platinum 107
CHAPTER 8: Considering Steel, Aluminum, Copper, and Other Metals 125
CHAPTER 9: Unearthing Top Mining Companies 141
CHAPTER 10: Trading Agricultural Products 151

Part 4: Choosing an Investment Approach 171
CHAPTER 11: Welcoming Commodities into Your Portfolio 173
CHAPTER 12: Investing in ETFs and Commodity Indexes 187
CHAPTER 13: Getting a Grip on Futures and Options 207
CHAPTER 14: Choosing a Professional and Trading Accounts 225

Part 5: The Part of Tens 245
CHAPTER 15: Ten Market Indicators You Should Monitor 247
CHAPTER 16: Ten Investment Vehicles for Commodities 253

Index 259

Table of Contents

INTRODUCTION...1

    About This Book 1

    Foolish Assumptions... 2

    Icons Used in This Book.. 3

    Where to Go from Here.. 4

PART 1: GETTING STARTED WITH COMMODITIES...............5

CHAPTER 1: **Investors, Start Your Engines! The Basics of Commodities**...7

    Defining Commodities and Their Investment Characteristics........ 8

    Going for a Spin: Choosing the Right Investment Vehicle............ 10

        The futures markets 10

        The equity markets.. 12

        Managed funds 13

        Physical commodity purchases.. 14

    Checking Out What's on the Menu... 14

        Energy... 15

        Metals... 16

        Agricultural products.. 17

CHAPTER 2: **The Pros and Cons of Commodities**.....................19

    Why the 21st Century Is the Century of Commodities 20

        Capitalizing on the global population explosion..................... 21

        Profiting from urbanization.. 21

        Benefiting from industrialization 22

    What Makes Commodities Unique 25

        Gaining from inelasticity 25

        Finding a safe haven.. 26

        Hedging against inflation 26

        Taking time to bring new sources online............................... 27

        Sell in May and go away? Definitely nay!............................... 28

    Commodities and the Business Cycle.. 28

    The Pitfalls of Using Leverage... 29

The Real Risks behind Commodities...30
    Sovereign government risk..30
    Geopolitical risk..31
    Speculative risk 32
    Corporate governance risk 33
Methods for Managing Risk 33
    Due diligence: Just do it..33
    Diversify, diversify, diversify 37

PART 2: IN POWER: MAKING MONEY IN ENERGY 39

CHAPTER 3: It's a Crude World: Investing in Crude Oil.............41
Seeing the Crude Realities...42
    Examining global reserve estimates.....................................43
    Looking at production figures 45
    Checking out demand figures 46
    Eyeing imports and exports..47
Going Up the Crude Chain 49
Making Big Bucks with Big Oil 51
    Oil companies: Lubricated and firing on all cylinders 52
    Get your passport ready: Investing overseas........................54

CHAPTER 4: What a Gas! Investing in Natural Gas 57
What's the Use? Looking at Natural Gas Applications 58
    Industrial uses of natural gas 58
    Natural gas in your home 61
    Natural gas's commercial uses..62
    Generating electricity with natural gas 62
    Natural gas and transportation 62
Liquefied Natural Gas: Getting Liquid Without Getting Wet........63
Investing in Natural Gas 64
    Natural selection: Trading nat gas futures 65
    Nat gas companies: The natural choice 66

CHAPTER 5: Investing in Renewable and Alternative Energy 69
Getting to Know Renewable Energy 70
    Sunny delight: Investing in solar energy 71
    Fast and furious: Trading in wind energy 73
    Betting on biomass...74

Digging Up Additional Energy Sources 75
    Reexamining coal 76
    Investing in nuclear power 82
    Trading electricity 84

CHAPTER 6: **Investing in Energy Companies** 89
    Bull's-Eye! Profiting from Oil Exploration and Production 90
        Going offshore 90
        Staying on dry land 92
        Servicing the oil fields 93
    Investing in Refineries 95
    Becoming an Oil Shipping Magnate 97
        Transportation supply and demand 98
        Crude oil ships ahoy! 99
        Petroleum shipping companies 100
        Avoiding industry risk 103
    The New Kids on the Block: EV Transportation Companies 103

PART 3: INVESTING IN METALS AND AGRICULTURAL PRODUCTS 105

CHAPTER 7: **All That Glitters: Investing in Gold, Silver, and Platinum** 107
    Going for the Gold 108
        Getting to know the gold standard 109
        Finding ways to invest in gold 112
    Investing in Silver 118
        Checking out the big picture on silver 118
        Getting a sliver of silver in your portfolio 119
    Adding Platinum to Your Investments 121
        Gathering platinum facts and figures 122
        Going platinum 123

CHAPTER 8: **Considering Steel, Aluminum, Copper, and Other Metals** 125
    Building a Portfolio That's as Strong as Steel 126
        Steely facts 126
        Investing in steel companies 128

Illuminating the Details of Aluminum 130
  Just the aluminum facts 130
  Aluminum futures 131
  Aluminum companies 131
Bringing Copper into Your Metals Mix 132
  Quick copper facts 132
  Copper futures contracts 133
  Copper companies 134
Palladium: A Metal for the New Millennium 135
Zooming In on Zinc 138
Investing in Nickel 138

CHAPTER 9: **Unearthing Top Mining Companies** 141
Considering Diversified Mining Companies 142
  BHP Billiton 142
  Rio Tinto 143
  Anglo-American 144
Checking Out Specialized Mining Companies 145
  Newmont Mining: Gold 145
  Wheaton Precious Metals: Silver 146
  Freeport-McMoRan: Copper 146
  Alcoa: Aluminum 147
  ArcelorMittal: Steel 148
Making Money during the Mining Merger Mania 149

CHAPTER 10: **Trading Agricultural Products** 151
Giving Your Portfolio a Buzz by Investing in Coffee 152
  Coffee: It's time for a break 152
  The coffee futures contract: It may be your cup of tea 153
  Ordering up investments in gourmet coffee shops 154
Warming Up to Cocoa 155
Investing in Sugar: Sweet Move! 156
Orange Juice: Refreshingly Good for Your Bottom Line 157
Investing in Corn 159
Wondering about Wheat 161
Trading Soybeans 163
  Soybeans 163
  Soybean oil 164
  Soybean meal 165
Holy Cow! Investing in Cattle 166
  Live cattle 166
  Feeder cattle 167

Checking Out Lean Hogs 168
Trading Frozen Pork Bellies...169

PART 4: CHOOSING AN INVESTMENT APPROACH 171

CHAPTER 11: **Welcoming Commodities into Your Portfolio**..173

The Color of Money: Taking Control of Your Financial Life 174
Looking Ahead: Creating a Financial Road Map 175
Figuring out your net worth...176
Identifying your tax bracket..178
Determining your appetite for risk................................179
Making Room in Your Portfolio for Commodities......................181
Fully Exposed: The Top Ways to Get Exposure to Commodities..181
Commodity futures..181
Commodity funds 183
Commodity companies 185

CHAPTER 12: **Investing in ETFs and Commodity Indexes**.........187

Getting to Know ETFs..188
Accessing Commodity Markets through ETFs............................190
Checking Out Commodity Indexes..192
Why indexes are useful..192
How to make money by using an index............................193
Uncovering the Anatomy of a Commodity Index.......................194
Noting the Five Major Indexes...195
The S&P Goldman Sachs Commodity Index.....................195
Reuters/Jefferies Commodity Research Bureau Index...........197
Dow Jones Commodity Index 199
Rogers International Commodities Index..........................201
Deutsche Bank Liquid Commodity Index.........................203
Determining Which Index to Use 205

CHAPTER 13: **Getting a Grip on Futures and Options**..................207

Taking the Mystery Out of Futures and Options 208
How to Trade Futures Contracts 208
Who trades futures?...210
Keeping track of all the pieces...212
Trading Futures on Margin...217

Figuring Out Where the Futures Market Is Heading...................218
    Contango...218
    Backwardation 219
Trading with Options 219
    Following options in action...220
    Understanding trader talk..222
    Selecting option traits..222

CHAPTER 14: **Choosing a Professional and Trading
Accounts**..225
Investing in Commodity Mutual Funds....................................226
    Asking the right questions 227
    Seeing what's out there..230
Mastering MLPs 231
    The ABCs of MLPs 231
    The taxman rings once..232
    Cash flow is king..233
    The nuts and bolts of MLP investing 234
    Heads up! Risk and MLPs..235
Relying on a Commodity Trading Advisor...............................235
Jumping into a Commodity Pool..238
Ready, Set, Invest: Opening an Account and Placing Orders......239
    Choosing the right account..240
    Placing orders..242

PART 5: THE PART OF TENS..245

CHAPTER 15: **Ten Market Indicators You Should Monitor** 247
Consumer Price Index 247
EIA Inventory Reports 248
Federal Funds Rate...248
Gross Domestic Product...249
London Gold Fix..249
Nonfarm Payrolls 250
Purchasing Managers Index...250
Reuters/Jefferies CRB Index 251
U.S. Dollar...251
WTI Crude Oil...251

CHAPTER 16: **Ten Investment Vehicles for Commodities**........253

Futures Commission Merchant...253
Commodity Trading Advisor..254
Commodity Pool Operator...254
Integrated Commodity Companies...254
Specialized Commodity Companies..255
Master Limited Partnerships..255
Exchange-Traded Funds..256
Commodity Mutual Funds...256
Commodity Indexes...256
Emerging-Market Funds..257

INDEX...259

Introduction

In the last two decades, commodities have grown into their own legitimate and respected asset class. Trade magazines and financial newsletters frequently include feature-length articles on the topic. Financial TV stations regularly report oil, gold, and copper prices on the crawling ticker. And no global macro money manager can claim continued success without constantly keeping a pulse on commodities.

Why are commodities, long regarded as an inferior asset class, quickly moving to the investing mainstream? Good performance. Investors like to reward good performance, and commodities have performed well in recent years. In addition, investors can more easily access these markets: Plenty of new investment vehicles, from exchange-traded funds (ETFs) to master limited partnerships (MLPs), have been introduced to satisfy investor demand.

Commodities are a complex asset class, with many different types of assets and many different vehicles through which to invest. As commodities have been generating more interest, there's a large demand for a product to help average investors get a grip on the market fundamentals. Commodities as an asset class have been plagued by a lot of misinformation, and it's sometimes difficult to separate fact from fiction or outright fantasy. The aim of this book is to help you figure out what commodities are all about and, more important, develop an intelligent investment strategy to profit in this market.

Keep in mind that disruptions are part of the market process. Investors who protect themselves through a "margin of safety" philosophy will be able to weather periods of extreme volatility. Using this book, you'll better equip yourself to avoid the pitfalls inherent in any investment activity.

About This Book

My aim in writing this book is to offer you a comprehensive guide to the commodities markets and show you a number of investment strategies to help you profit in them. You don't have to invest in just crude oil or gold futures contracts to benefit. You can trade ETFs, invest in companies that process commodities such as uranium, buy precious metals ownership certificates, or invest in MLPs. The commodities markets are global in nature, and so are the investment opportunities. My goal is to help you uncover these global opportunities and offer you investment ideas and tools to unlock and unleash the power of the commodities markets. Best of all, I do all of this in plain English!

Anyone who's been around commodities, even for a short period of time, realizes that folks in the business are prone to engage in linguistic acrobatics. Words like *molybdenum*, *backwardation*, and *contango* are thrown around like "hello" and "thank you." Sometimes these words seem intimidating and confusing. Don't be intimidated. Language is powerful, after all, and getting a grip on the concepts behind the words is critical, especially if you want to come out ahead in the markets. That's why I use everyday language to explain even the most abstract and arcane concepts.

Information that's interesting but not essential to understanding commodities is tucked into shaded sidebars. But if any technicalities make it into the main text, I give you a heads-up with a Technical Stuff icon. That's where you can skip over or speed read.

Keep in mind that when this book was printed, some web addresses may have needed to break across two lines of text. Wherever that's the case, rest assured that this book uses no any extra characters to indicate the break. So, when going to one of these web addresses, just type in exactly what you see in this book. Pretend that the line break doesn't exist.

Foolish Assumptions

In writing this book, I made the following assumptions about you:

>> You have some previous investing experience but are looking to diversify your holdings.

>> You're familiar with commodities trading, but you want to brush up on your knowledge.

>> Your traditional investments (stocks, bonds, mutual funds) haven't performed according to your expectations, and you're looking for alternatives to maximize your returns.

>> You're a new investor or someone with minimal trading experience, and you're interested in a broad-based investment approach that includes commodities and other assets.

>> You understand the attractiveness of commodities and want a comprehensive and easy-to-use guide to help you get started.

>> You're skeptical about the benefits of commodities, but you want to read about them anyway. Please do — I'm confident that this book will change your mind!

>> You have little or no investment experience but are eager to find out more about investing. This book not only explores investing in commodities, but also includes explanations of general investing guidelines that apply to any market.

Icons Used in This Book

One of the pleasures of writing a *For Dummies* book is that you get to use all sorts of fun, interactive tools to highlight or illustrate a point. Here are some icons that I use throughout this book.

REMEMBER

I use the Remember icon to highlight information that you want to keep in mind or that's referenced in other parts of the book.

TIP

When you see the Tip icon, make sure that you read the accompanying text carefully. It includes information, analysis, or insight that will help you successfully implement an investment strategy.

TECHNICAL STUFF

I explain more technical information with the Technical Stuff icon. The commodities markets are complex, and the vocabulary and concepts are quite tricky. You can skip these paragraphs if you just want a quick overview of the commodities world, but be sure to read them before seriously investing. They give you a better grasp of the concepts discussed.

WARNING

Investing can be an extremely rewarding enterprise, but it can also be a hazardous endeavor if you're not careful. I use the Warning icon to warn you of potential pitfalls. Stay alert for these icons because they contain information that may help you avoid losing money.

Where to Go from Here

I've organized this book in a way that gives you the most accurate and relevant information related to investing in general and commodity investing in particular. The book is modular in nature, meaning that although it reads like a book from start to finish, you can read one chapter or even a section at a time without needing to read the whole book to understand the topic that's discussed.

If you're a true beginner, however, I recommend that you read Part 1 carefully before you start skipping around in the chapters on particular commodities.

1

Getting Started with Commodities

Know why you should invest in commodities, check out the commodities markets, and find the best ways to invest in commodities.

Celebrate the advantages, acknowledge the downsides, and manage risk when investing in commodities.

Chapter **1**

Investors, Start Your Engines! The Basics of Commodities

The commodities markets are broad and deep, presenting both challenges and opportunities. Investors are often overwhelmed simply by the number of commodities out there: more than 30 tradable commodities to choose from. How do you decide whether to trade crude oil or gold, sugar or palladium, natural gas or frozen concentrated orange juice, soybeans or aluminum? What about corn, feeder cattle, and silver? Should you trade these commodities as well? And, if you do, what's the best way to invest in them? Should you go through the futures markets, go through the equity markets, or buy the physical stuff (such as silver coins or gold bullion)? And do all commodities move in tandem, or do they perform independently of each other?

With so many variables to keep track of and options to choose from, just getting started in commodities can be daunting. But have no fear — this book provides you with the actionable information, knowledge, insight, and analysis to help you grab the commodities market by the horns. Maybe you've heard a lot of myths and fantasies about commodities. I shatter some of these myths and, in the process, clear the way to help you identify the real moneymaking opportunities.

The commodities universe is large, and investment opportunities abound. In this book, I help you explore this world inside and out. By exploring this fascinating universe, not only do you get insight into the world's most crucial commodities — and catch a glimpse of how the global capital markets operate — but you also find out how to capitalize on this information to generate profits.

Defining Commodities and Their Investment Characteristics

REMEMBER

Just what exactly are commodities? Put simply, commodities are the raw materials humans use to create a livable world. Humans have been exploiting earth's natural resources since the beginning of time. They use agricultural products to feed themselves, metals to build weapons and tools, and energy to sustain themselves. Energy, metals, and agricultural products are the three classes of commodities and the essential building blocks of the global economy.

For the purposes of this book, I present commodities that fit a very specific definition, which I define in the following list. For example, the commodities I present must be raw materials. I don't discuss currencies — even though they trade in the futures markets — because they're not raw materials; they can't be physically used to build anything. In addition, the commodities must present real moneymaking opportunities to investors.

REMEMBER

All the commodities I cover in this book meet the following criteria:

>> **Tradability:** The commodity has to be tradable, meaning that there needs to be a viable investment vehicle to help you trade it. For example, I include a commodity if it has a futures contract assigned to it on one of the major exchanges, if a company processes it, or if an exchange-traded fund (ETF) tracks it. Uranium, which is an important energy commodity, isn't tracked by a futures contract, but

several companies specialize in mining and processing this mineral; by investing in these companies, you get exposure to uranium.

>> **Deliverability:** All the commodities have to be physically deliverable. I include crude oil because it can be delivered in barrels, and I include wheat because it can be delivered by the bushel. However, I don't include currencies, interest rates, and other financial futures contracts because they're not physical commodities.

COMMODITIES THROUGHOUT HISTORY

History reveals that the most devastating battles have been fought over crude oil, gold, uranium, and other precious natural resources (all covered in this book). When Francisco Pizarro's first expedition to South America in 1524 led him to the discovery of vast amounts of gold deposits, his conquistadors proceeded to wipe out the whole Inca civilization that stood between them and the gold. As a matter of fact, it's probably unlikely that Christopher Columbus would have come across to the North American continent in the first place were it not for an unquenchable desire to find the shortest and most secure route to transport spices and other commodities from India to Europe.

At the end of the 19th century, this continuous quest for commodities resulted in the deadly South African Boer Wars, which pitted the British Empire's armed forces against local fighters in a bloody battle over South Africa's precious metals and minerals. The 20th century, which heralded a new historical phase — the Hydrocarbon Age, shortly followed by the Nuclear Age — marks a turning point in humans' ability to utilize and exploit the earth's raw materials and the extent to which they will go to preserve this control. The Persian Gulf War of 1991, which, at its essence, was an effort to stabilize global oil markets after the Iraqi invasion of oil-rich Kuwait in the Middle East, is another manifestation of this historical reality.

To this day, international players in the geopolitical world consider access to the world's vast deposits of oil, gold, copper, and other resources. Commodities have, thus, determined the fate and wealth of nations throughout history and will continue to do so in the future.

>> **Liquidity:** I don't include any commodities that trade in illiquid markets. Every commodity in this book has an active market, with buyers and sellers constantly transacting with each other. Liquidity is critical because it gives you the option of getting in and out of an investment without having to face the difficulty of trying to find a buyer or seller for your securities.

Going for a Spin: Choosing the Right Investment Vehicle

The two most critical questions to ask yourself before getting started in commodities are the following: What commodity should I invest in? How do I invest in it? I answer the second question first and then examine which commodities to choose.

The futures markets

In the futures markets, individuals, institutions, and sometimes governments transact with each other for price-hedging and speculating purposes. An airline company, for instance, may want to use futures to enter into an agreement with a fuel company to buy a fixed amount of jet fuel for a fixed price for a fixed period of time. This transaction in the futures markets allows the airline to hedge against the volatility associated with the price of jet fuel. Although commercial users are the main players in the futures arena, traders and investors also use the futures market to profit from price volatility through various trading techniques.

TECHNICAL STUFF

One such trading technique is *arbitrage*, which takes advantage of price discrepancies between different futures markets. For example, in an arbitrage trade, you purchase and sell the crude oil futures contract simultaneously in different trading venues, for the purpose of capturing price discrepancies between these venues. I take a look at some arbitrage opportunities in Chapter 13.

REMEMBER

The futures markets are administered by the various commodity exchanges, such as the Chicago Mercantile Exchange (CME) and the Intercontinental Exchange (ICE). Investing through the futures markets requires a good understanding of futures contracts, options on futures, forwards, spreads, and other derivative products. I examine these products in depth in Chapter 13.

The most direct way of investing in the futures markets is to open an account with a *futures commission merchant* (FCM). The FCM is much like a traditional stock brokerage house (such as Schwab, Fidelity, or Merrill Lynch) except that it's allowed to offer products that trade on the futures markets. Here are some other ways to get involved in futures:

>> **Commodity trading advisor (CTA):** The CTA is an individual or company licensed to trade futures contracts on your behalf.

>> **Commodity pool operator (CPO):** CPOs are similar to CTAs, except CPOs can manage the funds of multiple clients under one account. This pooling provides additional leverage when trading futures.

>> **Commodity indexes:** A commodity index is a benchmark, similar to the Dow Jones Industrial Average or the S&P 500, that tracks a basket of the most liquid commodities. You can track the performance of a commodity index, which allows you to essentially "buy the market." A number of commodity indexes are available, including the Goldman Sachs Commodity Index and the Reuters/Jefferies CRB Index, which I cover in Chapter 12.

These examples are only a few ways to access the futures markets. Be sure to read Chapter 12 for additional methods.

A number of organizations regulate the futures markets, including the Securities and Exchange Commission (SEC) and the Commodity Futures Trading Commission (CFTC). These organizations monitor the markets to prevent market fraud and manipulation and to protect investors from such activity.

WARNING

Trading futures isn't for everyone. By their very nature, futures markets, contracts, and products are extremely complex and require a great deal of mastery by even the most seasoned investors. If you don't feel that you have a good handle on all the concepts involved in trading futures, don't jump into them; you could lose a lot more than your principal because of the use of leverage and other characteristics unique to the futures markets. If you're not comfortable trading futures, don't sweat it. You can invest in commodities in multiple other ways.

The equity markets

Although the futures markets offer the most direct investment gateway to the commodities markets, the equity markets also offer access to these raw materials. You can invest in companies that specialize in the production, transformation, and distribution of these natural resources. If you're a stock investor familiar with the equity markets, this may be a good route for you to access the commodities markets.

The only drawback of the equity markets is that you have to consider external factors, such as management competence, tax situation, debt levels, and profit margins, which have nothing to do with the underlying commodity. That said, investing in companies that process commodities still allows you to profit from the commodities boom.

Publicly traded companies

The size, structure, and scope of the companies involved in the business are varied, and I cover most of these companies throughout this book. I offer a description of the company, including a snapshot of its financial situation, future growth prospects, and areas of operation. I then make a recommendation based on the market fundamentals of the company.

You encounter the following types of companies in this book:

>> **Diversified mining companies:** A number of companies focus exclusively on mining metals and minerals. Some of these companies, such as Anglo-American PLC (Nasdaq: AAUK) and BHP Billiton (NYSE: BHP), have operations across the spectrum of the metals complex, mining metals that range from gold to zinc. I look at these companies in Chapter 9.

>> **Electric utilities:** Utilities are an integral part of modern life because they provide one of life's most essential necessities: electricity. They're also a good investment because they've historically offered large dividends to shareholders. Read Chapter 5 to figure out whether these companies are right for you.

>> **Integrated energy companies:** These companies, such as ExxonMobil (NYSE: XOM) and Chevron (NYSE: CVX), are involved in all aspects of the energy industry, from the extraction of crude oil to the distribution of liquefied natural gas (LNG). They give you broad exposure to the energy complex (see Chapter 6).

This list is only a sampling of the commodity companies I cover in this book. I also analyze highly specialized companies, such as coal-mining companies (Chapter 5), oil refiners (Chapter 6), platinum-mining companies (Chapter 7), and purveyors of gourmet coffee products (Chapter 10).

Master limited partnerships

Master limited partnerships (MLPs) invest in energy infrastructure such as oil pipelines and natural gas storage facilities. I'm a big fan of MLPs because they're a *publicly traded partnership.* They offer the benefit of trading like a corporation on a public exchange, while offering the tax advantages of a private partnership. MLPs are required to transfer all cash flow back to shareholders, which makes them an attractive investment. I dissect the structure of MLPs in Chapter 14 and introduce you to some of the biggest names in the business so you can take advantage of this unique investment.

Managed funds

Sometimes it's just easier to have someone else manage your investments for you. Luckily, you can count on professional money managers who specialize in commodity trading to handle your investments.

Consider a few of these options:

>> **ETFs:** ETFs are an increasingly popular investment because they're managed funds that offer the convenience of trading like stocks. In recent years, ETFs have appeared to track everything from crude oil and gold to diversified commodity indexes. Find out how to benefit from these vehicles in Chapter 12.

>> **Mutual funds:** If you've previously invested in mutual funds and you're comfortable with them, look into adding a mutual fund that gives you exposure to the commodities markets.

A number of funds are available that invest solely in commodities. I examine these commodity mutual funds in Chapter 14.

TIP

If you have a pet or a child, sometimes you hire someone to look after them. Before you hire this individual, you interview candidates, check their references, and examine their previous experience. When you're satisfied with the top candidate's competency, only then do you entrust that person with the responsibility of looking after your pet, child, or both. The same thing applies when you're shopping for a money manager. If you already have a money manager you trust and are happy with, stick with them. If you're looking for a new investment professional to look after your investments, you need to investigate that person as thoroughly as possible. In Chapter 14, I examine the selection criteria to use when shopping for a money manager.

Physical commodity purchases

The most direct way of investing in certain commodities is to actually buy them outright. Precious metals such as gold, silver, and platinum are great examples of this. Because the price of gold and silver has skyrocketed recently, you may have seen ads on TV or in newspapers from companies offering to buy your gold or silver jewelry. As gold and silver prices increase in the futures markets, they also cause prices in the spot markets to rise (and vice versa). You can cash in on this trend by buying coins, bullion, or even jewelry. I present this unique investment strategy in Chapter 7.

REMEMBER

This investment strategy is suitable for a limited number of commodities, mostly precious metals like gold, silver, and platinum. Unless you own a farm, keeping live cattle or feeder cattle to profit from price increases doesn't make much sense. And I won't even mention commodities like crude oil or uranium!

Checking Out What's on the Menu

I cover a number of commodities in this book. Here's a list of all the commodities you can expect to encounter while reading this book.

Energy

Energy has always been indispensable for human survival and makes for a great investment. Energy, whether fossil fuels or renewable energy sources, has attracted a lot of attention from investors as they seek to profit from the world's seemingly unquenchable thirst for energy. In this book, I present all the major forms of energy, from crude oil and coal to electricity and solar power, and show you how to profit in this arena.

>> **Crude oil:** Crude oil is the undisputed heavyweight champion in the commodities world. More barrels of crude oil are traded every single day (87 million and growing) than any other commodity. Accounting for 40 percent of total global energy consumption, crude oil provides some terrific investment opportunities.

>> **Natural gas:** Natural gas, the gaseous fossil fuel, is often overshadowed by crude oil. Nevertheless, it's a major commodity in its own right, used for everything from cooking food to heating houses during the winter. I also take a look at the prospects of LNG.

>> **Coal:** Coal accounts for more than 20 percent of total world energy consumption. In the United States, the largest energy market, 50 percent of electricity is generated through coal. Because of abundant supply, coal is making a resurgence.

>> **Uranium/nuclear power:** Because of improved environmental standards within the industry, nuclear power use is on the rise. I show you how to develop an investment strategy to capitalize on this trend.

>> **Electricity:** Electricity is a necessity of modern life, and the companies responsible for generating this special commodity have some unique characteristics. I examine how to start trading this electrifying commodity.

>> **Solar power:** For a number of reasons that range from environmental to geopolitical, demand for renewable energy sources such as solar power is increasing.

>> **Wind power:** Wind power is getting a lot of attention from investors as a viable alternative source of energy.

>> **Ethanol:** Ethanol, which is produced primarily from corn or sugar, is an increasingly popular fuel additive that offers investment potential.

The commodities landscape has retained its prominence in the last decade as a driver of global economic growth. And yet, within the commodities landscape, there have been major shifts, such as the rise of renewable energy and the advent of electric vehicles, which I highlight in this book.

Metals

Metallurgy has been essential to human development since the beginning of time. Societies that have mastered the production of metals have been able to thrive and survive. Similarly, investors who have incorporated metals into their portfolios have been able to generate significant returns. I cover all the major metals, from gold and platinum to nickel and zinc.

>> **Gold:** Gold is perhaps the most coveted resource on the planet. For centuries, people have been attracted to its quasi-indestructibility and have used it as a store of value. Gold is a good asset for hedging against inflation and for asset preservation during times of global turmoil.

>> **Silver:** Silver, like gold, is another precious metal that has monetary applications. The British currency, the pound sterling, is still named after this metal. Silver also has applications in industry (such as electrical wiring) that places it in a unique position of being coveted for both its precious metal status and its industrial uses.

>> **Platinum:** Platinum, the rich man's gold, is one of the most valuable metals in the world, used for everything from jewelry to the manufacture of catalytic converters.

>> **Steel:** Steel, which is created by alloying iron and other materials, is the most widely used metal in the world. Used to build everything from cars to buildings, it is a metal endowed with unique characteristics and offers sound investment potential.

>> **Aluminum:** Perhaps no other metal has the versatility of aluminum; it's lightweight yet surprisingly robust. These unique characteristics mean that it's a metal worth adding to your portfolio, especially because it's the second most widely used metal (right behind steel).

>> **Copper:** Copper, the third most widely used metal, is the metal of choice for industrial uses. Because it's a great conductor of heat and electricity, its applications in industry

are wide and deep, making this base metal an attractive investment.

>> **Palladium:** Palladium is part of the platinum group of metals, and almost half of the palladium that's mined goes toward building automobile catalytic converters. As the number of cars with these emission-reducing devices increases, the demand for palladium will increase as well, making this an attractive investment.

>> **Nickel:** Nickel is a ferrous metal that's in high demand because of its resistance to corrosion and oxidation. Steel is usually alloyed with nickel to create stainless steel, which ensures that nickel will play an important role for years to come.

>> **Zinc:** The fourth most widely used metal in the world, zinc is sought after for its resistance to corrosion. It's used in the process of *galvanization,* in which zinc coating is applied to other metals, such as steel, to prevent rust.

Agricultural products

Food is the most essential element of human life, and the production of food presents solid moneymaking opportunities. In this book, you find out how to invest in the agricultural sector in everything from coffee and orange juice to cattle and soybeans.

>> **Coffee:** In terms of physical volume, coffee is the second most widely produced commodity in the world, behind only crude oil. Folks just seem to love a good cup of coffee, which makes it a delicious investment opportunity.

>> **Cocoa:** Cocoa production, which is dominated by a handful of countries, is a major agricultural commodity, primarily because it's used to create chocolate.

>> **Sugar #11:** Sugar is a popular food sweetener, and it can be a sweet investment. Sugar #11 represents a futures contract for global sugar.

>> **Sugar #14:** Sugar #14 is specific to the United States and is a widely traded commodity.

>> **Frozen concentrated orange juice — type A:** FCOJ-A, for short, is the benchmark for North American orange juice

prices because it's grown in the hemisphere's two largest regions: Florida and Brazil.

>> **Frozen concentrated orange juice — type B:** FCOJ-B, like FCOJ-A, is a widely traded contract that represents global orange juice prices. This contract exposes you to orange juice activity on a world scale.

>> **Corn:** Corn's use for culinary purposes is perhaps unrivaled by any other grain, which makes this a potentially lucrative investment.

>> **Wheat:** According to archaeological evidence, wheat was one of the first agricultural products grown by humankind. It is an essential staple and makes for a great investment.

>> **Soybeans:** Soybeans have many applications, including as feedstock and for cooking purposes. The soybean market is a large one that presents some smart investment opportunities.

>> **Soybean oil:** Soybean oil, also known as vegetable oil, is derived from actual soybeans. It's used for cooking purposes and has become popular in recent years with the health-conscious dietary movement.

>> **Soybean meal:** Soybean meal is another derivative of soybeans that's used as feedstock for poultry and cattle. It may not sound enticing, but it can be a good investment.

>> **Live cattle:** For investors involved in agriculture, using the live cattle futures contract to hedge against price volatility is a good idea.

>> **Feeder cattle:** Whereas the live cattle contract tracks adult cows, the feeder cattle contract hedges against the risk associated with growing calves. The markets don't widely follow this area, but it's important to figure out how this market works.

>> **Lean hogs:** They may not be the sexiest commodity out there, but lean hogs are an essential commodity, making them a solid trading target.

>> **Frozen pork bellies:** Frozen pork bellies are essentially nothing more than good old bacon. This industry is cyclical and subject to wild price swings, which provides unique arbitrage trading opportunities.

IN THIS CHAPTER

» Profiting from global economic trends

» Considering the unique characteristics of commodities

» Investing in commodities across the business cycle

» Getting a grip on leverage

» Understanding real versus imagined risks

» Looking at tools to effectively manage risk

Chapter **2**

The Pros and Cons of Commodities

Commodities have traditionally been considered the black sheep in the family of asset classes. For several decades, no respectable money manager wanted anything to do with them. This traditional lack of interest (which no longer applies, by the way) has generated a lot of misinformation about commodities. As a matter of fact, probably no other asset class has suffered through so much misunderstanding and misconception.

Many investors are scared of venturing into the world of commodities. For one thing, it seems that every time the word *commodities* is uttered, someone pops up with a horrible story about losing their entire life savings trading soybeans, cocoa, or some other exotic commodity. Even though this negative perception is rapidly changing, commodities are still often misunderstood as an investment. I actually know some investors who invest in commodities (and who have made money off them) but don't understand the fundamental reasons they're such good long-term investments.

In this chapter, I show you why commodities are an attractive investment and why many investors are becoming more interested in this asset class. I also give you the goods on a number of global trends that are responsible for the recent run-up in commodity prices. Investors who are able to identify and navigate these trends are going to do extremely well. It's also important to note that no investment goes up in a straight line; any market has downturns, and that's to be expected. Identifying these trends is strategically important, but being able to tactically navigate them in the short term separates the winners from the losers.

WARNING

Sometimes events have a dramatic and unexpected effect on markets. Such was the case with the Global Financial Crisis (GFC) of 2008 and, more recently, the COVID-19 pandemic in 2020. These events had a profound impact on all markets, and commodities were no exception. The most astute investors, while perhaps not able to pinpoint the exact origins and effects of such events, can tactically adjust their portfolios to protect their downside.

Why the 21st Century Is the Century of Commodities

Since autumn 2001, commodities have been running faster than the bulls of Pamplona. The Reuters/Jefferies CRB Index (a benchmark for commodities) nearly doubled between 2001 and 2006. During this period, oil, gold, copper, and silver hit all-time highs (although not adjusted for inflation). Other commodities also reached levels never seen before in trading sessions. Since 2020, commodities have been front and center, driven by rapid performance, including a 100 percent increase between the pandemic lows and the time of this writing.

I believe that we're witnessing a long-term cyclical bull market in commodities. Because of a number of fundamental factors (which I go through in the following sections), commodities are poised for a rally that will last well into the 21st century — and possibly beyond that. It's a bold statement, I know. But the facts are there to support me.

WARNING

Although I'm bullish on commodities for the long term, I have to warn you that at times commodities won't perform well at all. This statement is simply the nature of the commodity cycle. Furthermore, in the history of Wall Street, no asset has ever gone up in a straight line. Minor (and, occasionally, major) pullbacks always happen before an asset makes new highs — if, in fact, it does make new highs.

There's a story behind the rise in commodities, and it's a pretty compelling one.

Capitalizing on the global population explosion

The 21st century is going to experience the largest population growth in the history of humankind. The United Nations (UN) estimates that the world will add a little less than 1 billion people during *each* of the first five decades of the 21st century. The global population will grow to about 9 billion people by 2050. (As of 2020, approximately 7.75 billion people lived on the planet.)

Also consider the following statistic: According to the UN, the average number of years it takes to add 1 billion people has shrunk from an average of 130 years in the 19th century to approximately 13 years in the 21st century. The rate at which the human population is increasing has reached exponential levels.

REMEMBER

So, how is this relevant to commodities? Put simply, significant population growth translates into greater global demand for commodities. Humans are the most voracious consumers of raw materials on the planet — and the only ones who pay for them. As the number of humans in the world increases, so will the demand for natural resources. After all, people need food to eat, houses to live in, and heat to stay warm during the winter; all of this requires raw materials. This large population growth is a key driver for the increasing demand for commodities, which will continue to put upward pressure on commodity prices.

Profiting from urbanization

Perhaps even more significant than population growth is the fact that it's accompanied by the largest urbanization movement the world has ever seen. In the early 20th century, according to the

UN, less than 15 percent of the world's population lived in cities; by 2005, that number jumped to 50 percent, and it shows no sign of decreasing. As a matter of fact, 60 percent of the world's population is expected to live in urban areas by the year 2030. The number of large metropolitan areas with 5 million or more people (known as *megacities*) is skyrocketing and will continue to climb for much of the century.

Urbanization is highly significant for commodities because people who live in urban centers consume a lot more natural resources than those who live in rural areas. In addition, more natural resources are required to expand the size of cities as more people move to them (rural to urban migration) and have more kids (indigenous urban population growth). More natural resources are required for the roads, cars, and personal appliances that are staples of city life.

TIP

Industrial metals such as copper, steel, and aluminum are going to be in high demand to construct apartment buildings, schools, hospitals, cars, and so on. So, investing in industrial metals is one possible way to play the urbanization card. Be sure to read Chapter 8 for more information on these metals.

The largest urbanization is taking place in the developing world, particularly in Asia. As more Asians move from the countryside to large urban areas, expect to see huge demand from that part of the world for raw materials to fuel this growth.

Benefiting from industrialization

The first industrial revolution, which took place in the 19th century, was a major transformational event primarily confined to Western Europe and North America. Major industrialization didn't spread to other corners of the globe until parts of the 20th century. Even then, it was only sporadic.

A new wave of industrialization is taking place in the 21st century, and it may be the most important one in history. This wave is transforming a large number of developing countries into more industrialized countries, and raw materials are fueling this transformation.

The BRIC countries

Although many developing countries are on the fast track to industrialization, four countries need to be singled out as the front-runners in this movement: Brazil, Russia, India, and China. They're collectively known as the *BRIC countries* or just the *BRICs*.

The BRIC countries, which are now on a path toward full industrialization, are scouring the globe to secure supplies of key natural resources such as oil, natural gas, copper, and aluminum — the raw materials necessary for a country to industrialize.

REMEMBER

As demand from the BRIC countries for natural resources increases, expect to see increasing upward price pressures on commodities.

China

Although all four of the BRIC countries are rapidly transforming themselves, no other country is doing so as rapidly and dramatically as China. Fittingly, the saying "May you live in interesting times" is said to be an old Chinese proverb. The 21st century is undoubtedly going to be an interesting century, and China will play an increasingly important role in global economic affairs.

China's gross domestic product (GDP) increased by 9 percent each year from 2000 to 2006. To sustain this growth, China has been consuming all sorts of commodities. Some of the highs that commodities such as oil, natural gas, cement, copper, and aluminum have experienced between 2003 and 2006 are a direct result of increased demand from China.

For example, in 2004, China gobbled up half the cement, one-third of the steel, one-quarter of the copper, and one-fifth of the aluminum produced in the world. In 2003, China overtook Japan to become the second-largest consumer of crude oil — right behind the United States. (For more information on global oil consumption, read Chapter 3.) In fact, in 2010, China surpassed Japan to become the world's second-largest economy, behind only that of the United States. More than a decade later, as of 2022, China has maintained its breakneck consumption of oil and now consumes more than 12.5 million barrels of oil per day, only behind the United States.

China is going to have a tremendous impact on the global economy in the 21st century and is expected to be the largest consumer of commodities in the world.

Brazil

Another BRIC country that is having and will continue to have a significant impact on commodities markets worldwide is Brazil, the largest country in South America in terms of GDP, landmass, population, and abundance of natural resources.

Brazil's geography, topography, and weather patterns make it a powerhouse in the commodities space. Consider a few of the natural resources in which Brazil is a world leader or has a dominant market share:

» Coffee

» Copper

» Corn

» Crude oil (offshore)

» Eucalyptus

» Gold

» Iron ore

» Livestock

» Silver

» Soybeans

» Sugar

» Sugarcane

Blessed with large amounts of arable land, the world's largest river basin drainage systems (the Amazon), and favorable geology, Brazil is a world leader in commodities, especially agricultural ones. Many companies are involved in the production and distribution of these natural resources, and as the world's demand for these products increases, I expect Brazil to do extremely well in the years and decades to come.

What Makes Commodities Unique

As an asset class, commodities have unique characteristics that separate them from other asset classes and make them attractive, whether as independent investments or as part of a broader investment strategy. I go through these unique characteristics in the following sections.

Gaining from inelasticity

In economics, *elasticity* seeks to determine the effects of price on supply and demand. The calculation can get pretty technical, but, essentially, elasticity quantifies how much supply and demand will change for every incremental change in price.

Goods that are elastic tend to have a high correlation between price and demand, which is usually inversely proportional: When prices of a good increase, demand tends to decrease. This relationship makes sense because you're not going to pay for a good that you don't need if it becomes too expensive. Capturing and determining that spread is what elasticity is all about.

REMEMBER

Inelastic goods, however, are goods that are so essential to consumers that changes in price tend to have a limited effect on supply and demand. Most commodities fall in the inelastic goods category because they're essential to human existence.

For instance, if the price of ice cream increased by 25 percent, chances are, you'd stop buying ice cream. Why? Because it's not a necessity, but more of a luxury. However, if the price of unleaded gasoline at the pump increased by 75 percent (as it did in 2022), you definitely wouldn't be happy about the price increase, but you'd still fill up your tank. The reason? Gas is a necessity — you need to fill up your car to go to work or school, run errands, and so on.

The demand for gasoline isn't absolutely inelastic, however; you won't keep paying for it regardless of the price. A point will come at which you'd decide that it's simply not worth it to keep paying the amount you're paying at the pump, so you'd begin looking for alternatives. (Read Chapter 5 for more information on alternative energy sources.) But the truth remains that you're willing to pay more for gasoline than for other products you don't need (such as ice cream); that's the key to understanding price inelasticity.

Most commodities are fairly inelastic because they're the raw materials that allow us to live the lives we strive for; they help us maintain a decent (and, in some cases, extravagant) standard of living. Without these precious raw materials, you wouldn't be able to heat your home in the winter. Actually, without cement, copper, and other basic materials, you wouldn't even have a house to begin with! And then there's the most essential commodity of all: food. Without food, we wouldn't exist. Because of the absolute necessity of commodities, you can be sure that as long as there are humans around, there's going to be a demand for these raw materials.

Finding a safe haven

During times of turmoil, commodities tend to act as safe havens for investors. These investors view certain commodities, such as gold and silver, as reliable stores of value, so they flock to these assets when times aren't good. When currencies slide, nations go to war, or global pandemics break out, you can rely on gold, silver, and other commodities for financial safety. For example, after the horrible acts of September 11, 2001, the price of gold jumped as investors sought safety in the metal.

It's a good idea to have part of your portfolio in gold and other precious metals so you can protect your assets during times of turmoil. Turn to Chapter 7 for more on investing in precious metals.

Hedging against inflation

One of the biggest factors to watch out for as an investor is the ravaging effects of inflation. Inflation can devastate your investments, particularly paper assets such as stocks. (I discuss inflation and other risks later in this chapter.) The central bankers of the world — smart people all — spend their entire careers trying to tame inflation, but inflation can still get out of hand. You need to protect yourself against this economic enemy.

Inflation has played a major role in the latest commodity price performance since 2020. Supply chain constraints have meant an increase in prices across the board. This, in turn, makes everything more expensive for consumers, especially when it comes to energy and food prices, which are essential blocks of global economies.

Ironically, one of the only asset classes that *benefits* from inflation is — you guessed it — commodities. Perhaps the biggest irony of all is that increases in the prices of basic goods (commodities such as oil and gas) actually contribute to the increase of inflation.

For example, there's a positive correlation between gold and the inflation rate. During times of high inflation, investors load up on gold because it's considered a good store of value.

TIP

One way to not only protect yourself from inflation, but also profit from it, is to invest in gold. I discuss the inflation-hedging opportunities that gold provides in Chapter 7.

Taking time to bring new sources online

The business of commodities is a time- and capital-intensive business. Unlike investments in high-tech companies or other "new economy" investments (such as e-commerce), bringing commodity projects online takes a lot of time.

For example, it can take up to a decade to bring new sources of oil online. First, a company must identify potentially promising areas to explore for oil. After locating an area, the company has to actually start drilling and prospecting for the oil. If it's lucky, this process of discovering significantly recoverable sources of oil takes only three to five years. The company must then develop infrastructure and bring in machinery to extract the oil, which must be transported to a refining facility to be transformed into consumable energy products such as gasoline or jet fuel. After it goes through the lengthy refining stage, the end product must finally be transported to consumers.

REMEMBER

So, what does all this mean to you as an investor? When you're investing in commodities, you have to think long term. If you're used to investing in tech stocks or if you're an entrepreneur involved in e-commerce, you need to radically change the way you think about investing when you approach commodities. If you're able to recognize the long-term nature of commodities, you'll be on your way to becoming a successful commodities investor.

Sell in May and go away? Definitely nay!

You may have heard the saying "Sell in May and go away." This is a Wall Street adage referring to stocks. The thinking goes that because the stock market doesn't perform well during the summer months, you should sell your stocks and get back into the game in the fall.

This adage doesn't apply to commodities because commodities move in different cycles than stocks. Some commodities perform really well during the summer months. For example, because summer is the heavy driving season, there's an increase in demand for gasoline products. Thus, all things equal, unleaded gasoline tends to increase in price during the summer.

I discuss the cyclical nature of commodities in the following section. For a more in-depth comparison between the performance of commodities and that of other assets, turn to Chapter 11.

Commodities and the Business Cycle

Commodities are cyclical in nature. Returns on commodity investments aren't generated in a vacuum — they're influenced by a number of economic forces. In other words, the performance of commodities, like that of other major asset classes, is tied to general economic conditions. Because economies move in cycles, constantly alternating between expansions and recessions, commodities react according to the current economic phase.

REMEMBER

The performance of commodities as an asset class is going to be different during economic expansions than during recessions. As a general rule, commodities tend to do well during periods of late expansions and early recessions. That's because, as the economy slows, key interest rates are decreased to stimulate economic activity, and this, in turn, tends to help the performance of commodities. Stocks and bonds, on the other hand, don't perform as well during recessions. As an investor seeking returns across all phases of the business cycle, opening up to commodities enables you to generate returns during good and bad economic times.

WARNING

The study of cycles, whether for commodities, stocks, or other assets, isn't an exact science. I don't recommend using cycles as the foundation of a trading or investment strategy. Instead, try to use the study of cycles to get a sense of what historical patterns have indicated and where an asset class is heading.

Although the historical pattern of commodities tends to show better performance during late expansions and early recessions, this in no way guarantees that commodities will keep following this pattern. Actually, during the latest commodity bull market, commodities have acted independently of the business cycle. This performance may be attributed to the fact that, for the reasons outlined in the earlier section "Why the 21st Century Is the Century of Commodities," this commodity bull market is a different beast than in previous cycles.

The Pitfalls of Using Leverage

In finance, *leverage* refers to the act of magnifying returns through the use of borrowed capital. Leverage is a powerful tool that gives you the opportunity to control large market positions with relatively little up-front capital. However, leverage is the ultimate double-edged sword because both your profits and your losses are magnified to outrageous proportions.

If you invest in stocks, you know that you're able to trade on margin. You have to qualify for a margin account, but when you do, you're able to use leverage (margin) to get into stock positions. You can also trade commodities on margin. However, the biggest difference between using margin with stocks and using margin with commodities is that the margin requirement for commodities is much lower than margins for stocks, which means the potential for losses (and profits) is much greater in commodities.

REMEMBER

If you qualify for trading stocks on margin, you need to have at least 50 percent of the capital in your account before you can enter into a stock position on margin.

The minimum margin requirements for commodity futures vary but, on average, are lower than those for stocks. For example, the margin requirement for soybeans in the Chicago Board of Trade is 4 percent. This means that, with only $400 in your account, you can buy $10,000 worth of soybeans futures contracts! If the trade goes your way, you're a happy camper. But if you're on the losing side of a trade on margin, you can lose much more than your principal since you'll receive the dreaded *margin call,* where your counterparty requires that you settle your position immediately.

Another big difference between stock and commodity futures accounts is that the balance on futures accounts is calculated at the end of the trading session. So, if you get a margin call, you need to take care of it immediately.

REMEMBER

When you're trading on margin, which is essentially trading on borrowed capital, you may get a margin call from your broker requiring you to deposit additional capital in your account to cover the borrowed amount. Because of the use of margin and the high amounts of leverage you have at your disposal in the futures markets, you need to be extremely careful when trading commodity futures contracts. To be a responsible investor, I recommend using margin only if you have the necessary capital reserves to cover any subsequent margin calls you may receive if the market moves adversely. For more on trading futures and margin requirements, turn to Chapter 13.

The Real Risks behind Commodities

Investing is all about managing the risk involved in generating returns. In this section, I lay out some common risks you face when investing in commodities and some small steps you can take to minimize these risks.

Sovereign government risk

In the era following the 2008 credit crisis, a more acute risk emerged: the sovereign government risk. This type of risk is more important than other types of risks because it involves the balance sheet of sovereign governments. During the financial crisis, banks were in a position to bail out consumers; when banks started to fail, governments began to bail out the banks. However, when governments start to fail, few institutions can bail them out.

This type of risk became more evident in the European countries, accustomed to single-digit GDP growth rates and relaxed lifestyles due to generous government programs and pensions. For a number of reasons (geographic, demographic, and economic), these countries no longer enjoy the place in the sun they once occupied, which is leading to the risk that these states may start defaulting. In addition to liquidity risks, these states pose a solvency risk — in other words, they simply can't pay back their borrowers.

Many countries in Europe — such as Greece, Portugal, Spain, Ireland, and, to some extent, Italy and France (Germany being the main exception) — are facing severe budget cuts and unprecedented decreases in government expenditure programs. This situation caused riots and violence across Europe in 2010. As their unfavorable demographic trends further accelerate and their manufacturing base is eroded by more competitive spheres in Asia and other emerging markets, expect to see more belt-tightening in Europe over the next five years. In a post-2008 world, you need to carefully examine the countries you're investing in.

Geopolitical risk

One of the inherent risks of commodities is that the world's natural resources are located on various continents, and the jurisdiction over these commodities lies with sovereign governments, international companies, and many other entities. The Russia–Ukraine War, which began in 2022, has certainly highlighted the geopolitical risk related to extracting natural resources in unstable parts of the world — in this case in the heart of Europe.

The war, which is still raging on as of the writing of this book, has disrupted a variety of key global commodities. And it's not just oil and gas, but agricultural products as well. As a result of the war, the United States and its allies have imposed sanctions on Russia. The sanctions prevented Russia from exporting its oil to many consumers around the world, which has increased the price of crude by 30 percent since the start of the war. Additionally, Russia decided to drastically reduce its pipeline exports of natural gas to its European customers, which have resulted in natural gas prices skyrocketing since the start of the war.

To make matters worse, both Ukraine and Russia are major wheat producers and exporters. As a direct result of the conflict, the price of wheat has increased dramatically. These actions have directly contributed to the raging inflation the world has experienced since the end of the pandemic lockdowns. Geopolitical risk can't be emphasized enough, especially since commodities represent building blocks of most major economies. Because of these supply-side disruptions, populations in Europe might not have enough gas to keep warm during the winter or enough bread to feed themselves; in addition, the price inflation threatens budgets and pocketbooks around the world.

TIP

So, how do you protect yourself from this geopolitical uncertainty? Unfortunately, you can't wave a magic wand to eliminate this type of risk. However, one way to minimize it is to invest in companies with experience and economies of scale. For example, if you're interested in investing in an international oil company, go with one that has an established international track record. A company like ExxonMobil, for instance, has the scale, breadth, and experience in international markets to manage the geopolitical risk it faces. A smaller company without this sort of experience faces more risk than a bigger one. In commodities, size does matter.

Speculative risk

Similar to the bond or stock markets, the commodities are populated by traders whose primary interest is making short-term profits by speculating whether the price of a security will go up or down.

REMEMBER

Unlike commercial users who are using the markets for hedging purposes, speculators are simply interested in making profits; thus, they tend to move the markets in different ways. Although speculators provide much-needed liquidity to the markets (particularly in commodity futures markets), they tend to increase market volatility, especially when they begin exhibiting what former Federal Reserve Chairman Alan Greenspan termed "irrational exuberance." Because speculators can get out of control, as they did during the dot-com bubble, you need to always be aware of the speculative activity going on in the markets. The amount of speculative money involved in commodity markets is in constant flux, but as a general rule, most commodity futures markets consist of about 75 percent commercial users and 25 percent speculators.

WARNING

Although I'm bullish on commodities because of the fundamental supply-and-demand story (which I present earlier in this chapter), too much speculative money coming into the commodities markets can have detrimental effects. I anticipate that, at times, speculators will drive the prices of commodities beyond the fundamentals. If you see too much speculative activity, it's probably a good idea to simply get out of the markets.

TIP

If you trade commodities, constantly check the pulse of the markets; find out as much as possible about who the market participants are so that you can distinguish between the commercial users and the speculators. One resource I recommend is the Commitment of Traders report, put out by the Commodity Futures Trading Commission (CFTC). This report, available online at www. cftc.gov/cftc/cftccotreports.htm, gives you a detailed look at the market participants.

Corporate governance risk

As if you didn't have enough to worry about, you also need to watch out for plain and simple fraud. The CFTC and other regulatory bodies do a decent job of protecting investors from market fraud, but the possibility of becoming a victim of fraud does exist. For example, your broker may hide debts or losses in offshore accounts, as was the case with Refco.

REMEMBER

One way to prevent being taken advantage of is to be extremely vigilant about where you're putting your money. Thoroughly research a firm before you hand over your money. I go through the due diligence process to follow when selecting managers in Chapter 14. Unfortunately, sometimes no amount of research or due diligence can protect you from fraud. It's just a fact of the investment game.

Methods for Managing Risk

You can't completely eliminate risk, but you can sure take steps to reduce it. In this section, I go through time-proven and market-tested ways to minimize risk.

Due diligence: Just do it

One way to minimize risk is to research all aspects of the investment you're about to undertake before you undertake it. Too often, investors don't start doing research until they've invested in commodities contracts or companies.

Many investors buy on hype; they hear a certain commodity mentioned in the press, and they buy just because everyone else is buying. Buying on impulse is one of the most detrimental habits you can develop as an investor. Before you put your money into anything, you need to find out as much as possible about this potential investment.

Because you have a number of ways to invest in commodities (which I discuss in Chapter 12), the type of research you perform depends on the approach you take. The following sections go over the due diligence to perform for each investment methodology.

Commodity companies

One way to get exposure to commodities is to invest in companies that process commodities. Although this is an indirect way to access raw materials, it's a good approach for investors who are comfortable in the equity environment.

Ask a few questions before you buy the company's stock:

>> What are the company's assets and liabilities?

>> How effective is the management with the firm's capital?

>> Where will the firm generate future growth?

>> Where does the company generate its revenue?

>> Has the company run into any regulatory problems in the past?

>> What is the company's structure? (Some commodity companies are corporations, whereas others act as limited partnerships. You can find more on limited partnerships in Chapter 14.)

>> How does the company compare with competitors?

>> Does the company operate in regions of the world that are politically unstable?

>> What is the company's performance across business cycles?

Of course, this list gives only a few questions to ask before making an equity investment. I go through a series of other facts and figures to gather about commodity companies in Chapter 6 (for energy companies) and Chapter 9 (for mining companies).

You can get the answers to these questions by looking through the company's annual report (Form 10-K) and quarterly reports (Form 8-K).

Managed funds

If you're not a hands-on investor or you simply don't have the time to actively manage your portfolio, you may want to choose a manager to do the investing for you. You can choose from a number of different managers, including the following:

>> **Commodity mutual fund:** Manager of mutual funds that invest in commodities

>> **Commodity pool operator:** Manager of group futures accounts

>> **Commodity trading advisor:** Manager of individual futures accounts

Before you invest with a manager, find out as much as you can about this person. Ask a few questions:

>> What's the manager's track record?

>> What's the manager's investing style? Is it conservative or aggressive, and are you comfortable with it?

>> Does the manager have any disciplinary actions against them?

>> What do clients have to say about the manager? (It's okay to ask a manager if you can speak to one of their existing clients.)

>> Is the manager registered with the appropriate regulatory bodies?

>> What fees does the manger charge? (Ask whether all fees are disclosed. Always watch for hidden fees!)

>> How much in assets does the manager have under management?

>> What are the manager's after-tax returns? (Make sure that you specify *after*-tax returns because many managers post returns only before considering taxes.)

>> Are minimum time commitments involved?

>> Are penalties assessed if you choose to withdraw your money early?

>> Are minimum investment requirements applied?

In Chapter 14, I go through other qualifying questions to ask before choosing a manager to invest money for you.

Futures market

The futures markets play an important role in the world of commodities. They provide liquidity and allow hedgers and speculators to establish benchmark prices for the world's commodities.

TIP

If you're interested in investing through commodity futures, you need to ask a lot of questions before you get started. Consider some of these:

>> On what exchange is the futures contract traded?

>> Is there an accompanying option contract for the commodity?

>> Is the market for the contract liquid or illiquid? (You want it to be liquid, just in case you're wondering.)

>> Who are the main market participants?

>> What's the expiration date for the contract you're interested in?

>> What's the open interest for the commodity?

>> Are there any margin requirements? If so, what are they?

To find out more about trading futures contracts, as well as options, be sure to read Chapter 13.

Commodity fundamentals

Whether you decide to invest through futures contracts, commodity companies, or managed funds, you need to gather as much information as possible about the underlying commodity itself. This caveat is perhaps the most important piece of the commodities puzzle because the performance of any investment vehicle you choose depends on the actual fundamental supply-and-demand story of the commodity.

Ask yourself a few questions before you start investing in a commodity, whether it's coffee or copper:

>> Which country or countries hold the largest reserves of the commodity?

>> Is the country politically stable, or is it vulnerable to turmoil?

>> How much of the commodity is actually produced on a regular basis? (Ideally, you want to get data for the daily, monthly, quarterly, and annual basis.)

>> Which industries or countries are the largest consumers of the commodity?

>> What are the primary uses of the commodity?

>> Are there any alternatives to the commodity? If so, what are they, and do they pose a significant risk to the production value of the target commodity?

>> Do seasonal factors affect the commodity?

>> What's the correlation between the commodity and comparable commodities in the same category?

>> What are the historical production and consumption cycles for the commodity?

REMEMBER

These questions are only a few to ask before you invest in a commodity. Ideally, you want to be able to gather this information before you start trading.

Diversify, diversify, diversify

One of the best ways to manage risk is to diversify. This strategy applies on a number of levels: both diversification *among* asset classes (such as bonds, stocks, and commodities) and diversification *within* an asset class (such as diversifying commodity holdings among energy and metals).

REMEMBER

For diversification to have the desired effects on your portfolio (to minimize risk), you want to have asset classes that perform differently. One of the benefits of using commodities to minimize your overall portfolio risk is that commodities tend to behave differently from stocks and bonds. For example, the performance of commodities and equities is remarkably different. This means that when stocks aren't doing well, you'll at least have your portfolio exposed to an asset class that *is* performing.

To find out more about how the performance of commodities compares to that of other assets and how this benefits you, check out Chapter 11.

2

In Power: Making Money in Energy

Invest in oil, know about key metrics, and brush up on market fundamentals and oil companies.

Understand the main uses of natural gas, figure out market signals, check out liquefied natural gas (LNG), and invest in natural gas companies and futures.

Examine renewable energy investing (including solar, wind, and biofuel) and check out coal, nuclear, and electricity.

Profit in investment in energy companies, from discoveries to refineries and shipping.

Chapter **3**

It's a Crude World: Investing in Crude Oil

C rude oil is undoubtedly the king of commodities in both its production value and its importance to the global economy. It's the most-traded nonfinancial commodity in the world today, and it supplies 40 percent of the world's total energy needs — more than any other single commodity. Despite many calls to shift energy consumption toward more renewable energy sources, the crude reality is that petroleum products are still the dominant resource worldwide. In fact, to this day, more barrels of crude oil are traded daily (90 million as of 2022, up from 87 million barrels by 2010 figures) than any other commodity. Crude oil's importance also stems from the fact that it's the base product for many indispensable goods, including gasoline, jet fuel, and plastics.

Oil is truly the lifeblood of the global economy. Without it, the modern world would come to a screeching halt. Drivers wouldn't be able to drive their cars, ships would have no fuel to transport goods around the world, and airplanes would be grounded indefinitely.

Because of its preeminent role in the global economy, crude oil makes for a great investment. In this chapter, I show you how to make money investing in what's arguably the world's greatest natural resource. However, the oil industry is a multidimensional, complex business with players that often have conflicting interests. Proceeding with a bit of caution and making sure that you understand the market fundamentals are both essential for success.

Seeing the Crude Realities

REMEMBER

Having a good understanding of the global consumption and production patterns is important if you're considering investing in the oil industry. Knowing how much oil is produced in the world, which countries are producing it, and which consumers are accepting the shipments allows you to develop an investment strategy that benefits from the oil market fundamentals.

I'm sometimes amazed at some of the misconceptions regarding the oil industry. For example, I was once speaking with students about energy independence and was shocked when a majority of them claimed that the United States got more than 50 percent of its oil from the Persian Gulf and Saudi Arabia, in particular; in fact, nothing could be further from the truth.

The United States is the top producer of crude oil in the world. It produces almost 19 million barrels a day, including oil products. In fact, the United States didn't become a net importer of oil until 1993; until that point, the United States produced more than 50 percent of the oil it consumed domestically.

The biggest oil exporter to the United States isn't a Middle Eastern country, but our northern neighbor. That's right, Canada is the largest exporter of crude oil to the United States! Persian Gulf oil makes up about 20 percent of imported oil to the United States.

My point here is that a lot of misinformation about this topic persists, and you need to be armed with the correct figures to be a successful investor. In the following sections, I introduce you to all the market participants (traders, major oil companies, and producing/consuming countries) and the metrics they monitor, such as global reserve estimates, daily production rates, daily consumption rates, daily export figures, and daily import figures.

I present you with the most up-to-date information regarding oil production and consumption patterns. Because these patterns are likely to change in the future because of supply and demand, I also tell you where you can go to get the latest information on the oil markets. Having the facts makes you a better investor.

Examining global reserve estimates

As an investor, knowing which countries have large crude oil deposits is an important part of your investment strategy. As demand for crude oil increases, countries that have large deposits of this natural resource stand to benefit tremendously. One way to benefit from this trend is to invest in indigenous countries and companies with large reserves of crude oil. (I go through this strategy in detail in the later section "Get your passport ready: Investing overseas.")

Oil & Gas Journal estimates that global proven crude oil reserves as of 2009 are 1,342 billion barrels (1.34 trillion barrels). Table 3-1 lists the countries with the largest proven crude oil reserves, according to 2010 data. These figures may change as new oil fields are discovered, as new technologies facilitate the extraction of additional oil from existing fields, and as a result of natural depletion.

TABLE 3-1 Largest Oil Reserves by Country, 2011

Rank	Country	Proven Reserves (Billion Barrels)
1	Venezuela	302
2	Saudi Arabia	266
3	Iran	202
4	Canada	172
5	Iraq	147
6	Kuwait	104
7	United Arab Emirates	98
8	Russia	80
9	Libya	74
10	United States	47

Source: Data from Oil & Gas Journal

In the last ten years or so, the proven reserves of the top ten countries have *increased* rather than decreased. This might seem counterintuitive considering that oil has remained flowing, thus depleting reserves; however, new technological breakthroughs have allowed for the discovery of additional oil fields and commercialization of previously difficult-to-access crude. Consider that Venezuela's reserves, according to the Organization of the Petroleum Exporting Countries (OPEC) and the International Energy Agency (IEA), more than *tripled* between 2010 and 2022 due to the discovery of large unconventional sources of oil.

REMEMBER

Having large deposits of crude doesn't mean that a country has exploited and developed all its oil fields. For example, although Iraq has the third-largest oil deposits in the world, it's not even among the top ten producing countries because of poor and underdeveloped infrastructure. There's a big difference between proven reserves and actual production, as you can see by comparing Tables 3-1 and 3-2.

TABLE 3-2 **Largest Producers of Crude Oil, 2021**

Rank	Country	Daily Production (Million Barrels)
1	United States	18.88
2	Saudi Arabia	10.84
3	Russia	10.78
4	Canada	5.54
5	China	4.9
6	Iraq	4.15
7	United Arab Emirates	3.79
8	Brazil	3.69
9	Iran	3.46
10	Kuwait	2.72

Source: U.S. Department of Energy

TIP

The calculation of proven, recoverable deposits of crude oil isn't an exact science. For example, *Oil & Gas Journal* figures are different from those of the U.S. Energy Information Administration (EIA), whose figures, in turn, are different from those of the IEA.

I recommend taking a big-picture approach to global reserve estimates and consulting all the major sources for these statistics. To keep up on updated figures and statistics on the oil industry, check out the following organizations and their websites:

>> **BP Statistical Review of World Energy:** www.bp.com/en/global/corporate/energy-economics/statistical-review-of-world-energy.html

>> **EIA:** www.eia.gov

>> **IEA:** www.iea.org

>> *Oil & Gas Journal:* www.ogj.com

Looking at production figures

Identifying the countries with large reserves is important, but it's only a starting point as you begin investing in the oil markets. To determine which countries are exploiting these reserves adequately, I recommend looking at another important metric: actual production. Having large reserves is meaningless if a country isn't tapping those reserves to produce oil. Table 3-2 lays out the top ten producers of crude oil.

A number of factors influence how much crude a country can pump out of the ground daily, including geopolitical stability and the application of technologically advanced crude-recovery techniques. Also note that daily production may vary throughout the year because of disruptions resulting either from geopolitical events such as embargos, sanctions, and sabotage that put a stop to daily production or from other external factors, like weather. For example, consider Hurricane Katrina and its devastating effect on the U.S. oil supply in summer 2005, as well as the BP Gulf of Mexico oil spill in 2010. In 2022, another major geopolitical event, the Russia–Ukraine War, has had a similar impact on the markets.

The big standout in daily production is the United States, which, over the past ten years, has seen an explosion of production come online, primarily driven by accommodating drilling policies, as well as the advent of fracking technology. Once a major importer of crude, the United States now not only is a large exporter but also produces almost double the amount of oil as Saudi Arabia!

You need to keep a close eye on global daily supply because any disruption in the production supply chain can have a strong impact on the current price of crude oil. Because there's a tight supply-and-demand equation, any disruption in supply can send prices for crude skyrocketing.

Traders in the commodity exchanges follow the daily crude oil production numbers closely. Supply numbers affect benchmark crude oil contracts such as both the West Texas Intermediate (WTI), traded on the Chicago Mercantile Exchange (CME), and the North Sea Brent, traded on the Intercontinental Exchange (ICE) in London. As a result, the market closely watches any geopolitical event or natural disaster that may reduce production. (Check out Chapter 13 for more on the crude oil futures contracts.)

If you're an active oil trader with a futures account, following these daily production numbers — which are available through the EIA website (www.eia.gov) — is crucial. The futures markets are particularly sensitive to daily crude oil production numbers, and any event that takes crude off the market can have a sudden impact on crude futures contracts. If you're a long-term investor in the markets, monitoring this number is also important because production figures can affect the general stock market performance as well. For example, if rebels seize a pipeline in Nigeria and 300,000 barrels of Nigerian crude are taken off the market, this will result in higher crude prices, which will have an impact on U.S. stocks. (They generally fall.) Thus, your stock portfolio holdings may be at risk because of daily crude oil production disruptions. Therefore, monitoring this statistic regularly is important for both short-term traders and long-term investors.

Checking out demand figures

The United States tops the list of oil consumers and has been the single largest consumer of crude oil for the past 25 years. Although a lot of folks pay attention to the demand increase from China and India, most of the demand for crude oil (and the resulting price pressures) still comes from the United States. Traders around the world closely watch supply, but demand figures are equally important because they indicate a steady and sustained increase in crude demand for the mid to long term. This is likely to maintain increased pressure on crude prices. I list the top ten consumers of crude oil in the world in Table 3-3.

TABLE 3-3 **Largest Consumers of Crude Oil, 2021**

Rank	Country	Daily Consumption (Million Barrels)
1	United States	20.54
2	China	12.71
3	India	4.92
4	Japan	3.74
5	Russia	3.7
6	Saudi Arabia	3.18
7	Brazil	3.14
8	Canada	2.6
9	South Korea	2.6
10	Germany	2.3

Source: U.S. Department of Energy

Over the past decade, the list of top oil-consuming countries hasn't changed by much. The United States is still the largest consumer; of note is that China's daily oil consumption doubled from 7 million barrels per day (mbd) in 2011 to 14 mbd in 2021. Even with doubling consumption over the past decade, China is still behind the United States.

Another noteworthy country is Germany, which saw the most drastic reduction in daily consumption, partly driven by the country's move away from oil and more toward natural gas and renewables. Another country of note is Saudi Arabia, which increased its daily consumption by 1 mbd over the past decade, driven by a drive toward domestic industrialization.

REMEMBER

Always design an investment strategy that will profit from long-term trends. This steady increase in global demand for crude oil is a good reason to be bullish on oil prices.

Eyeing imports and exports

When planning your investments in the oil market, another pair of numbers to keep close tabs on is export and import figures. Exports are different from production. A country can produce a lot of oil and consume most, if not all, of it, as the United States does. On the other end of the spectrum, a country can produce plenty of oil and export most of it, as is the case in the United Arab Emirates.

Identifying the top exporting countries allows you to zero in on the countries that are generating revenues from selling crude oil to other countries. Countries that are net exporters of crude stand to benefit tremendously from the oil boom, and you can get in on the action by investing domestically in these countries; I outline a strategy in the later section "Get your passport ready: Investing overseas." In Table 3-4, I list the top oil-exporting countries of 2020.

TABLE 3-4 Top Ten Oil Exporters, 2020

Rank	Country	Daily Oil Exports (Million Barrels)
1	Saudi Arabia	6.7
2	Russia	4.7
3	Iraq	3.4
4	Canada	3.1
5	Iran	2.7
6	United Arab Emirates	2.4
7	Nigeria	1.9
8	Kuwait	1.8
9	Norway	1.5
10	Kazakhstan	1.4

Source: U.S. Department of Energy

Traders pay a lot of attention to exports, but imports, which represent the other side of the equation, are equally important. Countries that are main importers of crude oil are primarily advanced, industrialized societies like Germany and the United States. These countries are rich enough that they can absorb crude oil price increases, but as a rule, the importers face a lot of pressure during any price increases. This pressure sometimes translates into lower stock market performances in the importing countries, which means you need to be careful if you're exposed

TABLE 3-5 Top Ten Oil Importers, 2020

Rank	Country	Daily Oil Imports (Million Barrels)
1	China	10.8
2	United States	5.8
3	India	4.1
4	South Korea	2.6
5	Japan	2.4
6	Germany	1.7
7	Spain	1.1
8	Italy	1.0
9	Netherlands	0.997
10	Taiwan	0.841

Source: United States Department of Energy

Going Up the Crude Chain

Crude oil by itself isn't very useful; it derives its value from its products. Only after it's processed and refined into consumable products such as gasoline, propane, and jet fuel does it become valuable.

TECHNICAL STUFF

Crude oil was formed over millions of years from the remains of dead animals and other organisms whose bodies decayed in the earth. Because of a number of geological factors, such as sedimentation, these remains were eventually transformed into crude oil deposits. Therefore, crude oil is literally a *fossil fuel* (a fuel derived from fossils). As a matter of fact, the word *petroleum* comes from the Latin words *petra*, which means "rock," and *oleum*, which means "oil." So, the word *petroleum* literally means "oil from the rocks."

TECHNICAL
STUFF

A barrel holds 42 gallons of crude oil or crude oil equivalents. (That's about 159 liters.) *Barrel* is abbreviated as *bbl*, and *barrels* is abbreviated as *bbls*.

Not all crudes are created equal. If you invest in crude oil, you need to realize right off the bat that crude oil comes in different qualities with different characteristics. You'd be surprised by how different that "black stuff" can be from region to region. Generally, crude oil is classified into two broad categories: light and sweet, and heavy and sour. Other classifications are used also, but these are the two major ones.

REMEMBER

The two criteria most widely used to determine the quality of crude oil are density and sulfur content:

>> **Density** usually refers to how much a crude oil yields in terms of products, such as heating oil and jet fuel. For instance, a crude oil with lower density, known as a *light crude,* tends to yield higher levels of products. On the other hand, a crude oil with high density, commonly referred to as a *heavy crude,* has lower product yields.

The density of a crude oil, also known as the *gravity,* is measured by a scale devised by the American Petroleum Institute (API). The higher the API number, expressed in degrees, the lower the density of the crude oil.

>> **Sulfur content** is another key determinant of crude oil quality. Sulfur is a corrosive material that decreases the purity of a crude oil. Therefore, a crude oil with high sulfur content, which is known as *sour,* is much less desirable than a crude oil with low sulfur content, known as *sweet.*

TIP

How is this important to you as an investor? If you want to invest in the oil industry, you need to know what kind of oil you're going to get for your money. If you're going to invest in an oil company, you need to be able to determine which type of crude it's processing. You can find this information in the company's annual or quarterly reports. A company involved in producing light, sweet crude will generate more revenue from this premium crude than one involved in processing heavy, sour crude. This distinction doesn't mean that you shouldn't invest in companies with exposure to heavy, sour crude; you just have to factor the type into your investment strategy.

Table 3-6 lists some important crude oils and their characteristics.

TABLE 3-6 **Crude Oil Grades**

Crude Oil Type	Density (API)	Sulfur Content
North West Shelf (Australia)	60	0.01
Arab Super Light (Saudi Arabia)	50	0.06
Bonny Light (Nigeria)	35.4	0.14
Duri (Indonesia)	21.5	0.14

TIP

As you can see, you can choose from a variety of crude oil products as investments. If you're interested in investing in a specific country, you need to find out what kind of crude oil it produces. Ideally, you want a crude oil with low sulfur content and a high API number as a density benchmark.

Making Big Bucks with Big Oil

The price of crude oil skyrocketed during the first decade of the 21st century. If this period is any indication of what's in store for oil, you definitely want to develop a winning game plan to take advantage of this trend. That said, crude remains a volatile commodity that's subject to external market forces. Specifically, the Global Financial Crisis of 2008 and its aftermath resulted in a price collapse of global crude oil markets during that period.

The period leading up to 2008 witnessed an overheating global economy, with excess liquidity, historically low interest rates, and increasing global trade. These forces and several others pushed oil prices to their record highs, approaching $150 per barrel. However, as the financial crisis struck Wall Street, Europe, and the rest of the world markets, oil prices experienced an asset price deflation similar to what most other assets were experiencing worldwide. Therefore, it's advisable to be mindful of economic forces operating outside internal market-specific considerations when trading oil markets. In other words, you must view spare capacity, production volumes, and other metrics inherent to the petroleum markets within the context of global market forces.

People are making a lot of money from the price fluctuations of crude and gasoline. Why shouldn't you be one of them? In this section, I show you how to profit from the prices at the pump.

Oil companies: Lubricated and firing on all cylinders

Oil companies get a bad rap. Whatever you may think of them, they make for a great investment. Oil companies are responsible for bringing precious energy products to consumers, and they're compensated handsomely for this service. Oil companies are for-profit companies that are run for the benefit of their shareholders. Instead of complaining about oil companies, why not become a shareholder of one (or more)?

In this section, I talk about the integrated oil companies, sometimes known as "big oil," "the majors," or "integrated oil companies." These are the oil companies involved in all the phases of the oil-production process, from exploring for oil to refining it and then transporting it to consumers. ExxonMobil, Chevron Texaco, and BP are all "big oil" companies.

TIP

Big oil companies aren't the only players in the oil business. Many other companies are involved in specific aspects of the transformational process of crude oil. For example, some companies, like Valero, are primarily involved in refining; others, such as General Maritime, own fleets of tankers that transport crude oil and products. I discuss how to invest in these companies — the refiners, transporters, and explorers — in Chapter 6.

Flying solo: Looking at individual oil companies

The major oil companies have been posting record profits in recent years. This success is a result of the increased global demand for crude oil and its products, as well as the technological and managerial efficiency practiced by the majors. As global demand continues and supplies remain limited, I expect big oil companies to keep generating solid revenues and profits. Earnings and revenues don't move in a straight line; you need to be able to tactically position your portfolio to profit from short-term market disruptions. In Table 3-7, I list some of the companies you may want to include in your portfolio.

This table is only a brief snapshot of some of the major integrated oil companies you can choose to add to your portfolio.

TABLE 3-7 **Major Integrated Oil Companies, 2021**

Oil Company	Ticker Symbol	Revenues
ExxonMobil	XOM	$285 billion
Shell	SHEL	$272 billion
Chevron	CVX	$162 billion
BP	BP	$157 billion
Marathon	MPC	$120 billion

REMEMBER

Most of these traditional oil companies have now moved into other areas in the energy sphere. These companies not only process crude oil into different products, but have vast petrochemicals businesses, as well as growing projects that involve natural gas and, increasingly, alternative energy sources. (To reflect this shift, for example, BP has changed its name from British Petroleum to Beyond Petroleum.) The bottom line is that investing in these oil companies gives you exposure to other sorts of products in the energy industry as well.

TIP

Although revenues and earnings are important metrics to look at before investing in these companies, you also need to perform a thorough due diligence that considers other important factors to determine a company's health. I introduce some of these key metrics in Chapter 6 to help you select the most suitable energy companies for your portfolio.

Oil company ETFs: Strength in numbers

If you can't decide which oil company you want to invest in, you have several other options that allow you to buy the market, so to speak. One option is to buy *exchange-traded funds* (ETFs) that track the performance of a group of integrated oil companies. I discuss ETFs in depth in Chapter 12, but here are a few oil company ETFs to consider:

>> **Energy Select Sector SPDR (AMEX: XLE):** The XLE ETF is the largest energy ETF in the market. It's part of the S&P's family of Standard & Poor's Depository Receipts (SPDR), commonly referred to as *spiders,* and tracks the performance of a basket of oil company stocks. Some of the stocks it tracks

include the majors ExxonMobil and Chevron; however, it also tracks oil services companies such as Halliburton and Schlumberger. You get a nice mix of integrated oil companies and other independent firms by investing in the XLE.

» **iShares Goldman Sachs Natural Resources Sector (AMEX: IGE):** The IGE ETF mirrors the performance of the Goldman Sachs Natural Resources Sector index, which tracks the performance of companies like ConocoPhillips, Chevron, and BP, as well as refiners such as Valero and Suncor. (I talk about refiners in Chapter 6.) Although most of this ETF is invested in integrated oil companies, it also enables you to play a broad spectrum of energy companies.

» **iShares S&P Global Energy Sector (AMEX: IXC):** This ETF mirrors the performance of the Standard & Poor's Global Energy Sector index. Buying this ETF exposes you to companies such as ExxonMobil, Chevron, ConocoPhillips, and Royal Dutch Shell. Launched at the end of 2001, the ETF has 35 percent aggregate returns for a three-year period.

Get your passport ready: Investing overseas

Another great way to capitalize on oil profits is to invest in an emerging-market fund that invests in countries that both sit on large deposits of crude oil and have the infrastructure in place to export crude oil.

Countries that export crude oil have seen their current account surpluses reach record highs. (*Current account* measures a country's balance of payments as they relate to trade.) These windfall profits are having a tremendous effect on the economies of such countries. The stock markets of some of these countries, particularly the Persian Gulf countries, known as the *Gulf Cooperation Council* (GCC), have had a remarkable run during the first decade of this century, averaging double-digit compounded annual returns. As their economies have grown from their hydrocarbon wealth, these countries have established sovereign wealth funds (SWFs) to diversify their earnings and holdings away from petroleum products.

Many Persian Gulf countries have large capital resources that they're deploying across global capital markets and asset purchases. Abu Dhabi, the city-state with the largest oil reserves in the United Arab Emirates, has established the Abu Dhabi Investment Authority (ADIA), the Abu Dhabi Investment Council (ADIC), and the International Petroleum Investment Corporation (IPIC) to invest its hydrocarbon receipts. This move has resulted in a broad and significant diversification of Abu Dhabi's economy away from petroleum and into other strategic sectors, such as technology and aerospace. The local stock markets are great ways to get exposure to these economies, and you can follow private equity opportunities as an investor.

WARNING

For the uninitiated, investing directly in emerging markets can be a risky proposition and requires a lot of research. Some countries have different regulatory rules than the United States, and you need to know those rules before you get involved in a foreign venture.

One way to play emerging markets while avoiding direct risks is to invest in emerging-markets funds located in the United States. These funds hire professionals who are familiar with the business environment in target countries and can navigate these foreign investment seas. These funds enable you to take advantage of booms in foreign countries, while remaining within the safe regulatory and investing environment of the United States.

TIP

A couple of emerging-markets funds give you indirect exposure to the booming oil-exporting countries:

>> Evergreen Emerging Markets Growth I (EMGYX)

>> Fidelity Emerging Markets (FEMKX)

For more information on how to choose the right mutual fund manager, turn to Chapter 14.

Chapter **4**

What a Gas! Investing in Natural Gas

If crude oil is the king of commodities, natural gas is sometimes said to be the queen. Although crude oil accounts for about 40 percent of total energy consumed in the United States (the biggest energy market in the world), approximately 25 percent of energy consumption comes from natural gas. Natural gas is, therefore, an important source of energy both in the United States and around the world, and it can offer tremendous moneymaking opportunities.

Similar to crude oil (see Chapter 3) and coal (see Chapter 5), natural gas is a *nonrenewable fossil fuel* found in large deposits within the earth. As a matter of fact, natural gas is sometimes found not too far away from crude oil deposits. Crude oil is the liquid fossil fuel, coal is the solid one, and natural gas is the gaseous one.

REMEMBER

People are sometimes confused by the term *natural gas* because they think (incorrectly) that it refers to the *gas* (gasoline) they use to fill their tanks. Although natural gas is sometimes used as a transportation fuel, the gasoline you buy at the gas station and natural gas have nothing to do with each other. The gasoline your car consumes is a product of crude oil, whereas natural gas is an entirely different member of the fossil fuel family, used primarily for heating, cooling, and cooking purposes.

Because of its importance as a source of energy, natural gas makes for a good investment. It's an important commodity with many applications. In this chapter, I present you with all the information you need to develop an investment strategy in the natural gas segment of energy. Because it's important to get all the facts up front about this commodity, I first provide you with hands-on information about the applicability of natural gas — how it's used and how you can profit from these uses. Then I give you a snapshot of the global natural gas market so you know who's producing it and who's consuming it. Identifying these patterns is a necessary part of developing a sound investment strategy. Finally, I show you how to actually start investing in and trading natural gas, as traders sometimes call it. Natural gas may not get the same kind of attention as crude oil, but it still makes for a great investment.

What's the Use? Looking at Natural Gas Applications

Because it's one of the cleanest-burning fossil fuels, natural gas has become increasingly popular as an energy source. In the United States alone, natural gas accounts for roughly a third of total energy consumption. Natural gas is second only to petroleum when it comes to generating energy in the United States.

So, who uses all this natural gas? The primary consumers of this commodity are the industrial sector, residential elements, commercial interests, electricity generation, and transportation.

Industrial uses of natural gas

The industrial sector is the largest consumer of natural gas, accounting for almost 40 percent of total consumption. Although industrial uses of natural gas have always played a major role in the sector, their significance has increased during the past several years and will continue to do so. The industrial sector has always accounted for a large part of natural gas use, and because this trend will continue, it's a good area to consider investing in. (Actually, demand for natural gas products as a whole will increase throughout the first quarter of the 21st century, for reasons I discuss in the next section.)

HOW DO YOU MEASURE NATURAL GAS?

Measuring natural gas can be confusing because multiple measurement methods exist. These measurements basically boil down to how much physical natural gas there is and how much energy the natural gas generates.

Whereas crude oil is measured in barrels (each barrel contains 42 gallons of oil), natural gas is measured in cubic feet. You may recall from chemistry class that a cubic foot is a measure of volume for a square prism with six sides, each 1 foot in length. (The technical name for this shape is a *regular hexahedron,* but you can simply think of it as the shape of a sugar cube.) Because natural gas is in a gaseous state, it's easier to measure it in cubic feet. Sometimes natural gas is converted into liquid form, known as liquefied natural gas (LNG), which I cover in the later section "Liquefied Natural Gas: Getting Liquid Without Getting Wet." LNG is also measured in cubic feet.

The abbreviation for cubic feet is *cf.* (Both letters are lowercase.) Therefore, 10 cubic feet is abbreviated as 10 cf. To have practical applications, cubic feet must be able to measure large amounts of volume. Consider the abbreviations for measuring larger volume amounts of cubic feet:

- **100 cubic feet:** 1 Ccf
- **1,000 cubic feet:** 1 Mcf
- **1 million cubic feet:** 1 Mmcf
- **1 billion cubic feet:** 1 Bcf
- **1 trillion cubic feet:** 1 Tcf

Note that cf is always in lowercase, and the first letter of the abbreviation is always capitalized. Many futures contracts based on natural gas are measured in cubic feet.

Natural gas can also be measured by the amount of energy it generates. This energy content is captured by a unit of measurement known as the *British thermal unit* (Btu). One Btu measures the amount of heat necessary to increase the temperature of 1 pound of water by 1°F. To put it in perspective, 1 cf is the equivalent of 1,027 Btu. British

(continued)

(continued)

thermal units, sometimes called *therms,* may appear on your gas bill to express the amount of natural gas your household consumed during a particular period.

For investment purposes, however, natural gas is generally quantified by using cubic feet.

Increased industrial demand should put upward price pressures on natural gas. One way to profit from this demand is by being long natural gas futures. (For more on going long on futures, flip to the later section "Natural selection: Trading nat gas futures.")

As an investor, looking at long-term trends helps you develop an investment strategy that takes advantage of the market fundamentals.

So, what specific parts of the industrial sector use natural gas? Natural gas is a truly versatile form of energy because it has many applications in industry. Consider a few industrial applications of natural gas products:

>> Feedstock for fertilizers

>> Food processing

>> Glass melting

>> Industrial boiler fueling

>> Metal smelting

>> Waste incineration

The chemical composition of natural gas consists primarily of *methane,* a hydrocarbon molecule. It also includes other hydrocarbons, such as *butane, ethane,* and *propane* — all gases that have important industrial uses.

When the industrial sector is firing on all cylinders, so to speak, demand for natural gas tends to increase. Keep an eye out for increased activity from the industrial sector because this is a bullish sign for natural gas. One indicator you can use to gauge the economic output from the industrial sector is the *Producer Price Index* (PPI). The PPI measures the average change in prices that producers get for their products, expressed as a percent change. The PPI, compiled by the Bureau of Labor Statistics (BLS), is a good measure of the health of the industrial sector. You can get the latest PPI reports at www.bls.gov/ppi.

Natural gas in your home

Residential use accounts for almost a quarter of total natural gas consumption. A large portion of homes in the United States, as well as other countries, use natural gas for both their cooking and heating needs — the two largest applications of natural gas in the home.

About 70 percent of households in the United States have natural gas ovens in the kitchen. The use of natural gas for cooking purposes has steadily increased as technological developments have allowed for an efficient and safe use of natural gas. How does this affect you as an investor? As long as folks need to cook, you can bet that natural gas will fill this important need. This essential usage ensures that demand from the residential sector for natural gas will remain strong — a bullish sign for nat gas.

TIP

More than 55 percent of homes in the United States use natural gas for heating purposes. One way to benefit from this particular application is to identify peak periods of natural gas consumption. Specifically, demand for natural gas for heating increases in the Northern Hemisphere during the winter seasons. Therefore, one way to profit in the natural gas markets is to calibrate your strategy to this cyclical, weather-related trend. In other words, all things constant, natural gas prices should go up during the winters as folks seek to stay warm.

TECHNICAL
STUFF

Although my aim in this book is to help you make money by *investing* in commodities such as natural gas, I'm going to take the liberty of showing you how to *save* money by using natural gas in your home. Natural gas is one of the cheapest energy forms, as measured by dollars per unit of energy generated. You get more energy from natural gas per dollar (as measured in British thermal units, the standard energy measurement unit) than from almost any other source. Using natural gas may save you some money during the winter, which you can then use to bulk up your commodities investments.

Natural gas's commercial uses

About 40 percent of the energy consumed by commercial users, such as hospitals and schools, comes from natural gas, accounting for about 15 percent of total natural gas consumption. Because commercial users include establishments such as schools, hospitals, restaurants, movie theaters, malls, and office buildings, demand for natural gas from these key drivers of the economy rises during times of increasing economic activity. This trend means that, all things equal, you need to be bullish on natural gas during times of economic growth.

TIP

One place to look for important economic clues that affect demand for natural gas is the U.S. Energy Information Administration (EIA), a division of the Department of Energy (DOE). The EIA provides a wealth of information regarding consumption trends of key energy products, such as natural gas, from various economic sectors. Visit www.eia.gov for more information.

Generating electricity with natural gas

Natural gas is quickly becoming a popular alternative for generating electricity, with just less than 25 percent of natural gas usage going toward generating electricity. Actually, natural gas is used to produce approximately 10 percent of electricity generation in the United States. That figure will increase dramatically in the coming years.

The long-term trend is that more natural gas will be required to generate electricity. This increased demand from a critical sector will keep upward pressures on natural gas prices over the long term. Keep this in mind as you consider investing in this commodity.

Natural gas and transportation

It's not a widely known fact, but natural gas is used in a number of vehicles (approximately three million worldwide) as a source of fuel. These vehicles, known simply as *natural gas vehicles* (NGVs), run on a grade of natural gas called *compressed natural gas* (CNG). This usage accounts for only about 5 percent of total natural gas consumption, but demand for CNG may increase as a viable (cheaper) alternative to gasoline (a crude oil derivative).

NGVs have become much more prevalent. As of 2010, more than 11 million NGVs were in circulation worldwide. The most dominant countries using NGVs are Pakistan, Argentina, Brazil, and Iran. Expect to see more of these vehicles on the road as countries continue their shift toward cleaner sources of transportation fuels. Fast-forward 12 years, and the number of NGVs worldwide has doubled, with more than 22 million NGVs in use today.

TIP

Keep a close eye on technological developments of natural gas in the transportation sector. If natural gas grabbed a slice of the transportation market, which now accounts for almost two-thirds of crude oil consumption, prices for natural gas could increase dramatically.

Liquefied Natural Gas: Getting Liquid Without Getting Wet

Liquefied natural gas is a recent development in the field. LNG is exactly what it says it is: natural gas in liquid form. The reason for this development is quite simple: As demand for natural gas increases, you need to be able to transport this precious commodity across vast distances (for example, across continents and through oceans). Transporting it is difficult to do when it's in a gaseous state. Enter LNG, which is easy to transport.

TECHNICAL
STUFF

Transforming natural gas from its gaseous state into a liquid one is a complex process. The natural gas must first be cooled to a temperature of –260°F to transform it to its liquid state. An additional advantage of LNG is that it takes up considerably less space — about 600 times less — which means that you can transport a lot more of it farther and more economically. When the natural gas is in a liquid state, it's usually transported in specially designed tankers to consumer markets. (I present some of the companies that transport energy products around the world in Chapter 6.) Before it's actually delivered to consumers, it goes through a regasification process.

REMEMBER

In the United States, most natural gas is transported through pipelines in a gaseous state. The natural gas pipeline system in the United States is one of the most extensive in the world — 300 million miles of pipeline — and it connects major natural gas–producing regions (such as the Gulf of Mexico) to large natural gas consumers (such as the East Coast). Although the pipeline remains the dominant method of transporting natural gas, LNG is quickly establishing itself as a viable source of natural gas, particularly as domestic production declines and imports increase. Some of the major operators of these pipelines that transport both natural gas and LNG are entities known as *master limited partnerships* (MLPs). The good news is that you can profit from moving natural gas across the United States by investing in MLPs, which I cover in Chapter 14.

In 2005, the United States received only about 1 percent of its total natural gas (170 Bcf) through LNG. By 2010, that figure had shifted dramatically upward, coming in at 452 Bcf. The top six exporters of LNG to the United States include Trinidad and Tobago, Egypt, Algeria, Nigeria, Norway, and Qatar. This trend is now well established and is set to increase in the coming years.

Investing in Natural Gas

The future for natural gas looks bright. The total natural gas consumption on a global scale in 2022 was approximately 4 trillion cubic meters (4 Tcm).

REMEMBER

Knowing that demand for natural gas will keep increasing until 2025 is an important piece of information for you as an investor. Perhaps even more important is figuring out which countries and companies will be meeting this demand. Determining who's going to be supplying this natural gas will help you devise an investment strategy to profit from this increased natural gas demand. Table 4-1 lists the countries with the largest reserves of natural gas in the world.

Global natural gas reserves are estimated at 6,040 Tcf, which is the equivalent of approximately 6 quadrillion cubic feet. (Quadrillion, not zillion, is the next figure above trillion.) You can get exposure to this huge natural gas market in a couple ways: by trading futures contracts or by investing in companies that are involved in the production and development of natural gas fields in some of the countries listed in Table 4-1. I discuss the pros and cons of each investment method in the following sections.

TABLE 4-1 Top Ten Natural Gas Reserves by Country, 2021

Rank	Country	Proven Reserves (Tcf)	Percent of World Total
1	Russia	1,680	24.3%
2	Iran	1,201	17.3%
3	Qatar	871	12.5%
4	United States	368	5.3%
5	Saudi Arabia	294	4.2%
6	Turkmenistan	265	3.8%
7	United Arab Emirates	215	3.1%
8	Venezuela	197	2.8%
9	Nigeria	180	2.6%
10	China	163	1.6%

Natural selection: Trading nat gas futures

The most direct method of investing in natural gas is to trade futures contracts on one of the designated commodities exchanges. The Chicago Mercantile Exchange (CME), the exchange for energy products, gives you the option to buy and sell natural gas futures and options.

REMEMBER

To trade futures, you need to have a futures account with a designated broker, known as the *futures commission merchant* (FCM). After you open a futures account, you can start trading these derivative products. For more on futures and options, turn to Chapter 13.

The natural gas futures contract is the second-most popular energy contract on the CME, right behind crude oil. It's traded under the ticker symbol NG, and it trades in increments of 10,000 metric million Btu (Mmbtu). You can trade it during all the calendar months, to periods up to 72 months after the current month.

The CME offers a mini version of this contract for individual hedgers and speculators. Check out the nat gas section of the CME website for more on this contract: www.cmegroup.com/markets/energy/natural-gas/natural-gas.html.

Trading natural gas futures contracts and options isn't for the fainthearted. Even by commodities standards, natural gas is a notoriously volatile commodity, subject to wild price fluctuations. If you're not an aggressive investor willing to withstand the financial equivalent of a wild roller-coaster ride, natural gas futures may not be for you.

Nat gas companies: The natural choice

Investing in companies that process natural gas is a positive investment choice because it offers you exposure to this market through the expertise and experience of industry professionals, without the volatility of the futures market. Some natural gas companies are involved in the production of natural gas fields; others are responsible for delivering natural gas directly to consumers.

I list companies that are *fully integrated* natural gas companies, which means they're involved in all the production, development, transportation, and distribution phases of natural gas. Investing in these companies gives you a solid foothold in this industry. Here's your hit list:

>> **Allegheny Energy (NYSE: AYE):** Provides natural gas–based electricity to consumers in the eastern United States, primarily in Pennsylvania, Virginia, and Maryland. This S&P 500 company is a good option if you want regional exposure to natural gas production.

>> **Alliant Energy (NYSE: LNT):** Provides consumers with natural gas and electricity derived from natural gas throughout the United States. This company is a good choice if you want exposure to the North American natural gas market.

>> **Nicor, Inc. (NYSE: GAS):** Nicor's operations are primarily centered in Illinois, where it provides natural gas to more than two million consumers. This company is another good regional investment.

QATARI NATURAL GAS

Qatar is a fascinating country in many respects. Surrounded by Saudi Arabia, the United Arab Emirates, and Iran, this Persian Gulf country is one of the largest producers of LNG in the world. It also has the third-largest proven reserve of natural gas globally, behind only Russia and Iran. Unlike many of its natural gas counterparts, which have populations in the tens of millions, Qatar has a population of about one million. The abundance of natural gas reserves, a booming economy, and a strategic location give this country one of the highest gross domestic product (GDP) rates in the world, about three times as high as the GDP per capita of the United States.

Strategic geographic location, abundance of natural resources (specifically, natural gas and oil), a highly educated workforce, and no income taxes (that's right — no corporate or personal income taxes in Qatar) make this country one of the most appealing places to invest and work. You can get direct exposure by investing in the Qatari stock market, which has several companies involved in the Qatari natural gas and power induwstries.

TIP

For a complete listing of companies involved in natural gas production and distribution, look at the American Gas Association website at www.aga.org.

IN THIS CHAPTER

» Profiting from solar power

» Considering wind energy

» Looking at biofuels

» Investing in coal

» Examining nuclear power

» Trading electricity

Chapter 5

Investing in Renewable and Alternative Energy

Two problems plague traditional sources of energy, such as oil, natural gas, and coal: their increasing monetary cost and their increasing opposition from environmentalists concerned about the hazards of burning these fuels. It's not hard to see that renewable sources of energy, such as solar and wind power, will attract more attention in the near future. In the 21st century, renewable energy as an industry has received a tremendous amount of media, social, and political coverage. Many factors account for this increased attention, least of all the calls for countries to reduce their fossil fuel consumption in light of the global environmental impact of burning such fuels.

About ten years ago, renewable energy accounted for about 7 percent of total energy use. Fast-forward to today, and that number has increased to 11 percent of total energy use. This pace isn't as fast as many would like, but it represents a steady increase amid widespread adoption, government subsidies, and industrial incentives. When you zoom in even further, the numbers are slightly more encouraging. Consider, for example, that renewable energy now accounts for a staggering 30 percent of global electricity generation. That's a massive jump, considering it was in the single digits in the 2000s.

The field of renewable energy is getting a lot of attention, and there's certainly potential to make some money in this field. In this chapter, I give you an overview of this dynamic industry and focus on specific fields — including solar energy, wind power, and biofuels — to help you develop an investment strategy rooted in the market fundamentals. I also go through the global energy scene and identify some of the major trends affecting it. I introduce you to alternative energy sources and show you how to profit from this segment of the energy market. Specifically, I provide you with investment opportunities in the following areas: coal, nuclear power, and electricity.

Getting to Know Renewable Energy

REMEMBER

In practical terms, *renewable energy* refers to sources of energy that are essentially always present, always available, and always renewable. The sun and wind are traditional sources of renewable energy because the sun always shines and the wind always blows, day in and day out. Harnessing these renewable sources of energy is beneficial for a couple reasons. First, they're always there. Second, they don't emit greenhouse gases, which means they're not increasing pollution output.

The benefits of renewable energy are obvious, but one of the big obstacles to implementing a large-scale, global industry is less obvious: cost. For instance, the cost of harnessing the power of the sun to generate electricity is extremely high and requires massive commitments of capital expenditures. The solar industry currently needs heavy government subsidies to be able to generate enough profits to remain competitive; the same applies to wind energy and other types of renewable energy, such as ethanol.

Renewable energy as a whole represents only a small fraction of the total energy landscape in the United States, which is also attributable to the broader global footprint. Getting exposure to some of these sectors from an individual portfolio perspective is difficult. For example, unless you own or operate geothermal plants, you have few direct methods for getting this kind of exposure. For this reason, in the following sections I focus only on renewable energy sources for which there are tradable, liquid, and transparent instruments — specifically, solar, wind, and biomass.

REMEMBER

Although it's currently challenging to get direct exposure to different renewable energy submarkets (such as geothermal), this will undoubtedly change in the future as more instruments are made available and as the market gains more breadth and credibility. In addition, you can adopt a creative approach to getting this kind of exposure; for example, if you want exposure to hydroelectric power generation, you can examine the electric utilities universe for companies that have hydroelectric power assets. (Find out more about electric utilities later in this chapter.) This strategy may not give you that direct investment route, but you can still manage to generate indirect exposure in your portfolio.

TIP

If you're interested in keeping up-to-date on the latest developments in the renewable energy space, I recommend that you check out the U.S. Department of Energy's Office of Energy Efficiency & Renewable Energy (EERE) at www.energy.gov/eere. For the official intergovernmental policy view on global warming and greenhouse gases from the United Nations, consult the Intergovernmental Panel on Climate Change (IPCC) at www.ipcc.ch.

Sunny delight: Investing in solar energy

Solar power currently accounts for only 1 percent of total renewable energy sources, but it's one of the fastest-growing areas in the space. Governments around the world are in the process of announcing massive infrastructure spending programs dedicated to harnessing the sun's power and turning it into electricity and other forms of energy.

India and China have been at the forefront of this trend, with $30 billion in projects announced in the 20 years ahead. Even countries that you may not associate with renewable energy are taking the lead on this matter. Saudi Arabia, the world's largest oil producer, and the United Arab Emirates have both dedicated large budgets to the development of solar power. Even the Kingdom of Morocco has jumped on the bandwagon, generating 3,934 megawatts as of 2022, and it has now updated its target to 10,000 megawatts by 2030.

Broadly speaking, solar power is the process by which energy from the sun is harnessed and channeled into a usable energy form — generally heat or electricity. Two different processes can transform solar power:

>> **Solar photovoltaic energy:** Don't be intimidated by this complicated name. It simply describes the method by which energy from the sun is captured and transformed into electricity.

>> **Solar thermal energy:** This method transforms the sun's energy into heat, which may be used for a number of different purposes, such as interior space heating or water heating. If you've ever seen flat-panel solar collectors mounted on homes or buildings, they're used for solar thermal energy purposes.

Many companies are trying to turn these two methods of transforming solar energy into a commercially viable enterprise, but they face some challenges. One of the biggest impediments to the commercial success of solar power is the sun itself. Specifically, the sun isn't a resource that you can control. For one thing, you can't manipulate the weather, so you're at the mercy of rain, fog, clouds, the earth's rotation, and other natural external factors that block the sun. For this reason, solar power accounted for a little less than 0.06 percent of total energy consumed in the United States during 2005.

TIP

Currently, the equity markets give you a direct way to get exposure to the solar industry. Following are two of the top names in the industry:

>> **First Solar, Inc. (Nasdaq: FSLR):** FSLR was one of the first solar companies to go public. It's involved in the manufacture and sales of photovoltaic solar panels to end users, including governments, corporate entities, and private individuals. Its two main revenue generators come from the components sector (selling parts for specific solar projects) and the systems segment (installation of solar farms). With net profit margins in excess of 22 percent (2010 figures), this company offers solid exposure to the photovoltaic market segment.

>> **Suntech Power Holdings (NYSE: STP):** Suntech is a world leader in the development, design, and implementation of solar photovoltaic systems and products. In addition to

providing construction services, the company offers engineering and maintenance services to its clients around the world. It has a global footprint, with operations in Germany, the United States, Australia, South Africa, Japan, and South Korea. For a truly diversified global exposure to the solar industry, be sure to consider Suntech.

Fast and furious: Trading in wind energy

Wind energy is another renewable resource that's getting increasing attention from investors. Energy is generated by huge wind machines (similar to traditional windmills), which are placed side-by-side in *wind farms.*

The challenge to wind energy is that it's dependent on the wind, which is unpredictable. Wind has traditionally held a small part in the energy generation spectrum, but it's increasing as it becomes a cost-effective solution. Currently, few publicly traded companies deal specifically in wind power.

That said, many industrial companies are beginning to implement large-scale investments in wind energy production. If you're looking for some indirect exposure to wind, you can always consider an investment in General Electric (NYSE: GE). Although GE is known for its large industrial footprint, it is becoming one of the leaders in the wind space and is the global leader in manufacturing and sales of wind turbines across dozens of markets.

NOOR MOROCCO

The Kingdom of Morocco has one of the highest rates of sunshine in the world, and the country has taken the lead in utilizing this reality by constructing one of the world's largest solar energy projects. With a cost of about $10 billion, the project known as Noor ("light" in Arabic) is equipped with a staggering 2,000 megawatts of solar generation capacity. Built over a span of 15 years, Noor will not only be responsible for almost 40 percent of the country's electricity, but also be connected to grids that will help power countries in the European Union and the United Kingdom.

TIP

With rising energy prices, wind energy may get more focus. If you're interested in investing in wind power and you want to stay on top of emerging trends, check out the American Clean Power Association at https://cleanpower.org. The site maintains a database of private companies involved in wind energy that may go public one day.

Betting on biomass

Biomass is currently the biggest component of the renewable energy industry, accounting for 53 percent of total production estimates. Scientifically speaking, biomass energy is produced by processing common wastes and transforming them into renewable energy through a biochemical conversion process.

Some common feedstock is used in this process:

>> Corn

>> Ethanol

>> Eucalyptus

>> Forestry crop residues

>> Industrial residues

>> Municipal solid wastes

>> Palm oil

>> Sugarcane

>> Vegetable oil

The raw material inputs are varied and come from an array of sources, which offers benefits and competitive advantages to the industry. Specifically, because such a large number of inputs are available, the process can be replicated across different markets, landscapes, and geographies. For example, agriculturally rich countries such as Brazil can process large amounts of agricultural wastes (such as ethanol and sugarcane waste) to generate energy; countries with large industrial apparatuses, such as Russia, can also take advantage of the biomass process by using industrial residues and municipal wastes as primary inputs. The process is thus versatile and scalable, which accounts for its ubiquity in the energy spectrum.

WHAT'S UP WITH ETHANOL?

Ethanol is an alcohol fuel used in transportation that can be made from corn, sugar, wheat, and other agricultural products. Because of its origins, ethanol is a renewable source of energy. In Brazil, the world's largest producer of ethanol fuel, ethanol is the primary automotive fuel. The United States has seen an increase in the use of ethanol as a transportation fuel, and that trend is likely to increase. One company involved in producing ethanol that I recommend is Pacific Ethanol (Nasdaq: PEIX). If you're interested in getting exposure to ethanol, PEIX is a good way to go.

For now, investors have no direct plays into the biomass and biofuels market; in the current industry structure, only privately held companies, municipalities, and other governmental institutions run biomass plants and operations.

However, a company located in Brazil, CPFL Energia (CPFL), is a world leader in biomass generation. CPFL generates, distributes, and sells electricity to the Brazilian domestic market. It derives a significant portion of its revenues from biomass generation — specifically, the transformation of sugarcane waste into electricity. The company trades on the Sao Paulo Stock Exchange (the BOVESPA) but recently listed its shares on the New York Stock Exchange (NYSE) under the ticker CPL, via an American depository receipt (ADR).

TIP

As a result, you can now get exposure to an exciting market that was nonexistent only a few years ago. I expect more companies involved in the biomass space to go public in the coming years, giving you a broader range of options to choose from. In the meantime, I encourage you to monitor CPFL.

Digging Up Additional Energy Sources

As the global population increases and emerging countries industrialize (see Chapter 2), the demand for energy products will rise throughout the first quarter of the 21st century. The U.S. Energy Information Administration (EIA) anticipates that global demand for energy products will increase drastically by 2030.

In 2009, fossil fuels (oil, natural gas, and coal) accounted for 85 percent of total energy consumption. Crude oil alone was responsible for almost 40 percent of global energy use. However, as the price of these traditional energy sources increases (driven by both strong demand and limited supply), the calls for new sources of energy are increasing as well. For example, in 2005, many members of Congress pushed for an alternative energy initiative to promote the use of solar, wind, and other renewable energy sources.

Despite all the political initiatives and public–private partnerships and investments in renewable energy, fossil fuels still account for 84 percent of world energy consumption in 2022. Some regions have certainly reduced their use of fossil fuels, but overall the world economy is very much still dependent on non-renewable energy sources.

REMEMBER

Despite numerous calls, however, the energy landscape is unlikely to change anytime soon, which means that fossil fuels will remain the dominant source of global energy for years to come. Alternative energies may generate a lot of attention, but how much actual progress will be made is still up in the air. Keep this in mind as you're looking at investing in these alternatives.

Despite the dominance of fossil fuels — particularly crude oil — the alternative space is a dynamic area and a fertile ground for investment opportunities. In the following sections, I cover three of these alternative energy sources.

Reexamining coal

Before the beginning of the 20th century, coal was truly the king of commodities. It was the dominant source of energy during the tumultuous Industrial Revolution. People still often associate the Industrial Revolution with images of coal mines. The beginning of the end of coal as the dominant energy source can be traced to a fateful day in 1912 when Winston Churchill, the First Lord of the Admiralty in the British Navy, ordered the conversion of all coal ships to oil. That move resulted in the rise of oil as the dominant global energy source, at the expense of coal.

Although Churchill's decision to switch the British Navy from coal to oil effectively dethroned coal as the fossil fuel of choice, coal still enjoys an elevated position in global energy markets. For example, in 2009 in the United States (the world's most important energy market), coal accounted for 23 percent of total fossil fuel consumption. In 2021, coal still accounted for 22 percent of electricity generation in the United States. Therefore, coal is still an important source of energy and can provide some good moneymaking opportunities. In this section, I show you how to make money in coal.

Coal hard facts

Coal is used primarily for electricity generation (steam coal) and steel manufacturing (metallurgical coal). Besides its practical uses in these two important areas, coal is an increasingly popular fossil fuel because of its large reserves. Specifically, companies in the United States have long touted the benefits of moving toward a more coal-based economy because the United States has the largest coal reserves in the world. I list in Table 5-1 the countries with the largest coal reserves.

TABLE 5-1 **Coal Reserves by Country, 2021**

Rank	Country	Reserves (Million Short Tons)	Percent of World Total
1	United States	250,219	24%
2	Russia	160,364	15%
3	Australia	147,435	14%
4	China	138,819	13%
5	India	101,363	10%
6	Indonesia	37,000	4%
7	Germany	36,103	3%
8	Ukraine	34,375	3%
9	Poland	26,479	3%
10	Kazakhstan	25,605	2%

Source: Data from World Energy Council

TECHNICAL STUFF

Coal is measured in short tons. One *short ton* is the equivalent of 2,000 pounds. In terms of energy, one short ton of *anthracite*, the coal of highest quality (see the later section "Paint it black"), contains approximately 25 million British thermal units (Btu) of energy.

TIP

If you're going to invest in companies that process coal, I recommend selecting a company with heavy exposure in one of the countries listed in Table 5-1. Specifically, because the United States, Russia, Australia, China, and India collectively hold more than 75 percent of the world's total coal reserves, investing in a coal company with large operations in any of these countries gives you exposure to this important segment of the market. I introduce some of these coal companies in the later section "It's a coal investment."

REMEMBER

Just because a country has large deposits of a natural resource, however, doesn't mean that it exploits them to full capacity. As such, there's a significant gap between countries with large coal reserves and those that produce the most coal annually. To give you a better idea of this market characteristic, I list in Table 5-2 the top coal-producing countries.

TABLE 5-2 **Hard Coal Production by Country, 2020**

Rank	Country	Production (Million Short Tons)
1	China	3,902
2	India	756
3	Indonesia	562
4	United States	484
5	Australia	476
6	Russia	400
7	South Africa	248
8	Kazakhstan	113
9	Poland	100
10	Germany	100

Demand for coal is expected to increase during the first quarter of the 21st century. Most of this growth will come from the emerging-market economies, particularly the economies of China and India, which will account for approximately 75 percent of the demand increase for coal. (China is currently the largest consumer of coal in the world, ahead of the United States, India, and Japan.)

An important note is that although the Organization for Economic Co-operation and Development (OECD) and G7 countries have been leading the charge against coal, it's the ultimate irony that coal production in OECD countries has skyrocketed over the past decade. For example, coal production in the U.S. increased from 335 tons to 484 tons per year in the past decade; similarly, Germany's output increased by 30 percent during the same period, from 73 tons to 100 tons per year; and Australia's production almost doubled from 250 tons to 476 tons.

Demand for coal has resulted in strong price movements in the commodity itself. Before the Global Financial Crisis of 2008, prices for coal experienced a major uptrend, going from $50 per short ton in 2006 to almost $200 per short ton in 2008. The financial crisis resulted in a severe quasi-crash scenario for coal prices, as was the case for several other important commodities. This correction was necessary because the rally was overdone on the way up; coal prices seem to have stabilized in the $100 range, but expect much more activity surrounding this commodity in the future.

Paint it black

As with other fossil fuels, coal comes in different qualities. Specifically, coal comes in four categories, classified by its carbon, sulfur, and ash content, as well as by the level of energy it releases.

Here are the four major categories of coal:

>> **Lignite:** Lignite contains the least amount of carbon and the most sulfur and ash of all coal types, so it's considered the least valuable. Sometimes called brown coal, it's primarily used in generating electricity.

>> **Sub-bituminous:** This type of coal contains a little more carbon than lignite and, thus, is considered to be of a higher quality. It also has lower levels of sulfur and ash than lignite. It's used mostly to heat water in electricity-generating steam turbines.

>> **Bituminous:** Because bituminous coal burns well and creates a lot of energy, it's of high value. The most common type of coal found in the United States, it's used to generate electricity and, in the steel industry, create high-quality steel.

» Anthracite: By far the most valuable type of coal, anthracite contains the highest levels of carbon and the least amount of sulfur and ash; it also provides the most energy on a per-unit basis. Because of its high value, anthracite is used for residential and commercial space heating.

Before you invest in companies involved in the coal business, find out which type of coal they produce. This information will help you better understand the company's business and profit margins. You can find this information in a company's annual and quarterly reports.

It's a coal investment

You can get access to the coal markets either by trading coal futures directly or by investing in coal companies.

As with other members of the fossil fuel family, coal has an underlying futures contract that trades on a commodity exchange — in this case, the Chicago Mercantile Exchange (CME). This coal contract gives commercial users — coal producers, electric companies, and steel manufacturers — the opportunity to hedge against market risk and offers speculators a chance to profit from this market risk. (For more on the CME and other commodity exchanges, turn to Chapter 14. Review Chapter 13 for more on futures contract specifications.)

The coal futures contract on the CME tracks the price of the Central Appalachian type of coal. Central Appalachian coal, known as CAPP, is a high-quality coal with low sulfur and ash content. The CAPP futures contract (which traders sometimes affectionately call "the big sandy" because it's produced in the area between West Virginia and Kentucky where the Ohio River flows) is the premium benchmark for coal prices in the United States.

The contract trades under the ticker symbol QL and is tradable during all the calendar months of the current year, in addition to all calendar months in the subsequent three years. Additional information on this futures contract is available on the CME website at www.cmegroup.com.

Although the coal futures contract does offer you exposure to coal, be warned that the market for this contract is fairly illiquid, meaning that the trading volume is low. Most of the traders involved in this market represent large commercial interests that transact with each other. A few speculators trade the coal futures markets, but they don't represent a significant portion of the market. You may not be able to get involved directly in this market without large capital reserves to compete with the commercial interests.

TIP

One of the best ways to invest in coal is to invest in a company that mines it. The following three companies are the best, in my opinion:

>> **Arch Coal (NYSE: ACI):** Arch Coal is smaller in size than its main competitors, Peabody and Consol, but I like it because the coal it produces is of very high quality. It operates more than 30 mines in the continental United States and controls more than 3 billion short tons of reserves. It has operations in the largest coal-producing regions in the United States, including in the Appalachians, the Powder River Basin (on the Montana/Wyoming border), and the Western Bituminous region (on the Colorado/Utah border).

>> **Consol Energy (NYSE: CNX):** With headquarters in Pittsburgh, Consol Energy has significant operations in the coal mines of Pennsylvania and nearby coal-rich states of West Virginia and Kentucky. As of 2009, it controlled 8 billion short tons of coal reserves, with operations in more than 17 mines across the United States. CNX is well positioned to take advantage of the booming domestic coal market.

>> **Peabody Energy (NYSE: BTU):** Peabody Energy is the largest coal company, with approximately 15 billion short tons of coal reserves. The coal it produces is responsible for generating approximately 10 percent of the electricity in the United States. With 2009 revenues exceeding $5 billion, Peabody Energy is the largest coal company out there today; it's the ExxonMobil of coal companies. I like the company because of its size and because it has mining operations in the United States as well as in Australia and Venezuela, two important coal markets.

TIP

If you want to invest in coal companies with more international exposure to markets in Russia, China, and other coal-rich countries, I recommend that you consult the World Coal Association at www.worldcoal.org.

Investing in nuclear power

When most people think of nuclear power, they tend to think of nuclear weapons and mushroom clouds. However, nuclear power has an important civilian role, too. Civilian and commercial nuclear power is an integral part of the global energy supply chain and is a valuable energy source for residential, commercial, and industrial consumers worldwide. In fact, nuclear power generates more than 20 percent of the electricity in the United States. In countries like France, nuclear power generates more than 75 percent of electricity!

Nuclear power currently accounts for about 5 percent of total global energy consumption, and it's expected to remain at these stable levels until 2030. But if the price of fossil fuels (oil, natural gas, and coal) rises dramatically enough to start affecting demand (creating what is called *demand destruction*), nuclear power may play an important role in picking up the slack.

TIP

One way you can profit from increased interest in nuclear power is to invest in uranium, the most widely used fuel in nuclear power plants. However, you're not likely to hear about this opportunity from your local financial media because uranium is a pretty obscure investment area. But sometimes as an investor, you need to be able to think creatively and look at opportunities that other investors haven't considered. Investing in uranium to benefit from the increased demand in nuclear power isn't a well-known or well-advertised investment play, but it can be profitable nevertheless.

SPLITTING ATOMS

The primary use of civilian nuclear power is in generating electricity. Electricity is generated by heating water to high temperatures to create steam that powers the turbines in a steam turbine. In a nuclear power plant, the water is heated through a process known as nuclear fission, in which atoms are split to release large amounts of energy. (This process is the opposite of nuclear fusion, in which atoms are fused.)

You may be surprised to find that the period of 2000–2008 saw a major bull market in uranium, with prices moving from $20 per pound to almost $140 per pound. The Global Financial Crisis brought some sense back into the market, because this commodity attracted many players of a speculative nature. Prices post-2008 went back to above pre-crisis levels, to a more reasonable $50 per pound, which presents a potential opportunity for the discriminating investor.

Uranium equities

TIP

Because uranium isn't a widely tradable commodity, the best way to profit from this trend is to invest in companies that specialize in the mining, processing, and distribution of uranium for civilian nuclear purposes. I like the following companies in this sector:

>> **Cameco Corporation (NYSE: CCJ):** Cameco is the marquee name in the uranium mining space. The company operates four uranium mines in the United States and Canada. The company mines uranium and is involved in refining and converting the uranium into fuel that's sold to nuclear power plants to generate electricity.

>> **Strathmore Corporation (Toronto: STM):** Strathmore specializes in the mining of uranium. The company, which trades on the Toronto Stock Exchange, operates in the Athabasca region in Canada, as well as in the United States.

>> **UEX Corporation (Toronto: UEX):** UEX is a Canada-based mining company that specializes in the exploration and mining of uranium in the Athabasca basin. The Athabasca basin in Canada is an important region in global uranium mining that accounts for about 30 percent of total world production. The company is currently still in exploration phases, but it could become a real moneymaker if it comes across large deposits of uranium. The company trades on the Toronto Stock Exchange.

Uranium ETF

In addition to getting direct equity exposure, you can invest in uranium companies with the convenience of an exchange-traded fund (ETF). In 2010, ETF provider Global X Funds out of New York launched the first-ever uranium-based ETF, the Global X Uranium ETF (NYSE: URA).

URA tracks a basket of the most actively traded uranium stocks, as measured by the Solactive Global Uranium Index, its underlying benchmark. As such, URA exposes you to some of the most high-profile names in the industry, including Cameco, Uranium One, Paladin Resources, Denison Mines, and Kalahari Minerals. If you're looking for broad-based exposure to the uranium equity markets, URA is a good choice for your investment objectives. For more information on URA, visit www.globalxetfs.com. Chapter 12 tells you how you can incorporate ETFs into your trading strategy.

Uranium futures

If you have a good grip on futures trading and are looking for a new instrument to add to your portfolio, I'm happy to report that you can invest directly in uranium itself. The CME offers the UxC (CME: UX), the first contract of its kind that gives you direct exposure to this precious resource. For more information on this contract, visit www.cmegroup.com.

Trading futures contracts involves a higher degree of risk due to the use of margin, volatility, and other factors. Make sure that you trade futures contracts only if you already have plenty of experience. For more on trading these instruments, turn to Chapter 13.

For more information on nuclear power, the EIA has an excellent website with all sorts of practical information on this industry at www.eia.gov/energyexplained/nuclear. The UxC is a great resource for everything regarding uranium and nuclear power; its website is at www.uxc.com.

Trading electricity

Benjamin Franklin may not have imagined what his kite experiment would mean for the world, but his experimentation paved the way for developments in electricity, which is now a necessity of modern life. Electricity is also a tradable commodity. In this section, I show you how to make money by investing in electricity.

Brushing up on current affairs

Have you ever wondered where the electricity that allows you to watch TV, use your air conditioner, or power your laptop comes from? Getting electricity to residential, commercial, and industrial consumers is a lengthy process. The electricity is first created in a generator at a power plant and is then sent through transmission lines at high voltages to a substation near consumers. The substation is equipped with a generator that transforms the high-voltage electricity into a low-voltage form, which is then sent to consumers via distribution lines. So how can you profit from it? It's quite simple.

Most of the electricity in the United States is generated through steam turbines. The water used to generate steam is heated to high temperatures using traditional energy sources such as coal, natural gas, and nuclear power, as well as other renewable sources (such as wind and solar).

TECHNICAL STUFF

Electricity is measured in watts, with 1 kilowatt equal to 1,000 watts and a megawatt equal to 1 million watts. In the power industry, watts are expressed in terms of hours of operation, where 1 kilowatt-hour (1 kWh) is 1,000 watts working for a period of 1 hour. Your electricity bill is measured in kilowatt-hours, and 1 kWh is the equivalent of 3,412 Btu. To put it in perspective, the United States consumed a grand total of 3,669 billion kWh of electricity in 2003.

Investing in the power industry

Investing in coal, as well as nuclear power, is one way to invest in electricity. But you can invest directly in the power industry in several other ways as well.

The most direct way of investing in electricity is to buy it. The CME offers a futures contract that tracks the price of electricity as administered by PJM Interconnection. PJM is a regional transmission organization (RTO) that oversees the largest electric grid system in the world and services more than 50 million customers in the United States. It's responsible for generating more than 700 million megawatt-hours of electricity across 55,000 miles of transmission lines. Because of its dominance in the U.S. electricity market, the PJM electricity futures contract on the CME/NYMEX provides you with a widely recognizable and tradable electricity benchmark. For more information on the CME/NYMEX and other commodity exchanges, flip to Chapter 14.

The PJM contract gives you the option of trading both *on-peak* and *off-peak* electricity hours. On-peak times are defined as Monday through Friday between 7 a.m. and 11 p.m., the times when the most electricity is consumed in the United States. Off-peak hours go from midnight to 7 a.m. local time Monday through Friday and include Saturday and Sunday as well. On-peak hours are usually more liquid because that's when most of the electricity is consumed.

TIP

The PJM contract is traded in units of 40 megawatt-hours (mWh) under the ticker symbol JM. For more information on this specific contract, check out the CME website, www.cmegroup.com. To find out more about futures contracts in general, turn to Chapter 13.

REMEMBER

Although most of the market participants in the electricity futures market are local and regional power providers and suppliers, the futures contract lends itself to being traded by individual speculators as well. In recent years, as interest in commodities as an asset class has increased, the number of speculative participants in the electricity market has grown as well.

Another investment option involves electric utilities. *Utilities* are the companies responsible for providing electricity to millions of folks in the United States and around the world. You probably get a letter from them every month, but you may have never given too much thought to the investment opportunities they present.

I like investing in utilities for a number of reasons, particularly for their high dividend payout. The industry has an average 3.5 percent dividend yield, one of the highest of any industry. However, remember when you're investing for dividend income that dividends are subject to market fluctuations. I list in Table 5-3 some utilities to consider, along with their dividend yield.

TABLE 5-3 **Publicly Traded Utilities, 2020 Dividend Yields**

Utility	Ticker	Dividend Yield
Great Plains Energy	NYSE: GXP	3.05%
Consolidated Edison	NYSE: ED	3.73%
Duke Energy Corp.	NYSE: DUK	3.84%
Dominion Resources	NYSE: D	4.04%
Entergy Corp.	NYSE: ETR	3.95%

REMEMBER

Dividends are a taxable source of income. Because of recent tax relief legislation, taxes on income generated through dividends are capped at 15 percent.

TIP

In addition to juicy dividend yields, utilities offer you solid capital appreciation opportunities. Consider these companies when implementing your utility trading strategy:

>> **Consolidated Edison (NYSE: ED):** If you live or have ever lived in New York, you're familiar with ConEd. ConEd is the main utility for New York State and New York City; its main line of business is regulated electric, gas, and steam delivery to wholesale and retail customers. ED provides electricity to more than 4.75 million clients and has a coverage of more than 650 square miles. This company is a good option if you're looking for exposure to the robust East Coast (especially New York) utility market.

>> **Duke Energy Corp. (NYSE: DUK):** Duke Energy is one of the main players in the U.S. utility market. With a staggering 50,000 MW electricity-generating-capacity, it has a footprint that spans the East Coast and the Midwest, and it has a portfolio in Latin America as well. In addition, Duke Energy owns and operates a natural gas–distribution business in Ohio and Kentucky, with an additional portfolio of renewable energy assets. I recommend this company for broad-based utility exposure in the Americas.

Chapter **6**

Investing in Energy Companies

O
ne way to play the energy markets is to invest in the companies involved in the production, transformation, and distribution of the world's most important energy commodities. In this chapter, I look at specialized energy and oil companies that are critical links in the global crude oil supply chain. This chain is long and convoluted, and these industries move in cycles, so identifying who does what allows you to develop a targeted investment strategy.

I show you how to profit from the first step of the oil industry (exploration and production), through the transformational process (refining), and through the delivery system (transportation). Each of the companies operating in these segments of the market offers unique investment opportunities.

Bull's-Eye! Profiting from Oil Exploration and Production

The exploration and discovery of oil is a lucrative segment in the oil business. So, how you can you strike it rich by discovering oil? Fortunately, you don't have to roll up your sleeves and go prospecting for oil in the Texas heartland. You can invest in companies that specialize in the exploration and production of oil fields, known in the business as E&P.

Oil wells are found in two places: on land and at sea. In recent years, offshore drilling has generated a lot of interest among investors, and a flurry of activity has been taking place in this sector because oil on land is becoming scarcer. In this section, I introduce you to some of the companies involved in this exciting segment of the market.

Going offshore

The offshore drilling business is a technology-heavy industry, and you want to be familiar with some of the associated terminology to make the most of your investments.

Because offshore drilling activity may take place in unforgiving locations, companies have to deploy specific vessels for specific drilling projects. These vessels are among the most technologically advanced structures created by humans. Some vessels are designed to withstand harsh winds and high waves. Others are more suited for shallow-water exploratory projects and need to move from location to location quickly.

Here are the names of some of the vessels you may come across as you start investing in offshore drilling companies:

>> **Drilling barge:** The drilling barge is one of the nimblest vessels in the market. It's a floating device usually towed by tugboat to target drilling locations. The drilling barge is primarily used inland, in still, shallow waters such as rivers, lakes, and swamps.

>> **Jack-up rig:** The jack-up rig is a hybrid vessel that's part floating barge, part drilling platform. The jack-up rig is towed to the desired location, usually in open, shallow waters

where its three "legs" are lowered and "jacked" down to the seafloor. When the legs are secured, the drilling platform is elevated to the desired levels to enable safe drilling.

>> **Submersible rig:** The submersible rig is similar to the jack-up rig in that it's primarily used for shallow-water drilling activity and is secured to the seabed.

>> **Semisubmersible rig:** Sometimes referred to as a *semi*, this structure is a feat of modern technological development. It's similar to a submersible except that it has the capacity to drill in deep waters under harsh and unforgiving weather conditions. The drilling platform is elevated and sits atop a floating structure that's semi-submerged in the water (hence, the name) and secured by large anchors that can weigh up to 10 tons each.

>> **Drill ship:** The drill ship is essentially a ship with a drilling platform. It's perhaps the most versatile drilling vessel because it can be easily dispatched to remote offshore locations, including drilling in deep waters.

>> **Offshore oil platform:** When one of the previous vessels discovers a commercially viable offshore oil field, a company may decide to build a permanent platform to exploit this discovery. Enter the offshore oil platform. These structures are a sight to behold and are truly man-made floating cities. They house personnel, include living quarters, and are often even equipped with heliports. They're ideally suited to harsh, deepwater conditions.

TIP

You can get information on an offshore drilling company's fleet in its annual report. Companies usually lease these vessels to customers — which may include independent oil and gas companies, national oil companies, and the major integrated oil companies — for a premium.

Some of the leading companies in the offshore drilling business include the following:

>> **Diamond Offshore Drilling (NYSE: DO):** With 15 offshore rigs, Diamond Offshore is one of the dominant players in the offshore drilling industry. Headquartered in Houston, Texas, DO has a wide global footprint, with deepwater drilling operations in Brazil, Scotland, Australia, and the Gulf of Mexico. The company has particular expertise in

ultra-deepwater drilling, with significant operations in Brazil through Petrobras, the state-owned oil company.

As easily accessible oil becomes scarcer, I expect national oil companies and the majors to make more use of DO's deepwater expertise.

>> **Noble Corporation (NYSE: NE):** Founded in 1921 in Texas, Noble is one of the oldest drilling contractors in the world. It has a fleet of more than 19 vessels and operations stretching from Brazil to the North Sea, and it has an edge in implementing technologically oriented solutions to meet customer demands.

>> **Transocean, Inc. (NYSE: RIG):** Transocean, whose company motto is "We're never out of our depth," is the ExxonMobil of the offshore drillers. It's the largest company in terms of market capitalization and the size and scope of its operations. The company has more than 37 offshore drilling units at its disposal and is an expert in operating under harsh and extreme weather conditions. It has offshore operations in the U.S. Gulf of Mexico, Brazil, South Africa, the Mediterranean Sea, the North Sea, Australia, and Southeast Asia. If you're looking for the largest and most diversified company in the group, Transocean is it.

If you want to dig deeper into this sector, you can check out www.rigzone.com, which includes up-to-date information on the offshore industry and the oil industry as a whole.

TIP

Staying on dry land

A large part of E&P activity takes place on dry land. Actually, the first commercially viable oil wells were discovered on land. Most industry insiders agree that the majority of onshore oil wells have been discovered, but you can still benefit by investing in companies that are involved in the exploitation and production of onshore oil fields.

You may consider investing in a couple of companies in this segment of the drilling market:

>> **Nabors Industries (NYSE: NBR):** Nabors is one of the largest land-drilling contractors in the world. It has a division that can perform heavy-duty and horizontal drilling activities.

>> **Patterson-UTI Energy Inc. (Nasdaq: PTEN):** Patterson-UTI is an onshore oil field drilling contractor that has extensive operations in North America. It operates in a number of segments, including drilling new wells and servicing and maintaining existing oil wells. It's part of the S&P MidCap 400 stocks.

Servicing the oil fields

Another area I recommend taking a close look at is companies that focus on oil field maintenance and services. The oil field services sector is dominated by technology-oriented and labor-intensive companies that seek to maximize an oil field's output by using sophisticated technological techniques, such as horizontal drilling and 3D mapping and imaging.

The major integrated oil companies or national oil companies generally hire oil field services companies for general oil field and oil well maintenance and extraction solutions. For example, Saudi Aramco, the largest oil company in the world in terms of proven reserves, may turn to an oil field services company for the maintenance of a particular oil field. The services company may get involved in actually extracting crude from the oil well, providing data and statistics on current and past usage and on potential future output, using technologically oriented techniques to extract hard-to-recover oil, and performing other specific and general oil field–management services.

REMEMBER

The added value of the oil field services companies is that they can improve oil recovery rates on existing fields and recover previously untapped oil pockets in old fields. As fewer oil fields are discovered, the world's major oil companies are looking for ways to maximize existing oil fields. Therefore, the role of the oil field services companies will become increasingly important in the future.

These companies make up your hit list if you're looking to invest in the oil field services space:

>> **Baker Hughes, Inc. (NYSE: BHI):** As with most oil field services companies, Baker Hughes is headquartered in Houston, Texas. The company operates both in the United States and internationally, with operations stretching from

the Persian Gulf to West Africa. Baker Hughes provides technologically oriented solutions to its customers to maximize oil field output efficiency. Baker Hughes isn't the biggest company in the group, but it's certainly a nimble competitor.

>> **Halliburton Co. (NYSE: HAL):** This company makes a lot of headlines (sometimes not very positive ones) because of the political nature of its work with the U.S. government and military. Besides its governmental contracts, the company is a leader in oil and gas field maintenance. It helps customers extract as much energy from existing wells as possible, while maintaining low costs. This makes Halliburton a knowledge-able company in the petroleum services sector.

Because of the nature of its political contracts, Halliburton is often a lightning rod for criticism. I recommend going beyond some of this criticism and directly analyzing the company's balance sheet, income statement, and other metrics to get a more accurate sense of the company's scope of operations. Although some of its work is political in nature (government contracts), that work represents only a fraction of its operational activities. More important, although Halliburton is the most notorious of the oil field services companies, it's certainly not representative of the other companies in the field. Many of the other players in this space focus exclusively on oil field maintenance and services and aren't involved in work of a political nature.

>> **Schlumberger Ltd. (NYSE: SLB):** Schlumberger may not be a household name, but it's well known and well regarded in the oil industry. The company is one of the most technologi-cally savvy services companies out there and can provide solutions regarding all aspects of oil field–management services, from exploration and extraction to maintenance and abandonment. It provides evaluations to help customers identify the short-term and long-term viability of an oil field and specializes in maximizing oil field output through technologically advanced solutions.

TIP

For more information on the oil field services sector and all the companies involved in it, I recommend checking out https:// finance.yahoo.com/industry/oil_gas_equipment_services.

Investing in Refineries

Crude oil by itself doesn't have many useful applications. It needs to be refined into consumable products such as gasoline and jet fuel. Refineries are a critical link in the crude oil supply chain because, after crude oil is discovered, that oil needs to be transformed into products before it's sent to consumers.

This list details some of the products that refineries derive from refining crude oil:

> > Asphalt

> > Automotive lubricating oil

> > Diesel fuel

> > Gasoline

> > Heating oil (commercial and residential)

> > Jet fuel (military and commercial aviation)

> > Kerosene

> > Petrochemicals

> > Propane

REMEMBER

Given the importance of these derivative products, you can imagine that you can make a lot of money investing in refineries. But before I give you a few company options, you need to look at three criteria when considering investing in companies that operate refineries:

> > **Refinery throughput:** The capacity for refining crude oil over a given period of time, usually expressed in barrels

> > **Refinery production:** Actual production of crude oil products, such as gasoline and heating oil

> > **Refinery utilization:** The difference between production capacity, the throughput, and what's actually produced

You can find this information in a company's annual or quarterly reports.

TIP

The largest refinery in the United States is located in Baytown, Texas, and is operated by ExxonMobil. It has a refining capacity of 626,000 barrels per day. Most major integrated oil companies have a large refining capacity. These include some of the majors, like ExxonMobil and BP. One way to get exposure to the refining space is to invest in these major companies. I discuss the majors, their scope of activity, and how to invest in them in Chapter 3.

Another, more direct, way to profit from refining activity is to invest in independent refineries. The marquee name in this area is a company called the Valero Energy Corporation (NYSE: VLO). Valero is the largest independent refining company in North America. It has a throughput capacity of 3.2 million barrels per day and operates the largest number of refineries in North America.

TIP

If you want to play the refinery card, Valero gives you one of the most direct ways to do so. The major integrated companies are a good play, but they're so big that you don't get the same kind of direct exposure you do from Valero.

Although Valero is the goliath in the refinery space, a number of smaller companies can offer you a lot of value. Take a look at a couple of these companies:

» **Sunoco, Inc. (NYSE: SUN):** Sunoco is the second-largest refiner in terms of total refinery throughput. It refines approximately 1 million barrels of crude oil per day into refined products, which it distributes primarily in the eastern United States.

   Sunoco, with headquarters in Philadelphia, operates refineries in Pennsylvania, Ohio, and New Jersey and has a wide distribution network across the East Coast.

» **Tesoro Corp. (NYSE: TSO):** Tesoro, headquartered in San Antonio, Texas, is one of the leading refiners in the midcontinental and western United States. Its refineries transform crude oil into gasoline that's distributed through a network of about 500 retail outlets in the western United States. It operates refineries in Utah, California, Washington, Alaska, and even Hawaii. This option is a good regional play. Tesoro has been acquired by Marathon and is a fully integrated subsidiary within the group.

Refiners operate in an extremely cyclical industry, which poses an inherent investment risk that favors only the savviest operators. An additional risk involves the very business model that refiners rely on. Independent refiners must purchase the raw material (crude oil) at market prices and resell the finished product (gasoline, heating oil, and so on) at market prices. However, many majors also operate internal refineries that compete aggressively with the independents; whereas the independents must purchase the raw material at market prices, however, internal refineries often get oil at subsidized prices. This market dynamic makes it extremely difficult for independents to compete on an equal footing with the majors. Keep this in mind as you're analyzing independent refiners.

The U.S. Energy Information Administration (EIA) compiles data on all U.S. refineries at www.eia.gov/energyexplained/oil-and-petroleum-products/refining-crude-oil-refinery-rankings.php.

Becoming an Oil Shipping Magnate

Commodities such as oil and gas would be useless if there were no way of transporting them to consumers. In fact, transporting commodities to consumers is probably as important as finding and processing them in the first place. Fortunately, as an investor, this need gives you fertile ground to make money in the transportation of commodities.

This statistic can put things in perspective for you: Two out of every three barrels of oil that are transported are moved around in ships. The remaining one-third is transported via pipelines. (For more on how to invest in pipeline infrastructure, consider master limited partnerships, which I discuss in Chapter 14.) Therefore, the shipping industry plays a crucial role in the integrated oil business.

In this section, I give you tools to help you invest in the oil-shipping business. I introduce you to the types of vessels that make up a modern oil tanker fleet, point out some of the major companies involved in the business, and offer you advice on pinpointing the right entry and exit points.

Transportation supply and demand

One of the most common questions I'm asked about the oil-shipping industry is the following: What's the relationship between the price of crude oil and oil tanker profit margins? As with many good questions, this one has no straight answer. It depends on a lot of factors.

Tanker spot rates — the bread and butter of the shipping industry — are determined by supply and demand. The supply side, in this case, consists of how many ships are available to transport crude and products to the desired destinations around the world. On the demand side is how much crude oil and products need to be shipped from point A to point B. In the global shipping business, these factors are the two you need to watch closely.

For example, recently tanker spot rates have experienced some supply-side pressure. Because of a series of environmental incidents, in 1997 the International Maritime Organization (www.imo.org), the global regulatory body of the shipping industry, ordered the phasing out of all single-hull ships to help prevent further oil spills.

Because of this regulation, the number of ships in the open sea transporting oil and products has decreased. A supply-side crunch arose, contributing to the increase in tanker spot rates from 2002 to 2004, the largest run-up in tanker spot rates during that period.

On the demand side of the equation, demand for crude oil and products worldwide remains robust. In 2010, the world consumed on average 87 million barrels of oil *per day*, and that number is growing. In 2021, world consumption increased to 96 million barrels per day.

TIP

Another important demand factor that many industry onlookers sometimes overlook is *oil import dependency*. Crude oil demand is critical, but if oil could be produced and consumed without the need to transport it across long distances on seaborne voyages, the oil-shipping industry would be out of business. The lifeblood of the global oil tanker business is the international flow of oil across countries and continents, or the dependence on oil imports. One key metric to help you gauge the level of activity in this area is global import and export data, which the EIA's energy statistics division monitors. Its website is www.eia.gov/petroleum.

As long as the supply of ships remains tight and the demand for crude oil seaborne transportation remains high, tanker spot rates will stay elevated. Now, to the extent that crude oil prices affect the demand of crude oil worldwide, crude oil prices will have an effect on tanker spot rates. Specifically, if crude oil prices go so high that folks are no longer willing to buy crude, thus causing demand destruction, the demand for shipping crude oil worldwide will also decrease (this is the notion of *elasticity*, which I cover in Chapter 2), causing tanker spot rates to go down as well. However, this rate drop is an indirect effect of rising oil prices, which is why the relationship between crude oil prices and tanker spot rates isn't easily quantifiable. Too many variables are at play.

At the end of the day, as long as there's a demand for crude to be transported from producers to consumers, you can rest assured that oil shippers will remain in business.

Crude oil ships ahoy!

One factor you need to consider as you're planning investments in the oil-shipping industry is the ships themselves. Before you invest in a tanker stock, closely examine the fleet of vessels it operates.

To help you with this examination, here are some of the types of vessels used in the global crude oil–shipping industry:

>> **Ultra-large crude carrier (ULCC):** This type of vessel is the largest vessel in the market. Used for long-haul voyages, it offers economies of scale because it can carry large amounts of oil across long distances.

>> **Very large crude carrier (VLCC):** The VLCC is the vessel of choice for long-distance seaborne voyages. It's ideally suited for intercontinental maritime transportation. Its areas of operation include the Persian Gulf to East Asia and West Africa to the United States, among other routes.

>> **Suezmax:** This vessel is named thus because its design and size allow it to transit through the Suez Canal, in Egypt. The Suezmax is among the vessels used to transport oil from the Persian Gulf to Europe, as well as to other destinations. It's ideally suited for medium-haul voyages.

>> **Aframax:** The Aframax, whose first four letters are an acronym for *average freight rate assessment,* is considered the workhorse in the tanker fleet. Because of its smaller size, it is ideally suited for short-haul voyages and can transport crude and products to most ports around the world.

>> **Panamax:** Like the Suezmax, the Panamax gets its name from its ability to transit through a canal — in this case, the Panama Canal. This vessel is sometimes used for short-haul voyages between the ports in the Caribbean, Europe, and the United States.

Besides their catchy names, these vessels are identified by how much crude oil and products they can transport on sea. The unit of measurement used to capture this capacity is known as the *dead weight ton* (DWT). DWT measures the weight of the vessel, including all cargo it's carrying. Most ships are constructed in such a way that 1 DWT is the equivalent of 6.7 barrels of oil.

Table 6-1 lists the DWT capacity of the vessels described previously, along with their equivalent in barrels of oil.

TABLE 6-1 **Vessel Capacity in DWT and Oil Equivalents**

Vessel Type	Dead Weight Tons	Oil Equivalent (Barrels)
ULCC	320,000 and up	2+ million
VLCC	200,000–320,000	2 million
Suezmax	120,000–200,000	1 million
Aframax	80,000–120,000	600,000
Panamax	50,000–80,000	300,000

Petroleum shipping companies

The companies responsible for transporting crude oil and petroleum products are an essential link in the global energy supply chain. This group is a diverse bunch, and each company provides a necessary and important service to this crucial industry. Some companies concentrate their operations regionally, such as in the Gulf of Mexico or the Persian Gulf. Others have extensive transportation capabilities with operations in all four corners of the globe. Some operate a small group of VLCC vessels, whereas others operate a large number of smaller vessels. Still others specialize in shipping only crude oil, and others focus on petroleum products such as gasoline.

With so many options to choose from, trying to identify which company to invest in can be confusing. In this section, I list all the major publicly traded oil-shipping companies, and I go through their operations and scope of activities so you can decide which one is right for your investment needs.

>> **Frontline Ltd. (NYSE: FRO):** Founded in 1948, Frontline is one of the oldest shipping companies in the world. It also operates one of the world's largest fleets of VLCC vessels, with more than 29 VLCCs. Frontline also owns more than 23 Suezmax vessels, making it one of the largest tanker companies in the world in terms of transportation capacity. Cumulatively, Frontline has the capacity of 18 million DWT. With operations in the Persian Gulf, Europe, the United States, and Asia, Frontline runs a tight ship, indeed!

>> **General Maritime Corp. (NYSE: GMR):** General Maritime focuses on the small and midsize segment of the tanker market. It operates a fleet of Suezmax and Aframax vessels, with operations primarily focused in the Atlantic basin. General Maritime links producers and consumers from Western Africa, the North Sea, the Caribbean, the United States, and Europe. If you're looking for exposure to the transatlantic oil seaborne trade, GMR is a good bet. The fact that GMR offers a $5 dividend per share also makes this an attractive tanker stock.

>> **Overseas Shipholding Group, Inc. (NYSE: OSG):** Unlike many of its competitors, which are incorporated in offshore locations such as Bermuda and the Bahamas, OSG is headquartered in New York City. Although it has an international presence, it's the only company with a large presence in the American shipping market. Its U.S. vessels are mainly engaged in transporting crude oil from Alaska to the continental United States, and products from the Gulf of Mexico to the East Coast. If you're interested in the domestic crude oil transportation market, take the plunge with OSG.

>> **Teekay Tankers (NYSE: TNK):** Teekay Shipping is one of the world's largest seaborne transporters of crude oil and crude oil products. It operates a fleet of more than 130 vessels,

including one VLCC that transports crude from the Persian Gulf and West Africa to Europe, the United States, and Asia; about 15 Suezmax vessels that connect producers in North Africa (Algeria) and West Africa to consumers in Europe and the United States; and more than 40 Aframax vessels that operate in the North Sea, the Black Sea, the Mediterranean Sea, and the Caribbean.

In addition to conventional tankers, Teekay operates a fleet of offshore tankers that are constructed to transport crude from offshore locations to onshore facilities. If you're interested in a truly global and diversified oil-shipping company, you can't go wrong with Teekay Shipping.

TIP

I give you here a snapshot of global tanker activities. If you do decide to invest in the global oil-shipping business, I recommend digging deeper into a target company's operations. You can find most of the information you need in a company's annual report (Form 10-K) or quarterly report (Form 10-Q). You can obtain additional information through third parties, such as analyst reports.

One of the best-kept secrets in this industry is the high dividend payout these companies issue. I'm a huge fan of dividends because they provide you with certainty in an uncertain investment world. And oil tanker stocks offer some of the highest dividend payouts out there. Table 6-2 gives you a group of shipping company stocks that offer some remarkable dividend payouts.

TABLE 6-2 **Oil Tanker Stocks, 2020 Dividend Yields**

Company	Ticker Symbol	Dividend Yield
Frontline	NYSE: FRO	8%
Knightsbridge Tankers	Nasdaq: NVLCCF	9%
Nordic American Tankers	NYSE: NAT	9.5%

TIP

Calculating dividend payouts can be tricky because a company isn't obligated to give back money to shareholders in the form of dividends. Some companies pay out high dividends one year but not the next; for others, paying dividends may be only a one-time event. One way to determine future dividend payouts is to examine the company's dividend payout history. Any good stock screener should have this information handy. I find that the Yahoo! Finance website (https://finance.yahoo.com) does the job.

Avoiding industry risk

As with most aspects of commodities, tanker spot rates and fixed rates, which provide the bulk of a shipping company's revenue stream, are highly cyclical. It's not extraordinary for shipping rates to fluctuate by 60 percent or 70 percent on a daily basis. Take a look at the tanker spot rate volatility.

So, how do you protect yourself from these extreme price volatilities? One way to hedge your positions is to invest in one of the large oil tanker stocks I mention in the preceding section. These companies have been in business a long time and have substantial experience managing these price swings.

Another factor to consider is global economic growth. The oil-shipping industry depends on a strong global economy with a healthy appetite for crude oil and crude oil products. If the global economy is thrown into a recession, you can expect the tanker stocks to take a hit. With everything else equal, if the world demand for oil products slows down, I recommend getting out of these tanker stocks.

TIP

If you're a more adventurous investor, you always have the option to short the stock of companies you know aren't going to do well. You can short a company's stock through various means, such as buying a put option or even selling a call option. I discuss short selling in Chapter 13.

The New Kids on the Block: EV Transportation Companies

One of the biggest developments in the industry in the last decade or so has been the advent of electric vehicles (EVs) in transportation. EVs have staked their claim as both new energy companies and transportation companies. Unlike traditional cars, EVs generate their power through an electric chargeable battery as opposed to the burning of fossil fuels.

The entrepreneur Elon Musk played a leading role in the development of EVs in 2008 by launching and spearheading the development of Tesla Motors (Nasdaq: TSLA). Tesla has become a dominant player in the manufacture and distribution of not only cars, but SUVs and trucks. Over the lifetime of these vehicles, they do reduce more emissions than traditional gas-powered vehicles. Expect to see a lot more of these vehicles on the road, and keep an eye out on this industry, as it will surely keep making headway. In Table 6-3, I list some EV companies to keep an eye on.

TABLE 6-3 ## Electric Vehicle (EV) Companies

Company	Ticker
Tesla Motors, Inc.	Nasdaq: TSLA
Rivian Automotive, Inc.	Nasdaq: RIVN
Lucid Group, Inc.	Nasdaq: LCID

3

Investing in Metals and Agricultural Products

Invest in gold, silver, and platinum.

Make money in steel, aluminum, copper, palladium, zinc, and nickel.

Check out mining companies and conglomerates and investigate their investment suitability.

Invest in coffee, cocoa, sugar, orange juice, corn, wheat, soybeans, cattle, hogs, and, last but not least, good ol' pork bellies.

Chapter **7**

All That Glitters: Investing in Gold, Silver, and Platinum

Metallurgy and civilization go hand in hand. The human ability to control metals has enabled the development of modern society and civilization. As a matter of fact, human prehistory is classified by using a three-age system based on the human ability to control metals: the Stone Age, the Bronze Age, and the Iron Age. Societies that have mastered the use of metals in weaponry and toolmaking have been able to thrive and survive. Societies without this ability have faced extinction.

Similarly, investors who have been able to master the fundamentals of the metals markets have been handsomely rewarded. In this chapter, I introduce you to the fascinating world of precious metals, which includes gold, silver, and platinum. These metals can play a role in your portfolio because of their precious-metal status, their ability to act as a store of value, and their potential to provide a hedge against inflation. Here, you discover all you need to know to incorporate precious metals into your portfolio.

REMEMBER

As a rule, metals are classified into two broad categories: *precious metals* and *base metals*. This classification is based on a metal's resistance to corrosion and oxidation. Precious metals have a high resistance to corrosion, whereas base metals (which I cover in Chapter 8) have a lower tolerance.

REMEMBER

Investing in companies that mine precious metals — or any other commodity, for that matter — doesn't give you direct exposure to the price fluctuations of that commodity. You need to be familiar with the fluctuations and patterns of the equity markets to profit from this investment methodology. You also need to consider any external factors that impact the performance of the company, such as management effectiveness, total debt levels, areas of operation, and other metrics that are specific to companies. That said, investing in the equity markets still gives you access to the commodities markets.

Going for the Gold

Perhaps no other metal — or commodity — in the world has the cachet and prestige of gold. For centuries, gold has been coveted and valued for its unique metallurgical characteristics. It was such a desirable commodity that it developed monetary applications, and a number of currencies were based on its value. In 1944, for example, 44 of the world's richest countries (including the United States) decided to peg their currencies to the yellow metal, in what is known as the Bretton Woods Agreement. Although former President Nixon removed the dollar from the gold standard in 1971, many countries still use gold as a global currency benchmark.

In addition, gold has applications in industry and jewelry that have resulted in increased demand for this precious metal. When I wrote the first edition of *Commodities For Dummies* in 2006, I strongly urged investors to invest in gold for the long term. Back when I first made this recommendation, gold was trading in the range of $500 per ounce; the gold price at the end of 2010 was $1,450 per ounce. Investors who acted on my recommendation would now be up approximately 300 percent at a time of increased volatility and reduced returns in the global market indexes. If you kept your investment when I wrote the second edition in 2011, you would've seen an additional $320 price increase in today's prices.

TIP

My outlook for gold during the next five years remains positive. Overall, I believe demand for gold will continue to increase, especially as a store of value, driven in part by the weakening paper currency environment that's a result of expansionary monetary policy in the Organization for Economic Co-operation and Development (OECD) countries. As paper currencies come under increased pressure, expect demand for gold to increase. Of course, no investment goes up in a straight line, so expect a bumpy ride and some periods of big pullbacks along the way.

Getting to know the gold standard

The increased demand for gold is linked to several factors. To profit from this increased demand, you need to be familiar with the fundamentals of the gold market.

First, you need to know what gold is used for. You may not be surprised to hear that jewelry accounts for a large portion of gold demand. However, did you know that dentistry also represents a significant portion of the gold market? Take a look at some of the uses of gold:

>> **Dentistry:** Because gold resists corrosion, it has wide application in dentistry. It's alloyed with other metals, such as silver, copper, and platinum, to create dental fixtures.

>> **Electronics:** Because of its ability to efficiently conduct electricity, gold is a popular metal in electronics. It's used as a semiconductor in circuit boards and integrated boards in everything from cellphones and TVs to missiles.

>> **Jewelry:** Since humans first discovered it thousands of years ago, gold has been used as an ornament and in jewelry. Today jewelry is the most important consumer use of gold in the world, accounting for more than 70 percent of total consumption.

>> **Monetary:** Many central banks hold reserves of gold. In addition, gold is one of the only commodities that's held in its physical form for investment purposes by the investing public (see the later section "Let's get physical" for more information). Another monetary use of gold, aside from central bank reserves and investor portfolios, is the use of gold in coinage. In countries such as Canada and South Africa, some gold coins are legal tender.

Many countries and banks hold reserve assets of gold. Over the past decade, the countries that have significantly boosted their gold reserves are China and India, each of which added more than 100 tons of gold to their reserves. During the same period, we've seen very little change in the top ten holders. I list in Table 7-1 the top ten holders of gold around the world.

TABLE 7-1 **World Gold Holdings in Tons, 2021**

Country/Entity	Reserves (Tons)
United States	8,133
Germany	3,359
International Monetary Fund	2,814
Italy	2,450
France	2,435
China	1,950
Switzerland	1,040
Japan	846
India	754
Netherlands	612

Source: Data from World Gold Council

What makes gold valuable

REMEMBER

Why is gold such an important metal? These traits can help you understand where gold derives its value:

>> **Ductility:** Gold is a very ductile metal. In metallurgy, *ductility* measures how much a metal can be drawn out into a wire. For example, 1 ounce of gold can be converted into more than 50 miles of gold wire! This gold wire can then be applied in electronics and used as an electric conductor.

>> **Malleability:** Pure gold (24 karat) is a very malleable metal and is prized by craftspeople around the world who shape it into jewelry and other objects of beauty. One ounce of gold can be transformed into more than 96 square feet of gold sheet.

>> **Quasi-indestructibility:** Gold has high resistance levels and doesn't easily corrode. Corrosive agents such as oxygen and heat have almost no effect on gold, which can retain its luster over thousands of years. The only chemical that can affect gold is cyanide, which dissolves gold.

>> **Rarity:** Gold is one of the rarest natural resources on earth. Most people don't realize this, but only about 150,000 tons of gold have ever been produced since humans first began mining it more than 6,000 years ago. To give you an idea of how little that is, all the gold in the world wouldn't even fill up four Olympic-size swimming pools! And because most gold is recycled and never destroyed, a majority of gold is still in use today. About 15 percent of gold is recycled every year.

How to measure gold

Gold, like most metals, is measured and weighed in *troy ounces*. One troy ounce is the equivalent of 31.1 grams. When you buy gold for investment purposes, such as through an exchange-traded fund (ETF) or gold certificates, troy ounce is the measurement of choice.

REMEMBER

When you want to refer to large quantities of gold, such as the amount of gold a bank holds in reserves or the amount of gold produced in a mine, the unit of measurement you use is *metric tons*. One metric ton is equal to 32,150 troy ounces.

If you've bought gold jewelry, you may have come across the following measurement: karats. *Karats* (sometimes spelled *carats*) measure the purity of gold. The purest form of gold is 24-karat gold (24K). Everything below that number denotes that the gold is alloyed, or mixed, with another metal. Table 7-2 shows what the different numbers of karats translate to in terms of gold's purity.

TIP

If you buy physical gold for either adornment (jewelry) or investment (gold coins/bars), you want to get the purest form of gold, 24K. If you can't get 24K gold, aim to get the purest form of gold you can get your hands on. Note that the purer the gold, the higher its value. Pure gold (24K) is always yellow in color. However, you've probably encountered white gold or even red gold — these other colors are created by alloying gold with metals such as nickel or palladium for a white color or with copper to create red gold. By definition, white and red gold aren't pure gold.

TABLE 7-2 **Purity of Gold, Measured in Karats**

Karats	Purity
24K	100%
22K	91.67%
18K	75%
14K	58.3%
10K	41.67%
9K	37.5%

TECHNICAL STUFF

Whereas purity measures how precious gold is in a percentage basis, *fineness* measures gold's purity expressed as a whole number. Fortunately, fineness and purity are so similar that gold with 91.67 percent purity has a fineness of 0.9167.

Finding ways to invest in gold

In this section, I introduce you to the different ways you can invest in gold: physical gold, gold ETFs, gold-mining companies, and gold futures contracts.

Let's get physical

Gold is unlike any other commodity because it's one of the few that can be physically stored to have its value preserved or increased over periods of time. One investment method unique to gold is to actually buy it — hard, physical gold. You can purchase gold bars, bullion, and coins and store them in a safe location as an investment. Perhaps no other commodity offers you this unique opportunity. (Storing physical coal or uranium for investment purposes just doesn't work, believe me!) In some countries, folks actually buy gold jewelry for the dual purpose of adornment and investment.

You can get your hands on these different forms of gold:

>> **Gold bars:** Gold bars have an undeniable allure. In pop culture, for example, gold is usually depicted as large gold bars. Much more than great movie props, gold bars are a great investment. Whereas gold coins are more suited for

smaller purchases, gold bars are ideal if you're interested in purchasing larger quantities of gold. Despite popular depictions, gold bars come in all shapes and sizes. They can be as small as 1 gram or as large as 400 troy ounces. Despite the size, most gold bars are high quality, with a fineness of 0.999 and above (24K).

For a comprehensive listing of gold bars, I recommend *The Industry Catalogue of Gold Bars Worldwide,* which you can find at https://goldbarsworldwide.com. Perhaps the only drawback of gold bars is their size, which makes them harder and more expensive to store. *Note:* Gold *bullion* is nothing more than large gold bars.

>> **Gold certificates:** Gold certificates are hybrid instruments that allow you to own physical gold without actually taking possession of it. As the name implies, gold certificates certify that you own a certain amount of gold, which is usually stored in a safe location by the authority that issues the gold certificates. Owning gold certificates is my favorite way of owning physical gold because they're safe and easy to store. When you own gold bars or coins, safety is always a concern — someone could literally steal your gold. Storage is another concern, particularly if you have large quantities of the stuff, because it can end up costing you a lot to store your gold in a bank vault or personal safe. The gold standard of gold certificates is the Perth Mint Certificate Program (PMCP).

The Perth Mint, Australia's oldest and most important mint, administers the PMCP. At one point, the Perth Mint had as much gold as Fort Knox. The PMCP is the only certificate program that a government guarantees — in this case, the government of Western Australia. The PMCP issues you a certificate and stores your gold in a secure government vault. You may retrieve or sell your gold at any point. For more on this program, check out the Perth Mint's website at www.perthmint.com.

>> **Gold coins:** One of the easiest ways to invest in physical gold is to buy gold coins. I like gold coins because they give you a lot of bang for your buck. Unlike large gold bars, gold coins allow you to purchase the yellow metal in smaller quantities and units. This flexibility offers two advantages:

- You don't have to put up as much money to buy a gold coin as you do to buy a gold bar.

- If you want to sell part of your gold holdings, you can easily sell five gold coins and keep five — that's not possible when you have only one gold bar.

Another reason I like gold coins is that you can easily and safely store them; they're more discrete than having large gold bullion. I also like gold coins because they're issued by a federal government and instantly recognized as such; in some countries (Canada and South Africa), they're even considered legal tender.

Here are the most popular types of gold coins, by country of issuance:

- **Gold eagle:** The U.S. government issues the gold eagle coin; it has the full backing of Congress and the U.S. Mint. It comes in various sizes, including 1 ounce, ½ ounce, ¼ ounce, and ¹⁄₁₀ ounce. At 22K, the gold eagle coin is a high-quality coin that you can use to fund an individual retirement account (IRA).

- **Gold Krugerrand:** The gold Krugerrand is issued by the South African government and is one of the oldest gold coins issued in the world. It has a fineness of 0.916.

- **Gold maple leaf:** You guessed it — the Canadian government backs the gold maple leaf. The Royal Canadian Mint issues it, and at 24K, it's the purest gold coin on the market.

TIP

If you want to purchase gold coins, bars, or even certificates, you need to go through a gold dealer. One gold dealer I recommend is Kitco (www.kitco.com). Before you do business with any gold dealer, though, find out as much information about the business (and business history) as possible. You can check out different gold dealers by consulting the Better Business Bureau at www.bbb.org.

Gold ETFs

ETFs that offer exposure to commodities are a popular investment gateway for folks who don't want to mess around with futures contracts. Signaling gold's importance, one of the first commodity ETFs to hit the market, is, you guessed it, a gold ETF.

I recommend these two gold ETFs:

>> **iShares COMEX Gold Trust (AMEX: IAU):** The iShares gold ETF holds a little more than 1.3 million ounces of gold in its vaults. The per-unit price of the ETF seeks to reflect the current market price in the spot market of the ETF gold.

>> **StreetTracks Gold Shares (NYSE: GLD):** The StreetTracks gold ETF is the largest gold ETF on the market today. Launched in late 2004, it holds about 12 million ounces of physical gold in secured locations. The price per ETF unit is calculated based on the average of the bid/ask spread in the gold spot market. This fund is a good way to get exposure to physical gold without owning it.

TIP

These ETFs must pay several entities to actually hold physical gold, so inquire about any storage fees. These fees are in addition to the general fund expenses, such as registration and administration fees. Carefully consider all expenses and fees because they have a direct impact on your bottom line. (For more on ETFs, turn to Chapter 12.)

TIP

Because both the StreetTracks and the iShares ETFs track the price of gold on the spot market, their performance is remarkably similar — at times, it's actually identical. Therefore, if you can't decide between the two, I recommend StreetTracks because it holds more physical gold and, more important, offers you more liquidity than the iShares ETF.

Stocks in gold companies

Another way to get exposure to gold is to invest in gold-mining companies. Numerous companies specialize in mining, processing, and distributing this precious metal. I recommend these companies:

>> **AngloGold Ashanti Ltd. (NYSE: AU):** AngloGold, which is listed in five stock exchanges around the world, is a truly global gold company. Based in South Africa, it operates more than 20 mines and has significant operations in Africa and South America, particularly in South Africa, Namibia, Tanzania, Ghana, Mali, Brazil, Argentina, and Peru, which have major gold deposits. It has additional operations in

Australia and North America. AngloGold is a wholly owned subsidiary of Anglo-American, the global mining giant (which I cover in Chapter 9).

>> **Barrick Gold Corporation (NYSE: ABX):** Barrick is a Canadian company with headquarters in Toronto. It's a premier player in the gold-mining industry and has operations in Argentina, Australia, Canada, Chile, Papua New Guinea, Peru, South Africa, Tanzania, and the United States. It also has a foothold in the potentially lucrative Central Asian market, where it has joint operations in Mongolia, Russia, and Turkey. Another reason I like Barrick is that it has one of the lowest production costs per ounce of gold in the industry.

>> **New Gold, Inc. (AMEX: NGD):** New Gold is a junior gold-mining company headquartered in Vancouver, British Columbia. It was founded in 2005 and currently operates three highly profitable mines in California, Mexico, and Australia; the cash costs per ounce for each of these mines are in the industry lows, translating into high margins. In addition, NGD is in the process of exploiting mines in Canada and Chile, two mining-friendly jurisdictions. The management team's successful track record in making acquisitions and operating mines makes this an indispensable investment for anyone looking for exposure to gold markets.

>> **Newmont Mining Corporation (NYSE: NEM):** Newmont, headquartered in Colorado, is one of the largest gold-mining companies in the world. It has operations in Australia, Bolivia, Canada, Indonesia, Peru, the United States (Nevada and California), and Uzbekistan. It's actually the largest gold producer in South America. Additionally, it has exploration programs in Ghana that may be very promising for the company. If you're looking for a truly global and diversified gold producer with real growth potential, you can't go wrong with Newmont.

Many other mining companies have gold-mining operations that are part of a general mining program that includes other metals, such as silver and copper. I selected these companies because their sphere of operations revolves almost exclusively around gold mining.

The performance of these companies isn't directly proportional to the spot or future price of gold. These companies don't give you the direct exposure to gold that gold certificates or bars do, for example. Also, by investing in these stocks, you're exposing yourself to regulatory, managerial, and operational factors.

Gold contracts

Gold futures contracts give you a direct way to invest in gold through the futures markets. You can choose from two gold futures contracts that are widely traded in the United States. (See Chapter 13 for the goods on futures contracts.)

>> **CME/CBOT Mini-Gold (CBOT: YG):** Launched in 2004, this gold contract, trading in the CBOT section of the Chicago Mercantile Exchange (CME), is a relative newcomer to the North American gold futures market. However, it's a popular contract because you can trade it online through the CME's electronic trading platform. In addition, at a contract size of 33.2 troy ounces, the Mini is popular with investors and traders who prefer to trade this smaller contract over the larger 100-ounce contract.

>> **CME/CBOT E-Micro Gold (CBOT: MGC):** Launched in 2010, this gold contract trades on the COMEX section of the CME. The contract is relatively new, and popularity has been growing each month with its electronic execution traded on the CME Globex platform. At a contract size of 10 troy ounces, the E-Micro is popular with investors and traders who prefer to trade a smaller contract over the Mini-Gold 33.2 troy ounce.

>> **CME/COMEX Gold (COMEX: GC):** The COMEX gold futures contract was the first such contract to hit the market in the United States (back in the 1970s). It's traded on the COMEX division of the CME, and it's the most liquid gold contract in the world. It's used primarily by large commercial consumers and producers, such as jewelry manufacturers and mining companies, for price-hedging purposes. However, you can also purchase the contract for investment purposes. Each contract represents 100 troy ounces of gold.

When investing in the futures markets, always trade in the most liquid markets. *Liquidity* is an indication of the number of contracts traded on a regular basis. The higher the liquidity, the more likely you are to find a buyer or seller to close out or open a position. You can get information on the volume and open interest of contracts traded in the futures markets through the Commodity Futures Trading Commission (CFTC) website at www.cftc.gov.

Investing in Silver

Silverware and jewelry aren't the only uses for silver. As a matter of fact, silverware is only a small portion of the silver market. A large portion of this precious metal goes toward industrial uses, such as conducting electricity; creating bearings; and welding, soldering, and brazing (the process by which metals are permanently joined). Because of its numerous practical applications and its status as a precious metal, investing in silver can bolster your portfolio. In this section, I introduce you to the ins and outs of the silver market and show you how to include silver in your portfolio.

Checking out the big picture on silver

Silver has multiple uses that make it an attractive investment. This list details the most important ones, which account for more than 95 percent of total demand for silver:

>> **Industrial:** The industrial sector is the single largest consumer of silver products, accounting for almost 55 percent of total silver consumption in 2022. Silver has numerous applications in the industrial sector, including creating control switches for electrical appliances and connecting electronic circuit boards. Because it's a good electrical conductor, silver will keep playing an important role in the industrial sector.

>> **Jewelry and silverware:** Many people incorrectly believe that the largest consumer of silver is the jewelry industry. Although silver does play a large role in creating jewelry and silverware, demand from this sector accounted for 30 percent of total silver consumption in 2022.

>> **Photography:** The photographic industry is also a major consumer of silver, accounting for about 10 percent of total consumption in 2022. In photography, silver is compounded with halogens to form *silver halide*, which is used in photographic film. Digital cameras, which don't use silver halide, are becoming more popular than traditional cameras.

TIP

Monitor the commercial activity in each of these market segments and look for signs of strength or weakness. A demand increase or decrease in one of these markets, such as photography, will have a direct impact on the price of silver.

Knowing where the silver comes from is always important to an investor, so I list the top producers of silver in the world in Table 7-3.

TABLE 7-3 ## Top Silver Producers, 2021

Country	Production (Measured in Tons)
Mexico	6,120
Peru	4,160
China	3,570
Russia	2,100
Poland	1,470
Chile	1,370
Bolivia	1,190
Australia	1,220
Argentina	1,020
United States	930

TIP

If you're interested in finding out more about silver and its invest-ment possibilities, the Silver Institute, a trade association for silver producers and consumers, maintains a comprehensive database on the silver market. Its website is www.silverinstitute.org.

Getting a sliver of silver in your portfolio

Silver can play an important role in your portfolio. Because of its precious metal status, you can use it as a hedge against inflation and to preserve part of your portfolio's value. In addition, because it has important industrial applications, you can use it for capital appreciation opportunities. Whether for capital preservation or appreciation, I believe any portfolio has room for some exposure to silver. In this section, I introduce you to the different ways you can invest in silver.

Buying physical silver

One of the unique characteristics of silver is that you can invest in it by buying it, just as you can buy gold coins and bars for investment purposes. Most dealers that sell gold generally offer silver coins and bars as well.

>> **100-ounce silver bar:** If you're interested in something substantial, you can buy a 100-ounce silver bar. Before buying it, check the bar to make sure that it's pure silver. (You want 99 percent purity or higher.)

>> **Silver maple coins:** These coins, which are a product of the Royal Canadian Mint, are the standard for silver coins around the world. Each coin represents 1 ounce of silver and has a purity of 99.99 percent, making it the purest silver coin on the market.

TECHNICAL STUFF

The term *sterling silver* refers to a specific silver alloy that contains 92.5 percent silver and 7.5 percent copper. (Other base metals are occasionally used as well.) Pure silver is sometimes alloyed with another metal, such as copper, to make it stronger and more durable. Just note that if you're considering silver jewelry as an investment, sterling silver won't give you as much value in the long term as pure silver.

Buying the silver ETF

One of the most convenient ways of investing in silver is to go through an ETF. The iShares Silver Trust (AMEX: SLV) holds silver bullion in a vault and seeks to mirror the spot price of that silver based on current market prices. This silver ETF is a testament to the increased demand by investors to include silver in their portfolios.

Looking at silver-mining companies

Another alternative investment route is to go through companies that mine silver. Although some of the larger mining companies (which I cover in Chapter 9) have silver-mining operations, you can get more direct exposure to the silver markets by investing in companies that specialize in mining this precious metal. These companies may not be household names, but they're potentially good investments nevertheless:

>> **Pan American Silver Corporation (Nasdaq: PAAS):** Pan American Silver, based in Vancouver, has extensive operations in the Americas. It operates 13 mines in some of the most prominent locations in the world, including Bolivia, Mexico, and Peru. If you're interested in a well-managed company to get exposure to Latin American silver mines, you won't go wrong with Pan American Silver.

>> **Wheaton Precious Metals Corp. (NYSE: WPM):** Wheaton is one of the only mining companies that generates all its revenues from silver-mining activity. Whereas other mining companies may have smaller interests in other metals, Wheaton focuses exclusively on developing and mining silver. It has operations in geographically diverse areas that stretch from Mexico to Sweden. If you're looking for a geographically diverse company to give you direct access to silver-mining activities, Wheaton is your best bet.

Checking out silver futures contracts

Similar to gold futures, silver futures contracts give you the most direct access to the silver market. Following are the most liquid silver futures contracts (see Chapter 13 for more on futures):

>> **CBOT Mini-Silver (CBOT: YI):** The Mini-Silver contract that trades on the CBOT division of the CME represents a stake in 1,000 troy ounces of silver with a purity of 99.9 percent. This contract is available for electronic trading.

>> **COMEX Silver (COMEX: SI):** The COMEX silver contract is the standard futures contract for silver. It's traded on the COMEX division of the CME and represents 5,000 troy ounces of silver per contract.

Adding Platinum to Your Investments

Platinum, sometimes referred to as "the rich man's gold," is one of the rarest and most precious metals in the world. Perhaps no other metal or commodity carries the same cachet as platinum, and for good reason: It's by far the rarest metal in the world. If you put all the platinum that has ever been mined into an Olympic-size swimming pool, that platinum wouldn't even cover your ankles!

Whereas precious and base metals such as gold and copper have been exploited for thousands of years, the human interest in platinum developed only in the 17th century, when the conquistadors discovered large amounts of the metal in South America. Platinum was soon discovered to have superior characteristics to most metals: It is more resistant to corrosion, doesn't oxidize in the air, and has stable chemical properties. Because of these characteristics, platinum is a highly desirable metal and can play an important role in your portfolio.

TIP

Platinum is also the name of the group of metals that includes platinum, palladium, osmium, ruthenium, rhodium, and iridium. In this section, I talk about the metal, not the group of metals, although I cover palladium in Chapter 8.

Gathering platinum facts and figures

Deposits of platinum ore are extremely scarce and, more important, geographically concentrated in a few regions around the globe, primarily in South Africa, Russia, and North America. South Africa has the largest deposits of platinum in the world and, by some accounts, may contain up to 90 percent of the world's total reserve estimates. Russia is also a large player in the production of platinum, currently accounting for 18.5 percent of total global production (2021 figures). North America also contains some commercially viable platinum mines, located mostly in Montana.

So, who uses platinum? Platinum has several uses, but these are the most important:

>> **Catalytic converters:** You may be surprised to find out not only that platinum is used in catalytic converters in transportation vehicles, but that this accounts for more than 55 percent of total platinum demand. Platinum's unique characteristics make it a suitable metal in the production of these pollution-reducing devices. As environmental fuel standards become more stringent, expect the demand from this sector to increase.

>> **Industrial:** Because it's a great conductor of heat and electricity, platinum has wide applications in industry. It's used in creating everything from personal computer hard drives to fiber-optic cables. Despite its relative value, platinum will continue to be used for industrial purposes.

>> **Jewelry:** At one point, jewelry accounted for more than 45 percent of total demand for platinum. Although that number has decreased, the jewelry industry is still a major purchaser of platinum metals for use in highly prized jewelry.

TIP

A change in demand from one of these industries will affect the price of platinum. The International Platinum Association maintains an updated database of the uses of platinum. Check out its website for more information on platinum supply and demand at www.ipa-news.com.

Going platinum

Platinum's unique characteristics as a highly sought-after precious metal with industrial applications make it an ideal investment. Fortunately, you can invest in platinum in several ways. I list a couple of these methods in the following sections.

The platinum futures contract

The most direct way of investing in platinum is to go through the futures markets. The CME offers a platinum futures contract. Due to platinum's uses in industry and as a store of value, it has experienced increased demand from investors; however, platinum is also a highly sensitive trading instrument and tends to react drastically to any price shocks, as was the case during the COVID-19 pandemic of 2020.

WARNING

Platinum can be subject to wide price swings, so it's not for the buy-and-hold investor; taking advantage of this opportunity requires quick and tactical trading strategies.

The CME platinum futures contract represents 50 troy ounces of platinum and is available for trading electronically. It trades under the ticker symbol PL.

Platinum-mining companies

Check out a couple of companies that give you direct exposure to platinum–mining activities:

>> **Anglo-American PLC (Nasdaq: AAUK):** Anglo-American is a diversified mining company that has activities in gold, silver, platinum, and other precious metals. I recommend Anglo-American because it has significant interests in South African platinum mines, the largest mines in the world. If you're looking for an indirect exposure to South Africa's platinum-mining industry, Anglo-American does the trick.

>> **Stillwater Mining Company (NYSE: SWC):** Stillwater Mining is headquartered in Billings, Montana, and owns the rights to the Stillwater mining complex in Montana, which contains one of the largest commercially viable platinum mines in North America. This option is a good play on North American platinum-mining activities.

Chapter 8

Considering Steel, Aluminum, Copper, and Other Metals

Steel, aluminum, and copper may not be as glamorous as their precious metal counterparts — gold, silver, and platinum, covered in Chapter 7 — but they're perhaps even more precious to the global economy. Gold, silver, and platinum do have industrial applications, but their primary value is derived from their ability to act as stores of value, in addition to their use in jewelry. Steel, aluminum, and copper are the most important *industrial* components of the metals complex, used to build everything from railcars to bridges. You may be surprised to hear that steel is the most widely used metal in the world — more than 1.95 billion tons of it were produced in 2022. Steel is closely followed by aluminum, which is closely followed by copper in terms of total global output. So, steel, aluminum, and copper — in that order — rank at the top of the metals complex, based on total output. The future looks bright for these metals. In this chapter, I help you develop a game plan for investing in these powerhouse metals.

In this chapter, I also go over a diverse group of metals: palladium, a precious metal, and two industrial metals, zinc and nickel. These metals are important components of the metals complex in their own right: palladium because of its precious metal status and as a part of the *platinum group of metals* (PGM), and nickel and zinc for their wide use in industry. These metals may not get much attention from the financial press, but you still need to consider including them in your portfolio because they're essential building blocks of the global economy.

Building a Portfolio That's as Strong as Steel

The development of steel, alongside iron, changed the course of human history. In fact, the last stage of prehistoric times, the *Iron Age*, is named thus because humans mastered the iron- and steel-making processes. This development allowed societies to build tools and weapons, which sped advancements in construction and technology. Steel was responsible for another revolution in the 19th century: the Industrial Revolution. Today, in a high-tech world dominated by software and technological gadgets, this age-old metal is still as reliable as ever. In fact, steel is making a resurgence as advanced developing countries — China, India, and Brazil — barrel down a path toward rapid industrialization not unlike the one the West experienced in the 19th century (see Chapter 2). *Steel*, which is iron alloyed with other compounds (usually carbon), is still the most widely produced metal in the world.

Note: Steel is measured in metric tons, sometimes abbreviated as MT. For global production and consumption figures, million metric tons (MMT) is used.

Steely facts

For a long time, the United States was the number-one producer of steel, but its dominance eroded largely because of competition from Asia (especially China and Japan) and partly for internal reasons (such as the high costs of running a steel mill in the United States). The United States is still an important player in the steel industry; other countries worth mentioning include Russia, Japan, and South Korea.

In Table 8-1, I list the top steel producers in the world in 2021. To put things in perspective, total global steel production in 2021 stood at 1,951 MMT, which means that steel production almost doubled in the previous ten years. What's more telling is that a big chunk of this growth originated in China, which grew its production by 40 percent, from 567 MMT in 2011 to 1,032 MMT in 2021!

TABLE 8-1 ## Top Steel-Producing Countries, 2021

Country	Production (Million Metric Tons)
China	1,032 MMT
India	118 MMT
Japan	96 MMT
United States	85 MMT
Russia	75 MMT
South Korea	70 MMT
Turkey	40 MMT
Germany	40 MMT
Brazil	36 MMT

Source: Data from World Steel Association

TIP

If you're interested in exploring additional statistical information relating to steel production and manufacturing, I recommend checking out the following resources:

>> **Association for Iron & Steel Technology:** www.aist.org

>> **Iron and Steel Statistics Bureau:** www.issb.co.uk

>> **World Steel Association:** https://worldsteel.org

Investing in steel companies

Although futures contracts are available for everything from crude oil to coffee, there's no underlying futures contract for steel. However, a number of exchanges have expressed interest in developing a steel futures contract, so keep an eye out for such a development.

TIP

For now, the best way to get exposure to steel is to invest in companies that produce steel, specifically globally integrated steel companies. The companies I list in Table 8-2 are global leaders in the steel industry.

TABLE 8-2 **Top Steel-Producing Companies, 2021**

Company	Production (Million Metric Tons)
Baowu Streel (China)	120
ArcelorMittal (Luxembourg)	79
Ansteel (China)	55
Nippon Steel (Japan)	49
Jiangsu Shagang (China)	44
POSCO (South Korea))	43
Hesteel Group (China)	41
Jianlong Steel (China)	36
Shougang (China)	35
Tata Steel (India)	30

Source: Data from World Steel Association

From Table 8-2, it's clear that China and its companies play a dominant role in the global production of steel. Chinese companies have always been competitive, but they've been able to cement their leadership position due to government subsidies and prioritization. I expect Chinese companies to maintain their leadership role in the years to come.

The companies in Table 8-2 are the world leaders in the industry. However, not all are available for investment. Some of them are private, and others trade on foreign exchanges that don't issue American depository receipts (ADRs; see Chapter 9). The following list represents good investments that not only are the best-run companies, but also display the greatest potential for future market dominance:

>> **ArcelorMittal (NYSE: MT):** ArcelorMittal resulted when the Indian company Mittal acquired the European Arcelor in 2006, in one of the biggest consolidation plays the industry has ever seen. Combining the number-one and number-two steel producers created a dominant leader with output almost double that of its nearest competitor. If you're looking for broad exposure to the steel industry, you can't go wrong with ArcelorMittal.

>> **Gerdau (NYSE: GGB):** Gerdau is a Brazilian vertically integrated steel producer with operations across several countries. Gerdau is a dominant player in the long steel category, with mills in Brazil, Argentina, Mexico, Colombia, and the United States. It brought in a net income of more than $15.4 billion in 2021, so you can remain confident that this company will generate long-term value for its shareholders.

>> **Nucor Corp. (NYSE: NUE):** The American steel industry remains a robust competitor on the global stage, despite the dominance of Chinese companies. Nucor operates almost exclusively in the United States; if you're interested in getting exposure to the American steel market, consider investing in it. Nucor is also one of the only companies to operate "minimills" domestically, which many people argue are more cost-efficient than the traditional blast furnaces.

>> **U.S. Steel (NYSE: X):** U.S. Steel, which was formed because of the consolidation of Andrew Carnegie's steel holdings in the early 20th century, is one of the oldest and largest steel companies in the world. By itself, U.S. Steel represents the whole history of the modern steel industry. At one point, it was the largest producer of steel in the world. Although it has scaled down its operations, it's still a significant player in the industry today. U.S. Steel is involved in all aspects of the steelmaking process, from iron ore mining and processing to the marketing of finished products.

Illuminating the Details of Aluminum

Aluminum is one of the most ubiquitous metals of modern society. Not just aluminum beverage cans account for its wide-spread use. Aluminum is also used in transportation (cars, trucks, trains, and airplanes), construction, and electrical power lines, to name just a few end uses. As a matter of fact, aluminum is the second most widely used metal in the world, right after steel. Because of its indispensability, you need to make room to include this metal in your portfolio. In this section, I show you how to do just that.

Note: Aluminum is generally measured in metric tons (MT).

Just the aluminum facts

Aluminum is a lightweight metal that's resistant to corrosion. Because of these characteristics, it's widely used to create numerous products, from cars to jets. Consider a few items made from aluminum:

>> **Construction:** Aluminum has industrial uses as well, including a role in the construction of buildings, oil pipelines, and even bridges. Building constructors are attracted to it because it's lightweight, durable, and sturdy.

>> **Packaging:** Almost a quarter of aluminum is used to create aluminum wrap and foil, along with beverage cans and rivets.

>> **Transportation:** Aluminum is used to create the body, axles, and, in some cases, engines of cars. In addition, large commercial aircrafts are built using aluminum because of its light weight and sturdiness.

Table 8-3 breaks down total aluminum consumption by sector.

TIP

If you're interested in finding out more about the aluminum industry, I recommend checking out the following organizations:

>> **The Aluminum Association:** www.aluminum.org

>> **International Aluminium Institute:** https://international-aluminium.org

TABLE 8-3 Aluminum Consumption by Sector, 2021

Industry	Aluminum Consumption (Percentage of Total)
Construction	25%
Transportation	23%
Electrical	12%
Foil stock and packaging	17%
Machinery	11%
Consumer goods	6%
Miscellaneous uses	6%

Source: Data from London Metal Exchange

Aluminum futures

You can invest in aluminum through the futures markets. The London Metal Exchange (LME) aluminum contract is the most liquid in the world. It represents a size of 25,000 tons, and its price is quoted in U.S. dollars. The underlying demand from rapidly industrializing nations, such as China and India, has resulted in upward price pressures on the metal.

Aluminum companies

Another way I recommend investing in aluminum is to invest in companies that produce and manufacture aluminum products. A couple of companies make the cut:

>> **Alcoa (NYSE: AA):** Alcoa is the world leader in aluminum production. It is involved in all aspects of the aluminum industry and produces primary aluminum, fabricated aluminum, and alumina. The company has operations in more than 52 countries and services numerous industries, from aerospace to construction. If you're looking to get the broadest exposure to the aluminum market, you can't go wrong with Alcoa.

>> **Aluminum Corporation of China (NYSE: ACH):** As its name implies, ACH is primarily engaged in producing aluminum in the Chinese market. I recommend this company, which trades on the New York Stock Exchange (NYSE), because it gives you a foothold in the aluminum Chinese market, which may potentially be the biggest such market in the future. Besides this competitive advantage, ACH is a well-run company with profit margins that, during the writing of this book, were larger than 40 percent.

Bringing Copper into Your Metals Mix

Copper, the third most widely used metal in the world, has applications in many sectors, including construction, electricity conduction, and large-scale industrial projects. Copper is sought after because of its high electrical conductivity, resistance to corrosion, and malleability. Copper played a huge role during the Industrial Revolution and in connecting and wiring the modern world. Because of the current trends of industrialization and urbanization across the globe (see Chapter 2), demand for copper has been — and will remain — very strong, making it a good investment.

Quick copper facts

Copper is used for a variety of purposes, from building and construction to electrical wiring and engineering. To get a better idea of its wide usage, check out the breakdown of copper use by sector in Table 8-4.

TABLE 8-4 **Copper Consumption by Sector, 2021**

Sector	Copper Consumption (Percentage of Total)
Building/construction	50%
Engineering	25%
Electrical	16%
Transportation	7%
Miscellaneous uses	2%

Source: Data from Copper Development Association

You probably come across items made from copper daily, but you may have never thought much about its ubiquity. These everyday items, among others, are made from copper:

>> Artistic items (bronze statues such as the Statue of Liberty)

>> Coinage (U.S. coins such as the quarter and the dime, which are more than 75 percent copper)

>> Construction tubes, pipes, and fittings

>> Doorknobs

>> Electrical wiring

>> High-speed internet cables

>> Industrial sleeve bearings

>> Musical instruments (brass instruments such as the trumpet and the tuba)

>> Plumbing tubes

Copper is often alloyed with other metals, such as nickel and zinc (both covered later in this chapter). When copper and nickel are alloyed, the resulting metal is *bronze;* when copper is alloyed with zinc, it results in *brass.* Ironically, the U.S. penny, the only U.S. coin that's a reddish/brown color (the color of copper), is the only coin that uses only 2.5 percent copper — 97.5 percent of the penny is made from zinc. The other coins in U.S. currency, which are all silvery/white, contain more than 90 percent copper.

TIP

If you're interested in finding out more about copper usage, I recommend that you consult the Copper Development Association at www.copper.org.

Copper futures contracts

Like most of the other important industrial metals, there's a futures market available for copper trading. Large industrial producers and consumers of the metal account for most of this market, although you also can use it for investment purposes. You have two copper contracts to choose from:

>> **CME/COMEX Copper (COMEX: HG):** This copper contract trades in the COMEX division of the Chicago Mercantile Exchange (CME). COMEX copper, which trades during the current month and subsequent 23 calendar months, is

traded both electronically and through the open outcry system. It represents 25,000 pounds of copper and trades under the symbol HG.

>> **LME Copper (LME: CAD):** The copper contract on the LME accounts for more than 75 percent of total copper futures activity. It represents a lot size of 25 tons. *Note:* Because the LME is in the United Kingdom, the British Financial Services Authority (FSA) regulates it.

Demand for copper from China, India, and other advanced developing countries is increasing, and that has put upward pressure on its price.

Copper companies

Another investment vehicle I recommend is companies that specialize in mining and processing copper ore. The companies I list here are leaders in their industry and are involved in all aspects of the copper supply chain. The only drawback of investing in companies is that you don't get direct exposure to the price fluctuations of the metals. Still, these companies are a good option if you don't want to venture into the futures markets.

>> **Freeport-McMoRan, Inc. (NYSE: FCX):** One of the reasons I like Freeport-McMoRan is that it's one of the lowest-cost producers of copper in the world. It has copper-mining and -smelting operations across the globe and has a significant presence in Indonesia and Papua New Guinea. The company specializes in producing highly concentrated copper ore, which it then sells on the open market. FCX also has some operations in gold and silver.

>> **Phelps Dodge Corporation (NYSE: PD):** Founded in 1834, Phelps Dodge is one of the oldest mining companies in the United States. It's also one of the largest manufacturers and producers of copper and copper products in the world. The company has a global presence in copper mining, with operations in the United States, South Africa, the Philippines, and Peru, among others. Because of its size and experience in the industry, Phelps Dodge is in a good position to capitalize on increased demand for copper.

I cover copper companies in depth in Chapter 9. I also examine integrated and diversified mining companies to help you design an investment strategy that effectively allows you to "buy the market."

Palladium: A Metal for the New Millennium

Palladium, which belongs to the PGM, is a popular alternative to platinum in the automotive industry and the jewelry industry. Its largest use comes into play in the creation of pollution-reducing catalytic converters. Palladium's malleability and resistance to corrosion make it the perfect metal for such use.

Aside from its usage in catalytic converters and jewelry, palladium is used in dentistry and electronics. Table 8-5 lists the main consumers of palladium.

TABLE 8-5 Palladium Consumption by Industry, 2021

Sector	Percentage of Total
Auto industry (catalytic converters)	70%
Jewelry	14%
Electronics	7%
Dentistry	5%
Other	4%

Source: Data from U.S. Geological Survey

TIP

Palladium has benefited from more stringent fuel emission standards established by the Environmental Protection Agency (EPA) and other international environmental organizations. When pollution-reducing regulation was established in the 1970s, demand for palladium skyrocketed. All things equal, if emissions standards are further improved and require a new generation of catalytic converters, demand for palladium will increase. Another reason to be bullish on palladium is that the number of automobiles, trucks, and other vehicles equipped with platinum- and palladium-made catalytic converters is increasing, particularly in China. If you invest in palladium, keep an eye on automobile-manufacturing patterns.

Two countries essentially dominate the palladium market: Russia and South Africa. These two countries account for more than 85 percent of total palladium production, as you can see in Table 8-6.

TABLE 8-6 **Top Palladium-Producing Countries, 2021**

Country	Production (Metric Tons)
Russia	81
South Africa	78
North America	32
Zimbabwe	12
Other	8

Source: Data from U.S. Geological Survey

Because these two countries dominate palladium production, any supply disruption from either country has a significant impact on palladium prices. Such was the case in early 2000, when the Russian government announced it would halt shipments of palladium and other platinum group metals for the year. The price of palladium almost doubled, partly in response to Russian supply-side disruptions.

The Russian government eventually announced a resumption of palladium-mining activity, and prices dropped back to normal levels in 2001. As a result of this price shock, mining companies have tried to diversify their activities beyond Russia and South Africa. However, there's no way around the fact that most of the world's reserves of palladium ore are located in these two countries. As a matter of fact, perhaps no two countries dominate a commodity as much as Russia and South Africa dominate palladium; it is as much a duopoly as you're going to get in the commodity markets.

WARNING

Keep in mind the unique market structure as you consider investing in this precious metal.

One of the best — albeit indirect — methods of getting exposure to the palladium markets is investing in companies that mine the metal. A number of companies specialize in this activity, but I recommend taking a look at these two:

>> **North American Palladium (AMEX: PAL):** North American Palladium, headquartered in Toronto, has a significant presence in the Canadian palladium ore–mining business. It's the largest producer of palladium in Canada. North American palladium is your entry into the lucrative Canadian palladium-mining sector.

>> **Stillwater Mining Company (NYSE: SWC):** Stillwater Mining, based in Montana, is the largest producer of palladium outside South Africa and Russia. Although it's involved in platinum and other PGM, its primary mining output is palladium. It produces approximately 1.2 million ounces of palladium a year, primarily through North American mines.

REMEMBER

Although these are the two largest companies that trade publicly on American exchanges, several international companies have significantly larger palladium–mining activities. Just make sure you're aware of the many regulatory differences between American and overseas markets before you invest in companies that trade in overseas stock markets.

You may also want to consider a couple of international palladium companies:

>> **Anglo Platinum Group (South Africa):** As its name suggests, Anglo Platinum Group invests in platinum group metals, but it's also one of the largest producers of palladium in the world. (This includes other PGM.) With its operations located primarily in South Africa, Anglo Platinum Group is your gateway to South African palladium. Its shares are traded in the Johannesburg Stock Exchange (JSE) and the London Stock Exchange (LSE).

>> **Norilsk Nickel (Russia):** Norilsk Nickel may not be a household name, but it's the largest producer of palladium in the world. It dominates the Russian palladium industry, which is the largest in the world. Beyond its large palladium-mining activities, the company is a major player in copper and nickel ore mining. The company's shares are available through the Moscow Interbank Currency Exchange (MICEX).

If you're comfortable in the futures markets (which I cover in Chapter 13), the CME offers a futures contract that tracks palladium. This contract represents 100 troy ounces of palladium and trades both electronically and during the open outcry session. It trades under the symbol PA.

Zooming In on Zinc

Zinc is the fourth most widely used metal, right behind iron/steel, aluminum, and copper (which I cover earlier in this chapter). Zinc has unique abilities to resist corrosion and oxidation and is used for metal *galvanization* (the process of applying a metal coating to another metal to prevent rust and corrosion). As you can see from Table 8-7, galvanizing metals (particularly steel) is by far the largest application of zinc.

TABLE 8-7 ## Zinc Consumption by Sector, 2020

Sector	Percentage of Market Consumption
Galvanization	50%
Brass and bronze coatings	16%
Zinc alloying	15%
Other	14%

Source: Data from London Metal Exchange

The best way to invest in zinc is to go through the futures markets. The LME offers a futures contract for zinc that has been trading since the early 1900s and is the industry benchmark for zinc pricing. The contract trades in lots of 25 tons and is available for trading during the current month and the subsequent 27 months.

Investing in Nickel

Nickel is a *ferrous metal,* which means it belongs to the iron group of metals. It's an important industrial metal that's used as an alloy with metals such as iron and copper, and it's sought after because of its ductility, malleability, and resistance to corrosion.

One of nickel's primary applications is in creating stainless steel. When steel is alloyed with nickel, its resistance to corrosion increases dramatically. Because stainless steel is a necessity of modern life, and a large portion of nickel goes toward creating this important metal alloy, you can rest assured that demand for nickel will remain strong. As you can see from Table 8-8, although nickel has many important uses, the creation of stainless steel remains its primary application.

TABLE 8-8 ## Nickel Consumption by Sector, 2021

Sector	Percentage of Market Consumption
Stainless steel	65%
Nonferrous alloys	12%
Ferrous alloys	10%
Electroplating	10%
Other	3%

Source: Data from London Metal Exchange

Australia has the largest reserves of nickel, and its proximity to the rapidly industrializing Asian center — China and India — is a strategic advantage. Another major player in the nickel markets is Russia; the Russian company Norilsk Nickel is the largest producer of nickel in the world. Nickel mining is a labor-intensive industry, but countries that have large reserves of this special metal are poised to do very well. Check out the countries with the largest reserves of nickel in Table 8-9.

The LME offers a futures contract for nickel. The nickel futures contract on the LME gives you the most direct access to the nickel market. It trades in lots of 6 tons, and its tick size is $5 per ton. As with zinc, it trades during the first month, as well as the 27 subsequent months.

TECHNICAL STUFF

The term *nickel*, used to denote the 5-cent coin, is misleading because the coin actually consists primarily of copper (75 percent). Nickel, the metal, makes up only 25 percent of nickel, the coin.

TABLE 8-9 Largest Nickel Reserves, 2021

Country	Million Tons
Indonesia	21
Australia	20
Brazil	16
Russia	6.9
Cuba	5.5
Philippines	4.8

Source: Data from U.S. Geological Survey

Chapter 9

Unearthing Top Mining Companies

Trading metals outright — through the futures markets — can be tricky for the uninitiated trader. You have to keep track of a number of moving pieces, such as contract expiration dates, margin calls, trading months, and other variables. In addition, metals on the futures markets can be subject to extreme price volatility, and you can set yourself up for disastrous losses. So, it's understandable if you don't want to trade metals futures contracts, which I cover in Chapter 13. But this doesn't mean that you should ignore the whole metals subasset class altogether, because you may miss out on some substantial returns.

One possible avenue for opening up your portfolio to metals is to invest in companies that specialize in mining metals and minerals. A number of such companies exist, and their performance has been stellar in recent years, especially as a result of increased demand for these metals post-pandemic. Although not all mining companies have had similar performances, ignoring such a large group of the market isn't advisable.

In this chapter, I look at the top mining companies — both the conglomerates and the specialized ones — to help you identify the best ones to include in your portfolio.

REMEMBER I provide you only a snapshot of recent financial performance here. Before you invest in any company, you want to look at a number of metrics to determine its financial health. Go through the balance sheet, income statement, and statement of cash flows — among other key financial statements — with a fine-tooth comb. Only if you determine that the company has a clean financial bill of health and is poised for growth should you proceed with your investment.

Considering Diversified Mining Companies

Like the large integrated energy companies — ExxonMobil and BP, covered in Chapter 3 — diversified mining companies are involved in *all* aspects of the metals production process. These companies, which often employ tens of thousands of people, have operations in all four corners of the globe. They're involved in excavating metals — both precious and base metals, ferrous and nonferrous — as well as transforming these metals into finished products and subsequently distributing the end products to consumers.

Investing in one of these companies gives you exposure not only to a wide variety of metals, but also to the whole mining supply chain. I've selected the "best of breeds," and I evaluate their investment suitability in the following sections.

BHP Billiton

BHP Billiton is one of the largest mining companies in the world. It formed as a result of the 2001 merger between Broken Hill Proprietary, an Australian company, and Billiton, an Anglo-Dutch company. BHP Billiton, headquartered in Melbourne, Australia, has mining operations in more than 30 countries, including Australia, Canada, the United States, South Africa, and Papua New Guinea. The company processes a large number of metals, including aluminum, copper, silver, and iron; it also has small oil and natural gas operations in Algeria and Pakistan. The company is listed on the New York Stock Exchange (NYSE) under the symbol BHP.

One of the reasons I like BHP Billiton is that it offers economies of scale, meaning large-scale exposure to various sectors of the supply chain, which enhances its pricing capabilities. This is a large company, by any standard. Here's a snapshot of the company's financial performance. (All figures are for 2021.)

>> **Revenues:** $65.4 billion

>> **Net income:** $30.9 billion

>> **Earnings before interest, taxes, depreciation, and amortization (EBITDA):** $37.6 billion

>> **Profit margins:** 47.2 percent

The company has benefited handsomely from the increasing prices of commodities such as copper and aluminum. Its solid financial profile is reflected in its stock price.

WARNING

Past results don't guarantee future performance. Commodity prices are cyclical in nature, and prices for metals such as copper, silver, and aluminum can't go up in a straight line forever. Make sure that you consider the cyclicality factor as you move forward with your commodity investments.

Rio Tinto

Rio Tinto is a mining company rich in both minerals and history. The Rothschild banking family founded the company in 1873 to mine ore deposits in Spain. Today Rio Tinto boasts operations in Africa, Australia, Europe, the Pacific Rim, North America, Australia, and South America. It's a true mining conglomerate that's involved in all facets of the mining supply chain, from extraction to transformation and distribution.

The company is involved in the production of a number of commodities, including iron ore, copper, aluminum, and titanium. In addition, Rio Tinto has interests in diamonds, manufacturing almost 30 percent of global natural diamonds, processed primarily through its mining activities in Australia.

By investing in Rio Tinto, you get not only a company that has extensive operations across the mining complex, but also one that's in a solid financial position. Check out some numbers the company posted in 2021:

>> **Revenues:** $63.5 billion

>> **Net income:** $21.1 billion

>> **EBITDA:** $33.6 billion

>> **Profit margins:** 33 percent

These strong numbers, which reflect increased demand for the commodities the company is involved in, have had a positive mid- to long-term impact on the company's stock. Rio Tinto trades on the NYSE under the ticker symbol RTP.

Anglo-American

Anglo-American PLC began mining gold in South Africa in 1917. It was a venture by British and American entrepreneurs (hence, the name) who saw an opportunity in developing South African mines. Ever since, it has played an important role in the development of South Africa's gold-mining industry. Today Anglo-American has operations in all four corners of the globe and operates in more than 20 countries. It's involved in producing and distributing a wide array of metals, minerals, and natural resources, including gold, silver, and platinum, but also diamonds and paper packaging. (It owns 45 percent of De Beers, the diamond company.)

I recommend Anglo-American as a long-term investment because it has been in the business for almost a century, it's involved in almost all aspects of the mining industry, and the scale of its operations is global.

The company is listed on the London Stock Exchange under the ticker symbol AAL. In addition, it has American depository receipts (ADRs) listed in the Nasdaq National Market that trade under the symbol AAUK.

TECHNICAL
STUFF

When a foreign company wants to access the American capital markets, it has the option of issuing its shares as ADRs. A domestic bank (such as the Bank of New York, which is the largest issuer of ADRs) issues ADRs to the American investing public, while the bank holds shares of the foreign company overseas. The advantage of the ADR is that it allows American investors to invest in foreign companies without going through foreign exchanges. The ADRs trade in such a way that they reflect the daily price movements of the underlying stock as it's traded in a stock exchange overseas. For more information, you can check out the BNY Mellon website on DRs at www.adrbnymellon.com.

Checking Out Specialized Mining Companies

The benefit of investing in diversified mining companies, like those profiled in the previous section, is that you get to "buy the market" in one fell swoop. However, what if you spot a rally in gold, copper, or another individual metal and want to profit from this specific trend? In this case, the most direct exposure through the equity markets comes by investing in companies that specialize in specific metals. I identify and evaluate some of these companies in this section.

Newmont Mining: Gold

Newmont is headquartered in Colorado but operates gold mines all over the world. It's the largest producer of gold in South America, one of the most important gold regions, and has wholly owned subsidiaries or joint ventures in Australia, Canada, and Uzbekistan.

I recommend Newmont because it's a premier player in the competitive gold-mining industry. It has some competitive advantages, including its control of 50,000 square miles of land containing more than 90 million equity ounces of gold. (*Equity ounces* is the amount of gold measured in troy ounces multiplied by the current market price of gold as measured in U.S. dollars.) In addition, it has a strong balance sheet and is in solid financial condition. Check out some of Newmont's numbers (2021 figures):

>> **Revenues:** $12.2 billion

>> **Net income:** $1.2 billion

>> **EBITDA:** $4.5 billion

>> **Profit margins:** 9.6 percent

If you're looking for a well-managed company with extensive experience and operations in the gold-mining industry, you can't go wrong with Newmont. (Be sure to read Chapter 7 for in-depth coverage of the gold industry.)

Wheaton Precious Metals: Silver

Wheaton Precious Metals Corporation (NYSE:WPM), formerly known as Silver Wheaton, focuses primarily on the production and commercialization of silver. Some mining companies have small operations in secondary metals, but WPM generates almost 100 percent of its revenues from silver mining. The company operates mines primarily in Mexico and Sweden. Its modus operandi is to purchase silver directly from the mines and sell it on the open market for a profit. As a result, the company has very little, if any, operating overhead. This results in strong revenues and cash flows, as you can see from 2021 operations:

>> **Revenues:** $1.2 billion

>> **Net income:** $754 million

>> **EBITDA:** $853 million

>> **Profit margins:** 63 percent

WPM may not generate the same kinds of revenues as Anglo-American or other large mining conglomerates, but it's a well-run company with high profit margins and stable revenues.

For more information on the silver industry, including the top producers, the largest-consuming segments, and an analysis of additional investment methodologies, turn to Chapter 7.

Freeport-McMoRan: Copper

Freeport-McMoRan (NYSE: FCX) is the largest independent copper producer in the world, besides having significant operations in gold mining. Freeport started operations in Texas and rapidly expanded to include other locations in the continental United States and, later, internationally; the company has a strong footprint in Asia.

Phelps Dodge had quite a history in the mining industry, having been in the copper business for more than 150 years. It started as a mining concern and played a key role in the industrialization of the United States. Copper was in high demand by the growing nation, and Phelps Dodge was there to supply it. The Phelps Dodge acquisition was a huge coup for Freeport, and today the combined company is the market leader in copper production, with significant operations in the production of molybdenum and molybdenum-based chemicals.

TECHNICAL STUFF

Molybdenum (pronounced mah-*lib*-den-um) is known as a transition metal because it's principally used as an alloy with a number of metals. It has wide applications in industry — for instance, it's used in the construction of oil pipelines, aircraft engines, and missiles.

Freeport is also known for operating the largest copper mine ever discovered, the Grasberg mine in Indonesia; the proceeds from Grasberg are so prolific that Freeport is the largest individual taxpayer to the Indonesian government. Freeport is large by any standards, as evidenced by its 2021 financial performance:

>> **Revenues:** $22.8 billion

>> **Net income:** $4.3 billion

>> **EBITDA:** $10.5 billion

>> **Profit margins:** 18 percent

Overall, Freeport's performance has been positive over the last five years, despite the slowdown that resulted from the COVID-19 pandemic.

You can find more information about the copper market and industry in Chapter 8.

Alcoa: Aluminum

Alcoa is a household name, and for good reason: It's the largest producer of aluminum, which is the most ubiquitous metal in the modern world. Cars, beverage cans, and fighter jets are all partly made from aluminum, and Alcoa is the primary supplier of this metal in the market today. Alcoa (an acronym that stands for Aluminum Company of America) is involved in all phases of the aluminum supply chain. It provides aluminum-based products to a wide range of customers, including the aerospace and automotive industries, individual and commercial enterprises, the manufacturing sector, and the military.

Another reason I like Alcoa is that it's making some aggressive moves overseas and signing strategic, long-term pacts with some of the top aluminum producers. It entered into a partnership with the Aluminum Corporation of China (NYSE:ACH), China's largest aluminum producer, and is positioning itself to capitalize on the Chinese market, possibly the largest aluminum market in the future. Alcoa has undergone some strategic changes and made some strategic acquisitions — such as purchasing its main competitor, Alcan — that have acted as a drag on its financial performance in the short term. Capturing these market synergies and experiencing some weakness in the aluminum market short term have pressured its profitability. That said, I believe these circumstances present a good opportunity to buy a solid company at a discount:

- **>> Revenues:** $12.1 billion
- **>> Net income:** $429 million
- **>> EBITDA:** $2.7 billion
- **>> Profit margins:** 3.5 percent

WARNING

The stock's performance has been choppy in recent years, so make sure that you research the company as much as possible before you take the plunge.

Be sure to read Chapter 8 for a close examination of the aluminum market.

ArcelorMittal: Steel

Mittal Steel, under the management of Indian-born steel magnate Lakshmi Mittal, launched an unsolicited bid to acquire Arcelor, the Luxembourg-based high-end steel manufacturer, in January 2006. After a five-month takeover battle, which involved *poison pill* and *white knight* takeover defense strategies (see the next paragraph), the boards of both companies agreed to a merger of equals. The combined entity created one of the largest independent steel companies in the world.

TECHNICAL
STUFF

In mergers and acquisitions (M&A), companies use a number of strategies to fend off hostile takeovers. One of the most popular defense strategies includes pursuing a merger or acquisition with a "friendly" company, known as a *white knight*. Another strategy, the *poison pill* strategy, takes a different approach; this option involves making the company unattractive to an acquirer, such as by increasing levels of debt or increasing the number of shares outstanding to dilute their value.

The new company combined the number-one and number-two steel producers in the world. ArcelorMittal is a truly global steel manufacturer, with operations in all four corners of the globe and across all stages of the steelmaking process.

Turn to Chapter 8 for an in-depth examination of the global steel industry.

Making Money during the Mining Merger Mania

Profiting from the merger activity in the mining industry can be a good investment strategy. Since the year 2000, a number of large companies have entered into merger agreements (the marriage of the Australian BHP and the British Billiton, which resulted in BHP Billiton, is a good example). This trend is likely to continue as mining companies seek to add new capacity by merging their activities or acquiring smaller rivals. In 2004, for instance, a total of 49 deals were made in the mining industry, valued at $5.6 billion; in 2005, the number of deals increased to 85, with a total value of $7.4 billion.

Due to the sustained levels of high commodity prices, mining companies have large cash reserves and are looking to spend them to beef up their operations by acquiring other companies. M&A present long-term value opportunities to these companies and their shareholders and are likely to continue in the years to come. In 2006, for example, Phelps Dodge (one of the largest copper-mining companies) launched a simultaneous double bid to acquire Inco and Falconbridge, both independent Canadian mining companies, in a synchronized transaction valued at more than $40 billion.

TIP

The caveat of profiting from merger announcements, of course, is identifying the "hunter" and the "hunted," the acquirer and the target. Doing so isn't easy; theoretically, any given sector has an infinite number of M&A combinations. The best plan is to regularly monitor the industry for news, special announcements, or unusual trading activity. Specifically, keep your eye out for any announcements by companies in Forms 8-K (filings with the U.S. Securities and Exchange Commission [SEC] that announce special situations); read news stories about the companies in the industry (I recommend reading *The Wall Street Journal*'s "Heard on the Street" column); and remain alert to any sudden and unusual movements in the companies' stock activity, such as an unusual spike in volume.

WARNING

Identifying possible merger announcements isn't an exact science, but it can yield some phenomenal returns. A lot of folks try to profit from insider information regarding merger deals, which is illegal and has led to some huge financial scandals. If you trade on information that's not public, you could end up going to jail, so don't do it! Also, keep in mind that, as a general rule, you want to buy the "hunted" before any merger announcements because the stock price of a target company tends to increase with any merger announcement, while that of the acquiring company decreases. The logic here is that the acquiring company is paying a premium for its acquisition and will have to bear the costs of incorporating this new entity within its corporate and operational structure.

Chapter **10**
Trading Agricultural Products

The commodities that kick off this chapter — coffee, cocoa, sugar, and frozen concentrated orange juice — are known as *soft commodities*. Soft commodities are usually commodities that are grown, as opposed to those that are mined (such as metals) or those that are raised (such as livestock). The *softs*, as they're sometimes known, represent a significant portion of the commodities markets. They're indispensable and cyclical, just like energy and metals, but they're also unique because they're edible and seasonal. *Seasonality* is a major distinguishing characteristic of soft commodities because they can be grown only during specific times of the year and in specific geographical locations — usually in tropical areas. (This is why these commodities are also known as *tropical commodities*.) In this chapter, I show you that there's nothing soft about these soft commodities.

In this chapter, I also look at some major agricultural commodities that trade in the futures markets. These commodities, sometimes simply known as *ags*, are a unique component of the broader commodities markets. They're labor intensive and subject to volatility because of underlying market fundamentals. However, they also present solid investment opportunities.

Livestock, like the tropical and grain commodities, is a unique category in the agricultural commodities subasset class. It's not a widely followed area of the commodities markets — unlike crude oil, for example, you're not likely to see feeder cattle prices quoted on the nightly news — but this doesn't mean that you can ignore this area of the markets. That said, these contracts are volatile, so venture into this area of the market only if you have an iron-clad grasp on the concepts behind futures trading — along with a high tolerance for risk. In this chapter, I analyze the markets for cattle (both live cattle and feeder cattle), lean hogs, and frozen pork bellies.

Giving Your Portfolio a Buzz by Investing in Coffee

Today, coffee is the second most widely traded commodity in terms of physical volume — behind only crude oil. Coffee is an important global commodity because folks just love a good cup o' joe.

Coffee: It's time for a break

As with a number of other commodities, coffee production is dominated by a handful of countries. Brazil has historically been the top producer of coffee in the world and has held this position for several decades. Traditionally, Colombia has held the number-two spot, but it has lost that position to up-and-comers such as Vietnam and Indonesia. Table 10-1 lists the largest coffee-producing countries.

Large-scale coffee production is measured in *bags*. One bag of coffee weighs 60 kilograms, or approximately 132 pounds.

If you want to further investigate the ins and outs of the coffee markets, visit these websites for more information:

>> **International Coffee Organization:** www.ico.org

>> **National Coffee Association of U.S.A.:** www.ncausa.org

TABLE 10-1 Top Coffee Producers, 2020

Country	Production (Millions of Bags)
Brazil	63.4
Vietnam	29
Colombia	14.3
Indonesia	12
Ethiopia	7.3
Honduras	6.1
India	5.7
Uganda	5.6
Mexico	4.0
Peru	3.8

Source: Data from International Coffee Organization

Just as choosing the right flavor is important when buying your cup of coffee, knowing the different types of coffees available for investment is crucial. The world's coffee production is pretty much made up of two types of beans:

>> **Arabica:** Arabica coffee is the most widely grown coffee plant in the world, accounting for more than 60 percent of global coffee production. Arabica is grown in countries as diverse as Brazil and Indonesia. It's the premium coffee bean, adding a richer taste to any brew, and, as a result, it's the most expensive coffee bean in the world. Because of its high quality, it serves as the benchmark for coffee prices all over the world.

>> **Robusta:** Robusta accounts for about 40 percent of total coffee production. Because it's easier to grow than Arabica coffee, it's also less expensive.

The coffee futures contract: It may be your cup of tea

The coffee futures markets determine the future price of coffee and, more important, protect producers and purchasers of coffee from wild price swings. (See Chapter 13 for more on futures contracts.) In addition to hedging opportunities, the coffee futures markets allow individual investors to profit from coffee price variations. The most liquid coffee futures contract is available on the Intercontinental Exchange (ICE), which assumed tradability of the coffee contract when it acquired the New York Board of Trade (NYBOT).

Take a look at its contract specs:

>> **Contract ticker symbol:** KC

>> **Contract size:** 37,500 pounds

>> **Underlying commodity:** Pure Arabica coffee

>> **Price fluctuation:** $0.0005 per pound ($18.75 per contract)

>> **Trading months:** March, May, July, September, and December

WARNING

Because of seasonality, cyclicality, and geopolitical factors, coffee can be a volatile commodity subject to extreme price swings. Be sure to research the coffee markets inside and out before investing.

Ordering up investments in gourmet coffee shops

Behind the relaxed, laid-back atmosphere of a gourmet coffee shop is a complex moneymaking operation. Coffee is serious business, and you can profit from the coffee craze that has gripped the United States (the largest consumer of coffee in the world) and is spreading throughout Europe and newly developing countries such as India and China: Simply invest in the companies that are capitalizing on this trend. Find out where your $4.50 for a cup of coffee is going, and profit from it.

Perhaps no other brand has come to represent an entire industry as Starbucks (Nasdaq: SBUX) has coffee. (The only other brands that come to mind are Kleenex with tissues and Xerox with photocopiers.) Starbucks is a cultural phenomenon, but more important, it's a financial juggernaut. This is a $100 billion company with about $30 billion in revenue (according to 2021 figures). Starbucks dominates the entire coffee supply chain, from purchasing and roasting to selling and marketing. It has more than 10,000 stores worldwide, primarily in the United States and Europe, but also in China, Singapore, and even Saudi Arabia.

Warming Up to Cocoa

Cocoa is a fermented seed from the cacao tree, which is usually grown in hot and rainy regions around the equator. As you can see in Table 10-2, African, South American, and Asian countries dominate the cocoa trade today.

TABLE 10-2 **Top Cocoa Producers, 2021**

Country	Production (Thousands of Tons)
Ivory Coast	2,034
Ghana	883
Indonesia	659
Nigeria	328
Cameroon	295
Brazil	235
Ecuador	205
Peru	121
Dominican Republic	86
Colombia	56

Source: Data from International Coffee Organization

Cocoa production for import and export purposes is measured in metric tons. To put things in perspective, almost 5 million tons of cocoa were produced worldwide in 2019, versus 3.6 million tons of cocoa in 2009. Due to increased population, demand for cocoa has increased significantly over the years, and I expect this trend to continue over the next decade.

TIP

For a more nuanced understanding of the cocoa market and the companies that control it, check out these resources:

>> **International Cocoa Organization:** www.icco.org

>> **World Cocoa Foundation:** www.worldcocoafoundation.org

The ICE offers a futures contract for cocoa. Consider some useful information regarding this cocoa futures contract, which is the most liquid in the market:

- **Contract ticker symbol:** CC
- **Contract size:** 10 metric tons
- **Underlying commodity:** Generic cocoa beans
- **Price fluctuation:** $1 per ton ($10 per contract)
- **Trading months:** March, May, July, September, and December

As with coffee, the cocoa market is subject to seasonal and cyclical factors that have a large impact on price movements. It can be pretty volatile.

Investing in Sugar: Sweet Move!

Sugar production reportedly started more than 9,000 years ago in southeastern Asia, where it was used in India and China for medicinal purposes. Today Latin American countries dominate the sugar trade; Brazil is the largest sugar producer in the world, as you can see in Table 10-3. In 2021, the top ten sugar producers accounted for 74 percent of global production.

If you're interested in investing in sugar, the ICE offers two futures contracts that track the price of sugar: sugar #11 (world production) and sugar #14 (U.S. production). Consider the contract specs for these two sugar contracts:

- **Sugar #11 (World)**
  - **Contract ticker symbol:** SB
  - **Contract size:** 112,000 pounds
  - **Underlying commodity:** Global sugar
  - **Price fluctuation:** $0.01 per pound ($11.20 per contract)
  - **Trading months:** March, May, July, and October

TABLE 10-3 Top Sugar Producers, 2021

Country	Production (Millions of Tons)
Brazil	37.3
India	26.6
China	11.4
Thailand	10
United States	7.6
Pakistan	6.1
Mexico	6
Russia	5.2
France	4.7

Source: Data from U.S. Department of Agriculture

>> **Sugar #14 (United States)**
- **Contract ticker symbol:** SE
- **Contract size:** 112,000 pounds
- **Underlying commodity:** Domestic (U.S.) sugar
- **Price fluctuation:** $0.01 per pound ($11.20 per contract)
- **Trading months:** January, March, May, July, September, and November

On a historical basis, sugar #14, produced in the United States, tends to be more expensive than sugar #11. However, sugar #11 accounts for most of the volume in the ICE sugar market.

Orange Juice: Refreshingly Good for Your Bottom Line

Orange juice is one of the only actively traded contracts in the futures markets that's based on a tropical fruit: oranges. Oranges are widely grown in the Western Hemisphere, particularly in

Florida and Brazil. As you can see in Table 10-4, Brazil is by far the largest producer of oranges, followed by China. The United States — primarily Florida — is in the top five.

TABLE 10-4 ## Top Orange Producers, 2021

Country	Production (Tons)
Brazil	14,710,000
China	7,500,000
European Union	6,500,000
Mexico	4,100,000
United States	4,000,000

Source: United Nations Statistical Database

Because oranges are perishable, the futures contract tracks *frozen concentrated orange juice* (FCOJ). This form is suitable for storage and fits one of the criteria for inclusion in the futures arena: that the underlying commodity be deliverable. This contract is available for trade on the ICE. The ICE includes two versions of the FCOJ contract: one that tracks the Florida/Brazil oranges and another based on global production.

Consider the contract specs of FCOJ on the ICE:

» **FCOJ-A (Florida/Brazil)**
- **Contract ticker symbol:** OJ
- **Contract size:** 15,000 pounds
- **Underlying commodity:** FCOJ from Brazil or Florida only
- **Price fluctuation:** $0.0005 per pound ($7.50 per contract)
- **Trading months:** January, March, May, July, September, and November

» **FCOJ-B (World)**
- **Contract ticker symbol:** OB
- **Contract size:** 15,000 pounds
- **Underlying commodity:** FCOJ from any producing country

- **Price fluctuation:** $0.0005 per pound ($7.50 per contract)

- **Trading months:** January, March, May, July, September, and November

WARNING

The production of oranges is sensitive to weather. For instance, the hurricane season common in the Florida region can have a significant impact on the prices of oranges both on the spot market and in the futures market. Be sure to consider weather and seasonality when investing in FCOJ futures.

Investing in Corn

Corn is an important food source for both humans and animals and, unlike other grains, can be grown in a variety of climates and conditions, making it an important cash crop for many countries. Corn isn't used just as a feedstock; it has other important applications and is processed into starches, corn oil, and even fuel ethanol. Corn is definitely big business.

REMEMBER

Corn, like other commodities, such as crude oil (see Chapter 3) and coffee (covered earlier in this chapter), comes in different qualities. The most important types of corn to be familiar with are *high-grade number 2* and *number 3 yellow corn*, both of which are traded in the futures markets.

The most direct way of investing in corn is to go through the futures markets. A corn contract, courtesy of the Chicago Mercantile Exchange (CME), helps farmers, consumers, and investors manage and profit from the underlying market opportunities. Take a look at the contract specs:

>> **Contract ticker symbol (open outcry):** C

>> **Electronic ticker (CME Globex):** ZC

>> **Contract size:** 5,000 bushels

>> **Underlying commodity:** High-grade no. 2 or no. 3 yellow corn

>> **Price fluctuation:** $0.0025 per bushel ($12.50 per contract)

>> **Trading hours:** 9:05 a.m. to 1 p.m. open outcry; 6:30 p.m. to 6 a.m. electronic (Central time)

REMEMBER

It's important to know the trading hours for corn and other commodities that trade both on the open outcry and through electronic trading. Open outcry hours are a legacy from the pre-internet age, when people traded all contracts on the trading floor; you can still participate in this trading method during the hours noted in this chapter. The electronic trading system is the latest addition and is much quicker, so you can be sure to get your orders placed quickly and efficiently. As of the writing of this book, the open outcry system is slowly being phased out; eventually, electronic trading will permanently replace it.

>> **Trading months:** March, May, July, September, and December

Corn futures contracts are usually measured in bushels (as with the corn contract the CME offers). Large-scale corn production and consumption is generally measured in metric tons.

Historically, the United States has dominated the corn markets — and still does, thanks to abundant land and helpful governmental subsidies. China is also a major player and exhibits potential for becoming a market leader in the future. Other notable producers include Brazil, Argentina, and Ukraine. Table 10-5 lists the top producers in 2021.

TABLE 10-5 Top Corn Producers, 2021

Country	Production (Millions of Tons)
United States	347
China	260
Brazil	101
Argentina	56
Ukraine	35
Indonesia	30
India	27
Mexico	27
Romania	17

Source: Data from U.S. Department of Agriculture

Similar to other agricultural commodities, corn is subject to seasonal and cyclical factors that have a direct, and often powerful, effect on prices. Prices for corn can go through roller-coaster rides, with wild swings in short periods of time.

TIP

For more information on the corn markets, check out the following sources:

>> **Corn Refiners Association:** https://corn.org

>> **National Corn Growers Association:** www.ncga.com

Wondering about Wheat

Today, wheat is the second most widely produced agricultural commodity in the world (on a per-volume basis), right behind corn and ahead of rice. World wheat production came in at 682 million metric tons in 2009, according to the U.S. Department of Agriculture.

Unlike other commodities that are dominated by single producers — Saudi Arabia and oil, the Ivory Coast and cocoa, Russia and palladium, for example — no single country dominates wheat production. As you can see from Table 10-6, the major wheat producers are a surprisingly eclectic group. The advanced developing countries of China and India are the two largest producers, and industrial countries like Canada and Russia also boast significant wheat-production capabilities.

TABLE 10-6 ## Top Wheat Producers, 2021

Country	Production (Millions of Tons)
China	134
India	107
Russia	85
United States	49
Canada	35

(continued)

TABLE 10-6 *(continued)*

Country	Production (Millions of Tons)
France	30
Pakistan	25
Ukraine	24
Germany	22
Turkey	20

Source: Data from U.S. Department of Agriculture

Wheat is measured in bushels for investment and accounting purposes. Each bushel contains approximately 60 pounds of wheat. As for most other agricultural commodities, metric tons are used to quantify total production and consumption figures on a national and international basis.

The most direct way of accessing the wheat markets, short of owning a wheat farm, is to trade the wheat futures contract. As with the other agricultural commodities discussed in this chapter, the CME offers a futures contract for those interested in capturing profits from wheat price movements — whether for hedging or speculative purposes. Here are the specs for the CME futures contract:

>> **Contract ticker symbol (open outcry):** W

>> **Electronic ticker (CME Globex):** ZW

>> **Contract size:** 5,000 bushels

>> **Underlying commodity:** Premium wheat

>> **Price fluctuation:** $0.0025 per bushel ($12.50 per contract)

>> **Trading hours:** 9:30 a.m. to 1:15 p.m. open outcry; 6:32 p.m. to 6 a.m. electronic (Central time)

>> **Trading months:** March, May, July, September, and December

Wheat production, like that of corn and soybeans, is a seasonal enterprise that's subject to various output disruptions. For instance, Kazakhstan, an important producer, has faced issues with wheat production in the past related to underinvestment in machinery and the misuse of fertilizers. This mismanagement of resources has an impact on the acreage yield, which then influences prices. Such disruptions on the supply side can have a magnified effect on futures prices.

TIP

Interested in finding out more about the wheat market? I recommend the following sources:

>> **National Association of Wheat Growers:** https:// wheatworld.org

>> **U.S. Wheat Associates:** www.uswheat.org

>> **Wheat Foods Council:** www.wheatfoods.org

Trading Soybeans

Soybeans are a vital crop for the world economy, used in everything from producing poultry feedstock to creating vegetable oil.

TIP

If you're interested in getting more background information on the soybean industry, check out the following reputable resources:

>> **American Soybean Association:** https://soygrowers.com

>> **Iowa Soybean Association:** www.iasoybeans.com

Soybeans

Although most soybeans are used to extract soybean oil (used as vegetable oil for culinary purposes) and soybean meal (used primarily as an agricultural feedstock), whole soybeans are also a tradable commodity. Soybeans are edible: If you've ever gone to a sushi restaurant, you may have been offered soybeans as appetizers, under the Japanese name *edamame*.

The United States dominates the soybean market, accounting for more than 50 percent of total global production. Brazil is a distant second, with about 20 percent of the market. The crop in the United States begins in September, and soybean production is cyclical.

The most direct way to trade soybeans is through the CME soybean futures contract. Here's the contract information:

>> **Contract ticker symbol (open outcry):** S

>> **Electronic ticker (CME Globex):** ZS

>> **Contract size:** 5,000 bushels

>> **Underlying commodity:** Premium no. 1, no. 2, and no. 3 yellow soybean bushels

>> **Price fluctuation:** $0.0025 per bushel ($12.50 per contract)

>> **Trading hours:** 9:30 a.m. to 1:15 p.m. open outcry; 6:31 p.m. to 6 a.m. electronic (Central time)

>> **Trading months:** January, March, May, July, August, September, and November

Soybean oil

Soybean oil is an extract of soybeans that you and I know as vegetable oil. Soybean oil is the most widely used culinary oil in the United States and around the world, partly because of its healthy, nutritional characteristics. It contains about 85 percent unsaturated fat and very little saturated fat, which makes it appealing to health-conscious consumers.

In addition to its gastronomic uses, soybean oil is becoming an increasingly popular additive in alternative energy sources technology, such as biodiesel. For example, an increasing number of cars in the United States and abroad are being outfitted with engines that allow them to convert from regular diesel to soybean oil during operation. Because of their economic fuel mileage and low environmental impact, these soybean oil-enabled cars, known as *frybrids*, are becoming more popular.

Demand for soybean oil has increased in recent years as demand for these cleaner-burning fuels increases and as the automotive technology becomes better able to accommodate the usage of such biodiesels. According to the Commodity Research Bureau (CRB), production of soybean oil increased from an average of 15 billion pounds in the mid-1990s to more than 35 billion pounds in 2009.

If you want to trade soybean oil, you need to go through the CME, which offers the standard soybean oil contract. Here's the contract information:

- >> **Contract ticker symbol (open outcry):** BO
- >> **Electronic ticker (CME Globex):** ZL
- >> **Contract size:** 60,000 pounds
- >> **Underlying commodity:** Premium crude soybean oil
- >> **Price fluctuation:** $0.0001 per pound ($6 per contract)
- >> **Trading hours:** 9:30 a.m. to 1:15 p.m. open outcry; 6:31 p.m. to 6 a.m. electronic (Central time)
- >> **Trading months:** January, March, May, July, August, September, October, and December

TIP

For more information on investing in soybean oil, turn to the National Oilseed Processors Association, an industry group, at www.nopa.org.

Soybean meal

Soybean meal, like soybean oil, is an extract of soybeans. Basically, whatever is left after soybean oil is extracted from soybeans can be converted to soybean meal. Soybean meal is a high-protein, high-energy-content food used primarily as a feedstock for cattle, hogs, and poultry. (I cover trading such livestock later in this chapter.)

To invest in soybean meal, you can trade the soybean meal futures contract on the CME. Here's the information to help you get started trading this contract:

- >> **Contract ticker symbol (open outcry):** SM
- >> **Electronic ticker (CME Globex):** ZM
- >> **Contract size:** 100 tons
- >> **Underlying commodity:** 48 percent protein soybean meal
- >> **Price fluctuation:** $0.10 per ton ($10 per contract)
- >> **Trading hours:** 9:30 a.m. to 1:15 p.m. open outcry; 6:31 p.m. to 6 a.m. electronic (Central time)
- >> **Trading months:** January, March, May, July, August, September, October, and December

TIP

You can get more information regarding soybean meal from the Soybean Meal Info Center at www.soymeal.org.

Holy Cow! Investing in Cattle

Cows are a special breed because they're low-maintenance animals with high-product output: They eat almost nothing but grass, yet they produce milk, provide meat, and, in some cases, create leather goods. This input-to-output ratio means that cows occupy a special place in the agricultural complex.

Two futures contracts exist for the cattle trader and investor: the live cattle and the feeder cattle contracts. Both trade on the CME.

Live cattle

The live cattle futures contract, traded on the CME, is unique because it was the first contract the CME launched to track a commodity that's actually alive. Before the live cattle futures, all futures contracts were for storable commodities, such as crude oil, copper, and sugar. The CME live cattle futures contract, launched in 1964, heralded a new era for the exchanges. Various market players, including cattle producers, packers, consumers, and independent traders, now widely trade this futures contract.

Consider the specs of this futures contract:

>> **Contract ticker symbol (open outcry):** LC

>> **Electronic ticker (CME Globex):** LE

>> **Contract size:** 40,000 pounds

>> **Underlying commodity:** Live cattle (55 percent choice, 45 percent select, Yield Grade 3 live steers)

>> **Price fluctuation:** $0.00025 per pound ($10 per contract)

>> **Trading hours:** 9:05 a.m. to 1 p.m. (Central time), electronic and open outcry

>> **Trading months:** February, April, June, August, October, and December

The live cattle contract is popular partly because it allows all interested parties to hedge their market positions to reduce the volatility and uncertainty associated with livestock production in general and live cattle growing in particular.

If you decide to trade this contract, keep the following market risks in mind: seasonality, fluctuating prices of feedstock, transportation costs, changing consumer demand, and threat of diseases (such as mad cow disease). The market for the live cattle contract can be fairly volatile.

Feeder cattle

The CME launched a feeder cattle futures contract in 1971, only a few years after the launch of the groundbreaking live cattle contract. The feeder cattle contract is for calves that weigh in at 650 to 849 pounds, which are sent to the feedlots to be fed, fattened, and then slaughtered.

Because the CME feeder cattle futures contract is settled on a cash basis, the CME calculates an index for feeder cattle cash prices based on a seven-day average. This index, known in the industry as the *CME Feeder Cattle Index*, is an average of feeder cattle prices from the largest feeder cattle-producing states in the United States, as compiled by the U.S. Department of Agriculture. These producing states are (in alphabetical order) Colorado, Iowa, Kansas, Missouri, Montana, Nebraska, New Mexico, North Dakota, Oklahoma, South Dakota, Texas, and Wyoming. You can get information on the CME Feeder Cattle Index through the CME website at www.cmegroup.com.

To get livestock statistical information, check out the U.S. Department of Agriculture's statistical division at www.marketnews.usda.gov/portal/lg.

Look over the specs of this futures contract:

>> **Contract ticker symbol (open outcry):** FC

>> **Electronic ticker (CME Globex):** GF

>> **Contract size:** 50,000 pounds

>> **Underlying commodity:** Feeder cattle (650- to 849-pound steers, medium-large #1 and medium-large #1–2)

>> **Price fluctuation:** $0.00025 per pound ($12.50 per contract)

>> **Trading hours:** 9:05 a.m. to 1 p.m. (Central time), electronic and open outcry

>> **Trading months:** January, March, April, May, August, September, October, and November

Two important traits characterize the feeder cattle contract:

>> Like many meat commodities, it's fairly volatile.

>> It's a thinly traded contract — in other words, it doesn't have as much liquidity as some of the other CME products.

Checking Out Lean Hogs

The lean hog futures contract (which is a contract for the hog's carcass) trades on the CME and is used primarily by producers of lean hogs — both domestic and international — and pork importers/exporters. Launched in 1997, the lean hog contract is a fairly new addition to the CME, intended to replace the live hog futures contract that was retired. The lean hog contract replaced the live hog contract because producers and consumers of these products don't transact the live animal (live hog); it made more sense for the futures contract to track the product traded in the marketplace.

Here are the contract specs for lean hogs:

>> **Contract ticker symbol (open outcry):** LH

>> **Electronic ticker (CME Globex):** HE

>> **Contract size:** 40,000 pounds

>> **Underlying commodity:** Lean hogs (hog barrow and gilt carcasses)

>> **Price fluctuation:** $0.00025 per pound ($10 per contract)

>> **Trading hours:** 9:10 a.m. to 1 p.m. (Central time), electronic and open outcry

>> **Trading months:** February, April, May, June, July, August, October, and December

Perhaps no other commodity, agricultural or otherwise, exhibits the same level of volatility as the lean hogs futures contract. One of the reasons is that, compared to other products, this contract isn't very liquid. It's primarily used by commercial entities seeking to hedge against price risk. Other commodities that are actively traded by individual speculators as well as the commercial entities (such as crude oil) are far more liquid and, therefore, less volatile.

Trading Frozen Pork Bellies

Essentially, the term *pork bellies* is the traders' way of referring to bacon. Physically, pork bellies come from the underside of a hog and weigh approximately 12 pounds. These pork bellies are generally stored frozen for extended periods of time, pending delivery to consumers.

As with most other livestock products, the CME offers a futures contract for frozen pork bellies. This contract, launched by the CME in 1961, is the first-ever contract on a commodity exchange for which the underlying deliverable commodity is a meat — albeit, dead meat. (The CME live cattle contract was the first contract based on a live animal; refer to that section earlier in this chapter for more information.)

Here are the specs for the CME frozen pork bellies futures contract:

>> **Contract ticker symbol (open outcry):** PB

>> **Electronic ticker (CME Globex):** GPB

>> **Contract size:** 40,000 pounds

>> **Underlying commodity:** Pork bellies, cut and trimmed (12- to 18-pound frozen pork bellies)

>> **Price fluctuation:** $0.00025 per pound ($10 per contract)

>> **Trading hours:** 9:10 a.m. to 1 p.m. (Central time), electronic and open outcry

>> **Trading months:** February, March, May, July, and August

The pork bellies market is a seasonal market subject to wild price fluctuations. Although production of pork bellies is a major determining factor of market prices, other variables have a significant impact on prices. A buildup in pork belly inventories usually takes place at the beginning of the calendar year, resulting in lower prices. But as inventories are depleted, the market moves to a supply-side bias, placing upward pressure on market prices. On the other side of the equation, consumer demand for bacon and other meats isn't easily predictable and fluctuates with the seasons.

WARNING

Because of the cyclicality of the supply-side model, coupled with the seasonality of the demand model, pork belly prices are subject to extreme volatility. As a matter of fact, the pork bellies futures contract is one of the most volatile contracts trading in the market today.

TIP

Demand for bacon and other high-fat, high-cholesterol foods appears to be waning as a result of the health-conscious eating trends sweeping the nation. These dietary changes could have an impact on the prices of frozen pork bellies and other meats. Be aware of the impact of these dietary trends on the prices of pork bellies and other meats before you invest.

4

Choosing an Investment Approach

Create your financial road map and design a portfolio that includes commodities.

Check out exchange-traded funds (ETFs), their pros and cons, how to choose a suitable product, and how to choose and invest in indexes.

Navigate futures contracts, trade on margin, spot market movements, and disentangle options contracts.

Invest in mutual funds, check out master limited partnerships (MLPs), work with commodity trading advisors and commodity pools, and trade on commodity exchanges.

Chapter **11**

Welcoming Commodities into Your Portfolio

Whether you're an experienced investor or a first-time trader, it's important to have a good grasp on how to use your portfolio to improve your overall financial situation. When designing your portfolio, you need to consider factors such as your risk tolerance, tax bracket, and level of liabilities. I start off this chapter by going through these basic portfolio management techniques so you can synchronize your portfolio with your personal financial profile.

Then I show you how to introduce commodities into your portfolio. I go through basic portfolio allocation methods and include an overview of the benefits of diversification. Finally, I list the different investment methods you have at your disposal to get exposure to commodities.

The Color of Money: Taking Control of Your Financial Life

You invest because you've realized that it's better to have your money working for you than to have it sit in a bank account earning so little interest that you end up losing money when you factor in inflation. Most people end up working for their money all their lives, and they get stuck in a vicious cycle where they become servants to it.

If you're caught in this vicious cycle, you want your relationship with money to do a 180-degree reversal: Instead of working hard for your money, you need to have your money work hard for you. Investing allows you to build and, more important, maintain your wealth.

Building wealth isn't easy, but with a little discipline and self-control, it can be a fun and rewarding process. If you're new to investing in general, check out Eric Tyson's *Personal Finance For Dummies* and *Investing For Dummies* (both published by Wiley) for foundational information and guidance.

REMEMBER

Often the accumulation phase isn't the biggest challenge to building wealth; many times being able to preserve wealth is more difficult. Keep in mind these factors that can negatively affect your bottom line:

>> **Inflation:** *Inflation,* an increase in prices or the money supply, which can result in a quick deterioration of value, is one of the most detrimental forces you face as an investor. Inflation keeps some of the brightest minds up at night; among them is the chairperson of the Federal Reserve, whose main priority is making sure the economy doesn't grow so fast that it creates bad inflation. When inflation gets out of control, the currency isn't worth the paper it's printed on. This state, known as *hyperinflation,* occurred in Weimar Germany in the 1920s. Conveniently, one way to protect yourself from inflation is to invest in commodities such as gold and silver. (Turn to Chapter 7 for more on using precious metals as a hedge against inflation.)

Since the COVID-19 pandemic lockdowns of 2020, inflation has run rampant in the world's major economies. Supply chain disruptions (as a result of the lockdown that ground factories to a halt), expansive monetary policy (as a result of the Federal Reserve and other major central banks providing liquidity), and the subsequent Russia–Ukraine War have resulted in the biggest inflation trends since the 1970s. Ironically, investors who are long on commodities can not only hedge themselves against inflation but also benefit from it.

>> **Business cycles:** In the world of investing, nothing ever goes up in a straight line. Minor turbulence always arises along the way, and most investments experience some drops before they reach new highs — that is, if they ever reach new highs. The economy moves in the same way, alternating between expansions and recessions. Certain assets that perform well during expansions, such as stocks, don't do so well during recessions. Alternatively, assets such as commodities do fairly well during late expansionary and early recessionary phases of the business cycle. As an investor interested in preserving and growing your capital base, you need to be able to identify and invest in assets that are going to perform and generate returns, regardless of the current business cycle. I discuss the performance of commodities across the business cycle in Chapter 2.

You can minimize these risks and others, such as risks posed by fraud, the markets, and geopolitics, with some due diligence and a few wise decisions. I look at risk as it relates to both commodities and investing in general in Chapter 2.

Looking Ahead: Creating a Financial Road Map

Achieving your financial goals takes a conscious and systematic effort. Of course, the first part is identifying and establishing your financial goals. These goals may be as diverse as amassing enough money to retire by age 50 and travel the world, to gathering enough money to pay for college, to making enough money to pass on to your children or grandchildren. Before you start investing in commodities or any other asset, sit down and figure out clear financial goals. Every individual has different needs and interests. In the following sections, I outline some key points to help you establish your financial goals.

After you identify your goals, you can begin figuring out how to use commodities to achieve those goals. I show you how in the later section "Making Room in Your Portfolio for Commodities."

Figuring out your net worth

You need to know where you are before you can determine where you want to go. From a personal finance perspective, you need to know how much you're worth so you can determine how much capital to allocate to investments, living expenses, retirement, and so on.

You calculate your net worth by subtracting your total liabilities from your total assets. (*Assets* put money in your pocket, whereas *liabilities* remove money from your pocket.)

Fill in the blanks in Table 11-1 to determine the total value of your assets.

TABLE 11-1 Total Assets

Assets	Value
Annuities	$_____
Bonds and other fixed income	$_____
Cash in all checking and savings accounts	$_____
Cash on hand	$_____
Certificates of deposit (CDs)	$_____
Commodity investments	$_____
Futures and options	$_____
Individual retirement accounts (IRAs)	$_____
Life insurance	$_____
Money-market funds	$_____
Market value of home	$_____
Market value of other real estate	$_____
Mutual funds	$_____
Pension plans — 401(k) or 403(b)	$_____

Assets	Value
Personal belongings (home furnishings, jewelry, and so on)	$_____
Stocks and other equity	$_____
Vehicles (car, boat, and so on)	$_____
Other investment assets	$_____
TOTAL VALUE OF ASSETS	$_____

Assets are only one part of the net worth equation. After you calculate your total assets, you need to determine how many liabilities you have. Use Table 11-2 to help you determine your total liabilities.

TABLE 11-2 ## Total Liabilities

Liabilities	Value
Car loans	$_____
College loans	$_____
Credit card loans	$_____
Mortgage(s)	$_____
Mortgage equity line	$_____
Other loans	$_____
TOTAL VALUE OF LIABILITIES	$_____

After you determine both your total assets and your total liabilities, use the following formula to determine your total net worth:

Total net worth = Total assets − Total liabilities

Determining your net worth on a regular basis is important because it allows you to keep track of the balance between your assets and your liabilities. Knowing your net worth allows you to then determine which investment strategy to pursue.

REMEMBER

Based on this simple mathematical formula, the key to increasing your net worth is to increase your assets while reducing your liabilities. Investing helps you increase your assets. Cutting down on living expenses may help you reduce your liabilities.

Identifying your tax bracket

Taxes have a direct impact on how much of your assets you get to keep at the end of the day. You must understand the implications that taxes can have on your portfolio.

How much you pay in taxes is based on your tax bracket. Table 11-3 lists the individual income tax brackets for 2022 to help you determine how much you'll end up paying in taxes based on your income.

TABLE 11-3 **2022 Income Tax Rate Schedule (Federal Level)**

Annual Taxable Income	Tax Level
$0–$10,275	10%
$10,276–$41,775	12%
$41,776–$89,075	22%
$89,076–$170,050	24%
$170,051–$215,950	32%
$215,951–$539,900	35%

The tax rate schedule in Table 11-3 is known as Schedule X, and it applies to you if you're filing your tax return as a single person. The Internal Revenue Service (IRS) has a number of different schedules, depending on how you're filing your returns.

>> **Schedule Y-1:** Married and filing jointly *or* qualifying widow(er)

>> **Schedule Y-2:** Married and filing separately

>> **Schedule Z:** Head of household

REMEMBER

Tax rates change depending on which schedule you file under. Visit the IRS website at www.irs.gov, or talk to your accountant to find out the tax rates under the different schedules. Because tax rates may change on an annual basis, inquire about these tax issues regularly.

Where you live can also have a big impact on how taxes affect your investments. Did you know that a number of states within the continental United States don't have income taxes? As a resident of one of these states, you pay federal income taxes but no state income taxes, so no one will blame you for considering relocation. These states have absolutely no income tax, which means you get to keep more of what you earn:

>> Alaska

>> Florida

>> Nevada

>> New Hampshire

>> South Dakota

>> Tennessee

>> Texas

>> Washington

>> Wyoming

WARNING

Out of the nine states that don't have personal income taxes, Florida does place a tax on intangible personal property; thus, items such as stocks, bonds, and mutual funds are subject to taxes. Also note that both New Hampshire and Tennessee tax income earned on interest and dividends.

REMEMBER

Investing in commodities, as in any other asset class, has tax implications. I'm not an accountant, and the aim of this book isn't to offer you tax advice, so I recommend that you talk to your accountant before you invest in commodities. Knowing the tax implications before you invest may save you a lot of heartache down the road.

Determining your appetite for risk

Risk is perhaps the single greatest enemy you face as an investor. How wonderful would life be if you could have guaranteed returns without risk? Because that's not possible (and has never been possible), you have to find how to manage, tame, and minimize risk. I cover managing risk related to commodities in Chapter 2, but I briefly discuss general portfolio risk in this section.

Your risk tolerance depends on a number of factors that are unique to you as an individual. The first step in determining your risk tolerance is deciding how much risk you're willing to take on. Although no equation or formula can determine risk (it would be nice if there were one), you can use a general rule to identify the percentage of your assets to dedicate to aggressive investments with an elevated risk/reward ratio.

REMEMBER

As a general rule, the younger you are, the higher the percentage of assets you should devote to higher-risk investments. This approach makes sense because if you lose a lot of value, you still have plenty of time ahead of you to recoup your losses. When you're older, however, you don't have as much time to get back your investments.

Table 11-4 gives you a simple guideline to help you determine the percentage of assets that should go into investments with higher returns (and risks), such as stocks, commodities, and real estate. This is *not* a percentage of how much of your portfolio you should invest in commodities; I discuss that percentage in the following section.

TABLE 11-4 Recommended Percentage of Assets in Growth Investments by Age Group

Age Group	Percentage in Growth Investments
21–30	81%–90%
31–40	71%–80%
41–50	61%–70%
51–64	45%–60%
65 and over	Less than 45%

WARNING

The rules in Table 11-4 aren't set in stone, but you can use them to approximate how much of your assets to place in investments that have a high risk/reward ratio. If your investments are increasing just fine with the percentages you're working with, don't change them. As the saying goes, if it ain't broke, don't try to fix it.

Making Room in Your Portfolio for Commodities

One of the most common questions I get from investors is, "How much of my portfolio should I have in commodities?" My answer is usually simple: It depends. To answer that question, you have to consider a number of factors to determine how much capital to dedicate to commodities.

Personally, my portfolio may include at any one point anywhere between 35 percent and 50 percent commodities. However, sometimes it's much lower than that — and sometimes almost 90 percent of my portfolio is in commodities.

TIP

If you're new to commodities, I recommend starting out with a relatively modest amount — anywhere between 3 percent and 5 percent of your portfolio — to see how comfortable you feel with this new member of your financial family. Test how commodities contribute to your overall portfolio's performance during one or two investing quarters. If you're satisfied, I recommend that you gradually increase your percentage.

Many investors who like the way commodities anchor their portfolios settle at about 15 percent exposure to commodities. I find that's a pretty good place to be if you're still getting used to commodities. When you see the benefits and realize how much value commodities can provide, I'll bet that number will steadily increase.

Fully Exposed: The Top Ways to Get Exposure to Commodities

You have several methods at your disposal, both direct and indirect, for getting exposure to commodities. In this section, I go through the different ways you can invest in commodities.

Commodity futures

The futures markets are the most direct way to get exposure to commodities. Futures contracts allow you to purchase an underlying commodity for an agreed-upon price in the future. I talk about futures contracts in depth in Chapter 13. In this section, I list some ways you can play the futures markets.

Commodity indexes

Commodity indexes track a basket of commodity futures contracts. Each index uses a unique methodology and performs differently than its peers. Commodity indexes are known as passive, long-only investments because they're not actively managed and they can only buy the underlying commodity; they can't short it. (For more on going long and going short, turn to Chapter 13.)

You can choose from these five major commodity indexes:

>> Deutsche Bank Liquid Commodity Index (DBLCI)

>> Dow Jones–AIG Commodity Index (DJ-AIGCI)

>> Goldman Sachs Commodity Index (GSCI)

>> Reuters/Jefferies Commodity Research Bureau Index (R/J-CRBI)

>> Rogers International Commodity Index (RICI)

I analyze the components, performance, and construction methodology of each of these indexes in Chapter 12.

Futures commission merchants

Don't be intimidated by the name. A *futures commission merchant* (FCM) is much like a regular stockbroker. However, instead of selling stocks, an FCM is licensed to sell futures contracts, options, and other derivatives to the public.

If you're comfortable trading futures and options contracts, opening an account with an FCM gives you the most direct access to the commodity futures markets. Make sure that you read Chapter 12 to find out the pros and cons of investing through an FCM.

Commodity trading advisors

A *commodity trading advisor* (CTA) is an individual who manages accounts for clients who trade futures contracts. The CTA may provide advice on how to place your trades, but this person may also manage your account on your behalf. Be sure to research the CTA's track record and investment philosophy so you know whether it squares with yours.

WARNING

CTAs may manage accounts for more than one client. However, they're not allowed to "pool" accounts and share all profits and losses among clients equally. (This is one of the main differences between a CTA and a CPO, discussed in the next section.)

Chapter 12 can help you identify key elements to look for when shopping for a CTA.

Commodity pool operators

The *commodity pool operator* (CPO) acts a lot like a CTA except that, instead of managing separate accounts, the CPO has the authority to "pool" all client funds in one account and trade them as if they were trading one account.

REMEMBER

Investing through a CPO offers two advantages over investing through a CTA:

>> Because CPOs can pool funds, they have access to more funds to invest. This pooling provides both leverage and diversification opportunities that smaller accounts don't offer. You can buy a lot more assets with $100,000 than you can with $10,000.

>> Most CPOs are structured as partnerships, which means that the only money you can lose is your principal. In the world of futures, this is pretty good because, due to margin and the use of leverage, you can end up owing a lot more than the principal if a trade goes sour. Be sure to read Chapter 13 for more on margin and leverage.

I walk through the pros and cons of investing through a CPO in Chapter 14.

Commodity funds

If you think delving into commodity derivatives isn't for you, you can access the commodity markets through funds. If you've invested before, you may be familiar with these two investment vehicles.

Commodity mutual funds

Commodity mutual funds are exactly like average, run-of-the-mill mutual funds except that they focus specifically on investing in commodities. You can choose from several funds, although the two biggest ones are the PIMCO and Oppenheimer funds. (I examine commodity mutual funds in Chapter 14.)

A 2005 ruling by the Securities and Exchange Commission (SEC) changed the way mutual funds account for qualifying income. This ruling has put some pressure on funds, particularly PIMCO, to come up with different accounting methods. Make sure you find out how such rulings affect your investments.

Exchange-traded funds

Exchange-traded funds (ETFs) have become popular with investors because they provide the benefits of investing in a fund with the ease of trading a stock. This hybrid instrument is becoming one of the best ways for investors to access the commodities markets.

You currently have at your disposal ETFs that track baskets of commodities through commodity indexes, as well as ETFs that track single commodities such as oil, gold, and silver. Here are some popular commodity ETFs:

>> **Deutsche Bank Commodity Index Tracking Fund (DBC):** Tracks the performance of the Deutsche Bank Commodity Index

>> **U.S. Oil Fund (USO):** Mirrors the movements of the West Texas Intermediate (WTI) crude oil on the NYMEX

>> **Street Tracks Gold Shares (GLD):** Tracks the performance of gold bullion

>> **iShares COMEX Gold Trust (IAU):** Tracks the performance of gold futures contracts on the COMEX

>> **iShares Silver Trust (SLV):** Tracks the performance of silver

Make sure you examine all fees associated with the ETF before you invest. Check out Chapter 12 for more information on this investment vehicle.

Commodity companies

Another route you can take to get exposure to commodities is to buy stocks of commodity companies. These companies are generally involved in the production, transformation, or distribution of various commodities.

This route is perhaps the most indirect way of accessing the commodity markets because, in buying a company's stock, you're getting exposure not only to the performance of the underlying commodity that the company is involved in, but other factors, such as the company's management skills, creditworthiness, and ability to generate cash flow and minimize expenses.

Publicly traded companies

Publicly traded companies can expose you to specific sectors of commodities, such as metals, energy, or agricultural products. Within these three categories, you can choose companies that deal with specific methods or commodities, such as refiners of crude oil into finished products or gold-mining companies.

If you're considering an equity stake in a commodity company, you need to determine how the company's stock performs relative to the price of the underlying commodity that company is involved in.

TIP

Although there's no hard rule, I've found a relatively strong correlation between the performance of commodity futures contracts and the performance of companies that use these commodities as inputs. So, investing in the stock of commodity companies actually gives you pretty good exposure to the underlying commodities themselves. However, you want to be extra careful and perform thorough due diligence before you invest in these companies. I show you some keys to look for before you invest in such companies in Chapters 6 and 9.

Master limited partnerships

A *master limited partnership* (MLP) is a hybrid instrument that offers you the convenience of trading a partnership like a stock. You get the best of both worlds: the liquidity that comes from being a publicly traded entity and the tax protection of being a partnership.

One of the biggest advantages of MLPs is that, as a unit holder, you're taxed at only the individual level. This structure is different from investing in a corporation because cash back to shareholders (in the form of dividends) is taxed at both the corporate level and the individual level. MLPs don't pay corporate tax, which is a huge benefit for your bottom line.

WARNING

For an MLP to qualify for these tax breaks, it must generate 90 percent of its income from qualifying sources that relate to commodities, particularly in the oil and gas industry.

Some of the popular assets that MLPs invest in include oil and gas storage facilities and transportation infrastructure such as pipelines. I cover MLPs in detail in Chapter 14.

Chapter **12**

Investing in ETFs and Commodity Indexes

Driven by growing investor demand for commodities, many financial institutions are now offering the commodities *exchange-traded fund* (ETF). This breed of fund enables you to buy into a fund that offers the diversification inherent in a mutual fund and the added benefit of being able to trade that fund like a regular stock. Thus, you get a powerful combination of diversification and liquidity. ETFs are becoming popular with investors because they provide the benefits of investing in a fund with the ease of trading a stock. This hybrid instrument is one of the best ways for investors to access the commodities markets, as you find out in this chapter.

Indexes, sometimes referred to as *liquid investing instruments*, are also useful tools in the world of investing. If investing were similar to driving a car, the index would be the equivalent of the speedometer — it tells you how fast the car (or the market) is going. Indexes exist for all sorts of assets. The two most well-known indexes track the top 30 blue-chip companies in the United

States (the Dow Jones Industrial Average) and the 500 largest companies (the S&P 500), but plenty of others await investors, too.

If you want to measure the performance of commodities, you also have at your disposal indexes that track baskets of commodities. These commodity indexes can be useful for two reasons:

>> You can use them as market indicators to help you gauge where the commodity markets are trading as a whole.

>> Because most indexes are tradable instruments (through ETFs and other investment vehicles), you can profit by investing directly in the index.

In this chapter, I give you the goods on commodity indexes and show you how to profit by using these powerful tools.

Getting to Know ETFs

ETFs offer many advantages to investors because they provide exposure to asset classes and specific investments that would otherwise be difficult for the average investor to access, such as uranium and palladium. In addition, they give you a broad diversification platform because they can track a basket of stocks or commodities. This characteristic is a major reason ETFs have become so popular in the past decade, increasing from several dozen to more than 7,600 ETF products, representing more than $7 trillion in assets.

Unlike a regular mutual fund, in which the net asset value (NAV) is generally calculated at the end of the trading day, the ETF enables you to trade throughout the day. Furthermore, you can go both long and short the ETF, something you can't do with regular mutual funds.

TIP

It's critical to perform extensive due diligence on any ETF product you're considering for your portfolio. You need a solid understanding of the underlying assets in the ETF. Often beginning investors simply browse the description without getting a good grip on what they're actually buying. For example, the current uranium ETF URA (NYSE: URA) isn't a product that tracks uranium metal prices; it tracks a basket of uranium-mining equities. Folks who don't get into the fine print may miss basic yet critical pieces of information regarding ETFs specifically and broader investment products in general. Make sure you go beyond the headlines and into the fine print.

TIP

ETFs aren't free, in the sense that they're actively managed products associated with a financial institution. ETF sponsors generally charge an added layer of fees for the convenience of using their products. Therefore, it's imperative to know the types of fees associated with each ETF you purchase. This information is conveniently located in the fund's prospectus.

Deutsche Bank launched the first commodity index ETF in the United States in February 2006. The Deutsche Bank Commodity Index Tracking Fund (AMEX: DBC) is listed on the American Stock and Options Exchange (AMEX) and tracks the Deutsche Bank Liquid Commodity Index (DBLCI). The DBLCI, in turn, tracks a basket of six liquid commodities:

>> Light, sweet crude oil (35 percent)

>> Heating oil (20 percent)

>> Aluminum (12.5 percent)

>> Corn (11.25 percent)

>> Wheat (11.25 percent)

>> Gold (10 percent)

The DBC is a superb indicator of the broader commodity markets. Since 2005, commodities have been characterized by a massive run-up in prices, driven partly by large consumption demands from emerging markets such as China and by speculative activity. That price run-up resulted in a massive bursting of asset bubbles in 2008 during the Global Financial Crisis. From 2008 until 2020, DBC accurately depicted the performance of commodities as an asset class, performance characterized by sideway-trending and downward-trending price movement. Not until 2020 did the index pick up steam. Now we're seeing a run-up in commodities prices driven by the post-pandemic economic boom.

The DBC ETF is structured as a commodity pool operator (CPO), and the fund invests directly in commodity futures contracts (see Chapter 14). To capture additional yields, the energy contracts are rolled monthly; the rest of the contracts are rolled annually. (Chapter 13 talks more about rolling futures contracts.) The fund also invests in fixed-income products, including the three-month Treasury bill, which provides an additional yield for investors. With an expense ratio of 1.5 percent, it's a reasonably priced investment.

Accessing Commodity Markets through ETFs

One of the downsides of investing in ETFs is that they can be fairly volatile because they track derivative instruments that trade in the futures markets. A downside of the DBC specifically (see the preceding section) is that it tracks a basket of only six commodities. However, more commodity ETFs are in the pipeline that will offer greater diversification benefits. In Table 12-1, I list some of the more common ETFs available. As you can see, you can now access a broad variety of commodity markets through ETFs, ranging from livestock and natural gas all the way to uranium and palladium.

TABLE 12-1 List of Commodity ETFs

ETF	Category	Ticker Symbol
Dow Jones–AIG Commodity Index Total Return	Broad index	NYSE: DJP
Deutsche Bank Commodity Index Tracking Fund	Broad index	NYSE: DBC
Goldman Sachs Commodity Index Total Return	Broad index	NYSE: GSG
Dow Jones–AIG Agriculture Total Return ETN	Agriculture index	NYSE: JJA
StreetTracks Gold Shares ETF	Gold	NYSE: GLD
iShares Gold Trust ETF	Gold	NYSE: IAU
iShares Silver Trust Fund	Silver	NYSE: SLV
Dow Jones–AIG Aluminum ETN	Aluminum	NYSE: JJU
United States Natural Gas Fund	Natural gas	NYSE: UNG

ETF	Category	Ticker Symbol
United States Oil Fund	Crude oil	NYSE: USO
Dow Jones–AIG Livestock Total Return ETN	Livestock index	NYSE: COW
ETFS Physical Palladium Shares ETF	Palladium	NYSE: PALL
ETFS Physical Platinum Shares ETF	Platinum	NYSE: PPLT
Global X Global Gold Explorers ETF	Gold exploration	NYSE: GLDX
Global X Global Silver Explorers ETF	Silver exploration	NYSE: SIL
Global X Lithium ETF	Lithium metal	NYSE: LIT
Global X Uranium ETF	Uranium metal	NYSE: URA
Emerging Global Energy Titans Index	Energy companies	NYSE: EEO

These ETFs are some of the most popular ones in the marketplace today:

>> **United States Oil Fund (AMEX: USO):** The United States Oil Fund (USO) is an ETF that seeks to mirror the performance of the West Texas Intermediate (WTI) crude oil futures contract on the New York Mercantile Exchange (NYMEX). Although the ETF doesn't reflect the movement of the WTI contract tick-by-tick, it does a good job of broadly mirroring its performance. It's a good way to get exposure to crude oil without going through the futures markets.

>> **SPDR Gold Shares (NYSEArca: GLD):** This ETF seeks to mirror the performance of the price of gold on a daily basis. The fund actually holds physical gold in vaults located in secure locations so investors can get exposure to physical gold without having to hold gold bullion.

>> **iShares Silver Trust (AMEX: SLV):** This ETF is the first ever to track the performance of the price of physical silver. Like the gold ETF, the silver ETF holds actual physical silver in vaults. It's a safe way to invest in the silver markets without going through the futures or physical markets.

TIP

Another ETF in the marketplace is the Aluminum ETF, launched by Dow Jones & AIG. Aluminum has always been an important metal because it's one of the building blocks of construction, industry, and infrastructure. With many important uses and applications, investors and traders worldwide closely follow this metal. I like this ETF for active traders because it's a fairly volatile metal. You can play the momentum in your favor by actively trading it.

Checking Out Commodity Indexes

A commodity index tracks the price of a futures contract of an underlying physical commodity on a designated exchange. When you invest through one of the commodity indexes I present in this chapter, you're actually investing in the futures markets. (For more on futures contracts, check out Chapter 13.)

REMEMBER

Indexes are known as passive, long-only investments for two reasons: No one is actively trading the index, and the index tracks only the long performance of a commodity. It doesn't track commodities that are *short* (a sophisticated strategy meant to profit when prices go down). For more on long and short positions, flip to Chapter 13.

Why indexes are useful

Using commodity indexes is a good way to determine where the commodity markets are heading. Just as stock indexes allow you to identify broad market movements (which then enable you to implement and update your investment strategy accordingly), commodity indexes give you a way to measure the broad movements of the commodities markets.

REMEMBER

In essence, a commodity index is a snapshot of the current state of the commodities market. You can use an index in one of three ways:

>> **Benchmark:** You can use a commodity index to compare the performance of commodities as an asset class with the performance of other asset classes, such as stocks and bonds.

>> **Indicator:** You can use the commodity index as an indicator of economic activity, possible inflationary pressures, and the state of global economic production.

>> **Liquid investment vehicle:** Because a commodity index tracks the performance of specific futures contracts, you can replicate the performance of the index by trading the contracts it tracks. You can invest in a commodity index both directly (by buying the contracts) and indirectly (via mutual funds). I discuss those options in depth in the following section.

How to make money by using an index

You can invest through a commodity index by using a number of methods. You can choose from five widely followed commodity indexes (covered later in this chapter), and each one is tracked and traded differently.

Consider a few ways you can invest through a commodity index:

>> **Own the futures contracts.** One of the most direct ways of tracking the performance of an index is to own the contracts the index tracks. To do this, you must have a *futures account*. (Refer to Chapter 13 to find out how to open a futures account.)

>> **Invest with a third-party manager.** Many money managers use commodity indexes as the basis of their investment strategy. Some of these vehicles include mutual funds, commodity pools, and commodity trading advisors. (For more on selecting the right manager, see Chapter 14.)

>> **Own futures contracts of the index.** A few commodity indexes have futures contracts that track their performance. When you buy the futures contract of the index, it's similar to buying all the commodity futures contracts the index trades.

>> **Make use of ETFs.** ETFs are a popular breed of investment that tracks the performance of a fund through the convenience of trading a stock. ETFs are a popular alternative for folks who don't want to trade futures. (Be sure to explore the benefits and drawbacks of ETFs earlier in this chapter.)

Uncovering the Anatomy of a Commodity Index

WARNING

As an investor interested in making money through index investing, you have five commodity indexes at your disposal. Although the composition and structure of every index is different, the aim is the same: to track a basket of commodities. Before you get into the specific commodity indexes, watch out for these pitfalls when you're shopping for an index:

>> **Components:** Each index follows a specific methodology to determine which commodities are part of the index. Some indexes, such as the S&P GSCI, include commodities based on their global production value. Other indexes, such as the DBLCI, include commodities based on their liquidity and representational value of a component class, such as picking gold to represent metals and choosing oil as a representative of the energy market.

>> **Weightings:** Some indexes follow a *production-weighted methodology,* in which weights are assigned to each commodity based on its proportional production in the world. Other indexes choose *component weightings* based on the liquidity of the commodity's futures contract. In addition, some weightings are fixed over a predetermined period of time, whereas others fluctuate to reflect changes in actual production values.

>> **Rolling methodology:** Because the index's purpose is to track the performance of commodities and not take actual delivery of the commodity, the futures contracts that the index tracks must be rolled over from the current-month contract to the *front-month contract* (the upcoming trading month). Because this rolling process provides a *roll yield* (a yield that results from the price differential between the current and front months), you need to examine each index's policy on rolling. You can find this information in the index brochure.

>> **Rebalancing features:** Every index reviews its components and their weightings on a regular basis to maintain an index that reflects actual values in the global commodities markets. Some indexes rebalance annually; others rebalance more frequently. Before you invest in an index, find out when it's rebalanced and what methodology it uses to do so.

Although each index is constructed differently, all indexes must follow certain criteria to determine whether a commodity will be included:

>> **Tradability:** The commodities have to be traded on a designated exchange and must have a futures contract assigned to them.

>> **Deliverability:** The contracts that go into the index must be for an underlying commodity that has the potential to be delivered. This eliminates the inclusion of futures contracts that represent financial instruments, such as economic indicators, interest rates, and other "financials."

>> **Liquidity:** The market for the underlying commodity has to be liquid enough to allow investors to move in and out of their positions without facing liquidity crunches, such as not being able to find a buyer or seller.

Noting the Five Major Indexes

In the following sections, I go through each of the five major commodity indexes you can invest in. Each one is unique, so you can be sure to find one that best suits your needs.

The S&P Goldman Sachs Commodity Index

The S&P Goldman Sachs Commodity Index (S&P GSCI) is one of the most closely watched indexes in the market. Launched in 1992 by the investment bank Goldman Sachs, it tracks the performance of 24 commodity futures contracts. In 2007, Standard & Poor's (S&P) purchased the original GSCI from Goldman Sachs, and S&P is now responsible for its operations. The S&P GSCI is the most heavily tracked index. As of 2006, investors had poured in $50 billion to track it; by 2010, that figure was $65 billion.

The S&P GSCI is a production-weighted index because it assigns different weights to commodities proportional to their current global production quantity, a method known as *global production weighting*. As such, the index assigns more weight to crude oil than cocoa to reflect actual world production figures — there's a lot more crude oil produced in the world than cocoa.

REMEMBER

The bulk of the S&P GSCI is tied to energy contracts because energy products dominate global commodity production. The S&P GSCI is currently overweight energy, but this can always change in the future. If energy production decreases on a global scale, the index reflects this change. The index reviews its weightings annually and reassigns weights to the index in January.

Table 12-2 lists the actual commodity futures contracts that make up the S&P GSCI, along with their correspondent weighting in the index. It also lists the exchange on which they trade in case you want to purchase these contracts.

TABLE 12-2 **S&P GSCI Components**

Commodity	Exchange	Weight
WTI crude oil	CME	30.05%
Brent crude oil	ICE	13.81%
Natural gas	CME	10.3%
Heating oil	CME	8.16%
Unleaded gas	CME	7.84%
Gas–oil	ICE	4.41%
Aluminum	LME	2.88%
Live cattle	CME	2.88%
Chicago wheat	CME	2.47%
Corn	CME	2.46%
Copper	LME	2.37%
Lean hogs	CME	2%
Soybeans	CME	1.77%
Gold	CME	1.73%
Sugar	CSC	1.3%
Cotton	NYC	0.99%
Kansas wheat	KBOT	0.9%

Commodity	Exchange	Weight
Nickel	LME	0.82%
Coffee	CSC	0.8%
Feeder cattle	CME	0.78%
Zinc	LME	0.54%
Lead	LME	0.29%
Cocoa	CSC	0.23%
Silver	CME	0.2%

Because futures contracts have an expiration date, they must be rolled on a regular basis. Contracts such as the crude oil futures are rolled monthly because they expire every month. However, some contracts have contract expiration dates only during certain months of the year. (I discuss monthly contract tradability in Chapter 13.) These contracts, such as those for cotton or gold, are rolled according to the available monthly contract trade.

TIP

The S&P GSCI has a futures contract that tracks the index's performance. You can buy this contract on the Chicago Mercantile Exchange (CME). If you have a futures trading account, you can simply buy this contract for direct access to the S&P GSCI. The ticker symbol for the S&P GSCI on the CME is GI.

Another way to access the S&P GSCI is to invest in a managed fund that tracks its performance. One such fund is the Oppenheimer Real Asset Fund, which I discuss in Chapter 14. The Oppenheimer Fund mirrors the performance of the S&P GSCI. However, as a general rule, managed funds don't identically replicate the performance of an index because you have to consider external factors such as loads, management fees, and other expenses related to the management of the fund.

Reuters/Jefferies Commodity Research Bureau Index

Created in 1957 as the Commodity Research Bureau's official commodity-tracking index, this index is the oldest commodity index in the world. The original index received its most recent makeover in 2005 when it was renamed the Reuters/Jefferies Commodity Research Bureau Index (CRB) — quite a mouthful!

REMEMBER

The CRB index is widely followed by institutional investors and economists. Of all the indexes, it's perhaps the most widely used as an economic benchmark, although the S&P GSCI and the DJ/AIGCI (introduced in the next section) are also widely used references.

The CRB index has performed well since 2002. Table 12-3 lists the total annual returns of the CRB index.

TABLE 12-3 Annual Returns of the CRB Index, 2015-2022

Year	Total Return
2015	–21.7%
2016	29.8%
2017	15.6%
2018	–10.4%
2019	18.97%
2020	4.14%
2021	30.3%
2022	15.2%

The key to investing in these types of liquid instruments is time: The longer your investment horizon, the better the returns you're going to generate. If you're able to hold on when experiencing a drawdown of over 20 percent in 2015, then you'll certainly be happy to be rewarded with subsequent returns of almost 30 percent and more than 15 percent the two subsequent years.

REMEMBER

The CRB index tracks all the major commodity component classes. The CRB index currently tracks a basket of 19 commodities, which are selected based on their liquidity and production value. This index is unique because it's the only one that uses a *tiered methodology* of distributing weights to commodities. This hybrid approach gives a production value weight to energy products, while assigning fixed weights to other commodities. The components and their weightings are reviewed annually. Table 12-4 lists the index tiers and the commodities the index tracks.

TABLE 12-4 CRB Index Tiers and Components

Tiers	Commodity	Weight	Exchange
Tier I	WTI crude oil	23%	CME
	Heating oil	5%	CME
	Unleaded gas	5%	CME
Tier II	Natural gas	6%	CME
	Corn	6%	CME
	Soybeans	6%	CME
	Live cattle	6%	CME
	Gold	6%	CME
	Aluminum	6%	LME
	Copper	6%	CME
Tier III	Sugar	5%	ICE
	Cotton	5%	ICE
	Cocoa	5%	ICE
	Coffee	5%	ICE
Tier IV	Nickel	1%	LME
	Wheat	1%	CME
	Lean hogs	1%	CME
	Orange juice	1%	ICE
	Silver	1%	CME

Dow Jones Commodity Index

The Dow Jones Commodity Index (DJCI) is one of the most widely followed indexes in the market. The DJCI places a premium on liquidity but also chooses commodities based on their production value.

The DJCI is one of the few indexes that place a *floor* and *ceiling* on individual commodities and component classes. For example, no component class (such as energy or metals) is allowed to account for more than 33 percent of the index weighting. Another rule is that no single commodity may make up less than 2 percent of the index's total weighting. The DJCI follows these rules to ensure that all commodities are well represented and that no commodity or component class dominates the index.

The component weightings are rebalanced annually. Currently, the index tracks a group of 19 publicly traded commodities, listed in Table 12-5.

TABLE 12-5 DJCI Components

Commodity	Weight
WTI crude oil	12.78%
Natural gas	12.32%
Soybeans	7.76%
Aluminum	6.9%
Gold	6.22%
Live cattle	6.09%
Copper	5.88%
Corn	5.87%
Wheat	4.77%
Lean hogs	4.35%
Unleaded gas	4.05%
Heating oil	3.84%
Cotton	3.16%
Sugar	2.96%
Coffee	2.93%
Soybean oil	2.76%
Zinc	2.7%
Nickel	2.66%
Silver	2%

TIP

One way to access the commodities listed in the DJCI is to invest in a mutual fund that tracks it. One of the largest commodity mutual funds, the PIMCO Commodity Real Return Fund, uses the DJCI as its benchmark. Therefore, you get a high correlation between the performance of the index and the performance of the fund. Turn to Chapter 14 to find out more about the PIMCO fund.

TIP

Another way to access the DJCI is through the CME, which offers a futures contract that tracks the performance of the DJCI. This is similar to the S&P GSCI contract on the CME. The ticker symbol for the DJCI on the CME is AI.

Rogers International Commodities Index

With a total of 36 listed commodities, the Rogers International Commodities Index (RICI) tracks the most commodities among the different indexes. The RICI is the brainchild of famed commodities investor Jim Rogers, who launched the index to achieve the widest exposure to commodities.

As with the other commodity indexes, the RICI includes traditional commodities such as crude oil, natural gas, and silver. But it also includes quite exotic commodities, including silk and adzuki beans. If you're looking for the broadest exposure to commodities, the RICI is probably your best bet.

The RICI was launched in 1998 and has performed extremely well. Between 1998 and 2022, its total return was 473.85 percent. The RICI is a production-weighted index, assigning weightings to component classes based on their actual global production value and rebalancing the index every December. Table 12-6 lists the RICI components and their index weighting.

TIP

If you want to invest in the RICI, you can do so through the RICI TRAKRS that the CME offers. *TRAKRS* (pronounced "trackers") are similar to the futures contracts the CME offers. To trade the RICI TRAKRS on the CME, use the ticker symbol RCI.

TABLE 12-6 RICI Components

Commodity	Weight
Crude oil	35%
Wheat	7%
Corn	4.75%
Aluminum	4%
Copper	4%
Cotton	4%
Heating oil	3.75%
Unleaded gas	3.75%
Gold	3%
Natural gas	3%
Soybeans	3%
Coffee	2%
Lead	2%
Live cattle	2%
Silver	2%
Soybean oil	2%
Sugar	2%
Zinc	2%
Platinum	1.8%
Cocoa	1%
Live hogs	1%
Lumber	1%
Nickel	1%
Rubber	1%

Commodity	Weight
Tin	1%
Soybean meal	0.75%
Canola	0.67%
Orange juice	0.66%
Adzuki beans	0.5%
Oats	0.5%
Rice	0.5%
Palladium	0.3%
Barley	0.27%
Silk	0.05%

Deutsche Bank Liquid Commodity Index

Launched in 2003 by Deutsche Bank, the Deutsche Bank Liquid Commodity Index (DBLCI) is the new kid on the index block and has the most distinct approach to tracking commodity futures contracts. The DBLCI tracks just six commodity contracts: two in energy, two in metals, and two in agricultural products. Table 12-7 shows the weighting of each of these component classes.

The weighting of the DBLCI is done at the end of the year, and it seeks to reflect global production values. Hence, as with the other production-weighted indexes (such as the S&P GSCI), it's also overweight energy because this reflects the current production values in the world.

REMEMBER

With so few underlying commodities, you may ask whether the DBLCI offers a broad and diverse enough exposure to the commodities markets. One of the advantages of the DBLCI is that it chooses only the most *liquid* and *representative* commodities in their respective component classes.

TABLE 12-7 **DBLCI Components**

	Index Weight	Contract Months	Exchange
Energy			
WTI crude oil	35%	Jan–Dec	NYMEX
Heating oil	20%	Jan–Dec	NYMEX
Precious Metals			
Gold	10%	Dec	COMEX
Industrial Metals			
Aluminum	12.5%	Dec	LME
Grains			
Corn	11.25%	Dec	CBOT
Wheat	11.25%	Dec	CBOT

For example, the WTI Crude Oil contract is indicative of where the energy complex is moving. So, instead of including unleaded gas, propane, natural gas, and other energy contracts, the DBLCI relies on WTI as a benchmark to achieve representation in the energy market as a whole. This approach is unique in the world of commodity indexes; the index can track the commodities markets by monitoring the performance of only a small number of commodities. This "less is more" approach is also helpful for individual investors who prefer to track indexes by buying the index contracts; instead of buying 19 contracts, you have to buy only 6 contracts to mirror the index's performance.

The energy contracts of the DBLCI are rolled monthly; the metal and agricultural contracts are rolled annually.

TIP

The DBLCI is the first commodity index to have its performance tracked by an ETF. You can buy the ETF and get exposure to the DBLCI on the American Stock and Options Exchange (AMEX). Deutsche Bank also manages this fund, whose ticker symbol is DBC. I discuss this ETF in depth earlier in this chapter.

Determining Which Index to Use

With so many indexes, how do you decide which one to follow? Generally, the S&P GSCI is the most tracked index in the market — it has the most funds following, or tracking, its performance. As of 2022, more than $150 billion in assets tracked its performance, and this number is growing monthly. The index is pretty popular with institutional and, increasingly, individual investors. It's also perhaps the easiest one to follow because you can track it by investing through the Oppenheimer Real Asset Fund, as well as through the S&P GSCI futures contracts on the CME.

Although the S&P GSCI is the most widely tracked index, the most closely *watched* index is the Reuters/Jefferies CRB Index. The CRB Index is a global benchmark for what the commodities markets are doing. As such, it's the equivalent of the Dow Jones Industrial Average in the commodity world: When investors want to gauge where the commodity markets are heading, they usually turn to the CRB Index. In addition, when analysts or journalists discuss the performance of the commodities markets, they usually refer to the CRB Index.

Investors who don't trade futures or don't feel comfortable investing in an index through a mutual fund can always choose to invest in an index through ETFs, which offer the convenience of trading complex financial instruments with the ease of trading stocks. Currently, the DBLCI is the only index tracked by an ETF, the DBC. Buying the DBC is as simple as logging into your brokerage account or calling your broker and placing an order for the number of DBC units you want to purchase. An ETF is in the works to track the S&P GSCI, and I expect to see more ETFs that track these commodity indexes as more investors seek access to this area of the market.

Chapter **13**
Getting a Grip on Futures and Options

S ome investors think that "futures and options" and "commodities" are basically the same, but they're not. *Commodities* are a class of assets that includes energy, metals, agricultural products, and similar items. *Futures* and *options* are investment vehicles through which you can invest in commodities. Think of it this way: If commodities were a place, futures and options would be the vehicle you'd use to get there. In addition to commodities, futures and options allow you to invest in a variety of other asset classes, such as stocks, indexes, currencies, bonds, and even interest rates, often referred to as *financial futures.*

REMEMBER

In Wall Street lingo, futures and options are known as *derivatives* because they derive their value from an underlying financial instrument such as a stock, bond, or commodity. However, futures and options are different financial instruments with singular structures and uses — but I'm getting ahead of myself.

My aim in this chapter isn't to make you an expert in trading these sophisticated financial instruments, but to introduce you to these vehicles so you have a working knowledge of what they are.

Taking the Mystery Out of Futures and Options

By their very nature, futures and options are complex financial instruments. It's not like investing in a mutual fund, where you mail your check and wait for quarterly statements and dividends. If you invest in futures and options contracts, you need to monitor your positions daily — or even hourly. You have to keep track of the expiration date, the premium paid, the strike price, margin requirements, and other shifting variables. (I discuss these in the later section "Keeping track of all the pieces.")

That said, understanding futures and options can be beneficial to you as an investor because they're powerful tools. They give you leverage and risk-management opportunities that your average financial instruments don't offer. If you can harness the power of these instruments, you can dramatically increase your leverage — and performance — in the markets.

WARNING

The futures markets are only one way for you to get involved in commodities. Because they're fairly volatile, it's important that you have a solid understanding before you jump in.

How to Trade Futures Contracts

The futures market is divided into two segments: one that's regulated and another one that's not. Trading in the regulated portion of the futures market is done through designated commodity futures exchanges such as the New York Board of Trade (NYBOT) — now part of the Intercontinental Exchange (ICE) — and the Chicago Mercantile Exchange (CME), which I cover in Chapter 14. Trading in the unregulated portion of the futures market is done by individual parties outside the purview of the exchanges. This is known as the *over-the-counter* (OTC) *market.*

The futures market is the opposite of the cash market, often known as the *spot market* because transactions take place right away, or on the spot.

A *futures contract* is a highly standardized financial instrument in which two parties enter into an agreement to exchange an underlying security (such as soybeans, palladium, or ethanol) at a mutually agreed-upon price at a specific time in the future — which is why it's called a futures contract.

Futures contracts, by definition, trade on designated commodity futures exchanges, such as the London Metal Exchange (LME) or the CME. The exchanges provide liquidity and transparency to all market participants. However, the structure of the futures market is such that only about 20 percent of market activity takes place in the exchange arena. The overwhelming majority of transactions in the futures markets take place in the OTC market. The OTC market isn't regulated or monitored by the exchanges, and it usually involves two market participants that establish the terms of their agreements through forward contracts. *Forwards* are similar to futures contracts, except that they trade in the OTC market and, thus, allow the parties to come up with flexible and individualized terms for their agreements. Generally, the OTC market isn't suitable for individual investors who seek speculative opportunities because it consists primarily of large commercial users (such as oil companies and airlines) who use it solely for hedging purposes.

Note: In this chapter, I focus on derivatives that trade on the commodity exchanges. I don't focus on the OTC market because it doesn't lend itself to trading by individual investors. So, when I refer to the "futures market" in this chapter, I'm talking about the trading activity in the designated commodity futures exchanges.

Despite the fact that futures contracts are designed to accommodate delivery of physical commodities, such delivery rarely takes place because the primary purpose of the futures markets is to minimize risk and maximize profits. The futures market, unlike the cash or spot market, isn't intended to serve as the primary exchange of physical commodities. Instead, it's a market where buyers and sellers transact with each other for hedging and speculative purposes. Out of the billions of contracts traded on commodity futures exchanges each year, only about 2 percent of these contracts result in the actual physical delivery of a commodity.

In the land of futures contracts, both the buyer and the seller have the right *and* the obligation to fulfill the contract's terms. This process works differently than in the realm of options. With options, the buyer has the right but *not* the obligation to exercise the option, and the seller has the obligation but *not* the right to fulfill their contractual obligations. This scenario can get a little confusing, I know. I dig deeper into these issues in the later section "Trading with Options."

Who trades futures?

Essentially, two types of folks trade futures contracts. The first are commercial producers and consumers of commodities who use the futures markets to stabilize either their costs (in the case of consumers) or their revenues (in the case of producers). The second group consists of individual traders, investment banks, and other financial institutions who are interested in using the futures markets as a way of generating trading profits. Both groups take advantage of the futures markets' liquidity and leverage (which I discuss in the following sections) to implement their trading strategies.

If you ever get involved in the futures markets, it's important to know who you're up against. I examine the role of these hedgers and speculators in the following sections so you're ready to deal with the competition.

Getting over the hedge

Hedgers are the actual producers and consumers of commodities. Both producers and consumers enter the futures markets with the aim of reducing price volatility in the commodities they buy or sell. Hedging gives these commercial enterprises the opportunity to reduce the risk associated with daily price fluctuations by establishing fixed prices of primary commodities for months, sometimes even years, in advance.

Hedgers can be on either side of a transaction in the futures market: the *buy side* or the *sell side*. Consider a few examples of entities that use the futures markets for hedging purposes:

>> Farmers who want to establish steady prices for their products use futures contracts to sell their products to consumers at a fixed price for a fixed period of time, thus guaranteeing a fixed stream of revenues.

>> Electric utility companies that supply power to residential customers can buy electricity on the futures markets to keep their costs fixed and protect their bottom line.

>> Transportation companies whose business depends on the price of fuel get involved in the futures markets to maintain fixed costs of fuel over specific periods of time.

To get a better idea of hedging in action, consider a hedging strategy that the airline industry uses. One of the airline executives' biggest worries is the unpredictable price of jet fuel, which can vary wildly from day to day on the spot market. Airlines don't like this kind of uncertainty because they want to keep their costs low and predictable. (They already have enough to worry about with rising pension and health-care costs, fears of terrorism, and other external factors.) So, how do they do that? They hedge the price of jet fuel through the futures market.

Southwest Airlines (NYSE: LUV) is one of the most active hedgers in the industry. At any one point, Southwest may have up to 80 percent of a given year's jet fuel consumption fixed at a specific price. Southwest enters into agreements with producers through the futures markets, primarily through OTC agreements, to purchase fuel at a fixed price for a specific period of time in the future.

The benefit for Southwest (and its passengers) is that the company has fixed its costs and eliminated the volatility associated with the price fluctuation of jet fuel. This action has a direct impact on Southwest's bottom line. The advantage for the producer is that it now has a customer who's willing to purchase the product for a fixed time at a fixed price, thus guaranteeing a steady stream of cash flow.

However, unless prices in the cash market remain steady, one of the two parties that enters into this sort of agreement may have been better off without the hedge. If prices for jet fuel increase, the producer has to bear that cost and deliver jet fuel to the airline at the agreed-upon price, which is now below the market price. Similarly, if prices of jet fuel go down, the airline would've been better off purchasing jet fuel on the cash market. But because these are unknown variables, hedgers still see a benefit in entering into these agreements to eliminate unpredictability.

The truth about speculators

For some reason, the term *speculator* carries some negative connotation, as if speculating is a sinful or immoral act. In reality, speculators play an important and necessary role in the global financial system. In fact, whenever you buy a stock or a bond, you're speculating. When you think prices are going up, you buy. When they're going down, you sell. The process of figuring out where prices are heading and how to profit from this is the essence of speculation. So, we're all speculators really.

In the futures markets, speculators provide much-needed liquidity that allows the many market players to match their buy and sell orders. Speculators, often simply known as *traders,* buy and sell futures contracts, options, and other exchange-traded products through an electronic platform or a broker to profit from price fluctuations. A trader who thinks that the price of crude oil is going up will buy a crude oil futures contract to try to profit from their hunch. This action adds liquidity to the markets, which is valuable because liquidity is a prerequisite for the smooth and efficient functioning of the futures markets.

When markets are liquid, you know that you'll be able to find a buyer or a seller for your contracts. You also know that you'll get a reasonable price because liquidity offers you a large pool of market participants competing for your contracts. Finally, liquidity means that when a number of participants are transacting in the marketplace, prices aren't going to be subject to extremely wild and unpredictable price fluctuations. This doesn't mean that liquidity eliminates volatility, but it certainly reduces it.

Keeping track of all the pieces

Trading futures contracts takes a lot of discipline, patience, and coordination. One of the biggest deterrents to participating in the futures markets is the number of moving pieces you have to constantly monitor. In this section, I go through the many pieces you have to keep track of if you decide to trade futures.

Because futures contracts can be traded on only designated and regulated exchanges, these contracts are highly standardized. *Standardization* simply means that these contracts are based on a uniform set of rules. For example, the CME crude oil contract is standardized because it represents a specific grade of crude (West Texas Intermediate) and a specific size (1,000 barrels). Therefore, you can expect all CME crude contracts to represent 1,000 barrels of West Texas Intermediate crude oil. In other words, the contract you purchase won't be for 1,000 barrels of Nigerian Bonny Light, another grade of crude oil.

The regulatory bodies that are responsible for overseeing and monitoring trading activities on commodity futures exchanges are the Commodity Futures Trading Commission (CFTC) and the National Futures Association (NFA). I discuss these at length in Chapter 14.

REMEMBER

The buyer of a futures contract is known as the *holder;* when you buy a futures contract, you're essentially "going long" the commodity. The seller of a futures contract is referred to as the *underwriter* or *writer.* If you sell a futures contract, you're holding a short position. Keep in mind that "going long" simply means you're on the buy side of a transaction; conversely, "going short" means you're on the sell side. In other words, when you "go long," you expect prices to rise, and when you "go short," you expect prices to decrease.

Underlying asset

The *underlying asset* is the financial instrument that the futures contract represents. The underlying asset can be anything from crude oil to platinum to soybeans to propane. Because futures contracts are traded on designated exchanges, every exchange offers different types of assets you can trade. For a list of these assets, be sure to read Chapter 14.

REMEMBER

Futures contracts can be used to trade all sorts of assets, not just traditional commodities like oil and gold. Futures can be used to trade interest rates, indexes, currencies, equities, and a host of other assets. Some futures contracts even allow you to trade weather!

TIP

Before you place your order, make sure that you're clear about the underlying commodity you want to trade. Specify on which exchange you want your order executed. This is important because you have contracts for the same commodities that trade on different exchanges. For example, aluminum futures contracts are traded on both the CME and the LME. When you're placing an order for an aluminum contract, it's important to specify where you want to buy the contract: either on the COMEX or on the LME.

Underlying quantity

The contract size, also known as the *trading unit,* is how much of the underlying asset the contract represents. To meet certain standards, all futures contracts have a predetermined and fixed size. For example, one futures contract for ethanol traded on the Chicago Board of Trade is the equivalent of one rail car of ethanol, which is approximately 29,000 gallons.

The light, sweet crude oil contract on the CME represents 1,000 U.S. barrels, which is the equivalent of 42,000 gallons. The futures contract for frozen pork bellies represents 40,000 pounds of pork.

Make sure that you know the exact amount of underlying commodity the contract represents before you purchase a futures contract.

Because more individual investors want to trade futures contracts, many exchanges are now offering contracts with smaller sizes, which means that the contracts cost less. The CME, for instance, now offers the miNY Light Sweet Crude Oil contract, which represents 500 barrels of oil and is half the price of its traditional crude oil contract.

Product grade

Imagine that you placed an order for a Ford Mustang and instead got a Ford Taurus. You'd be pretty upset, right? To avoid unpleasant surprises if delivery of a physical commodity actually takes place, exchanges require that all contracts represent a standard product grade. For instance, gasoline futures traded on the CME are based on contract specifications for New York Harbor Unleaded Gasoline. This grade is a uniform grade of gasoline widely used across the East Coast, which is transported to New York Harbor from refineries on the East Coast and in the Gulf of Mexico. Thus, if delivery of a CME gasoline futures contract takes place, you can expect to receive New York Harbor Unleaded Gas.

If your sole purpose is to speculate and you're not intending to have gasoline or soybeans delivered, knowing the product grade isn't as important as if you were taking physical delivery of the commodity. However, it's always good to know what kind of product you're actually trading.

Price quote

Most futures contracts are priced in U.S. dollars, but some contracts are priced in other currencies, such as the British pound sterling or the Japanese yen. The price quote really depends on which exchange you're buying or selling the futures contract from. Keep in mind that if you're trading futures in a foreign currency, you're potentially exposing yourself to currency exchange risks.

Price limits

Price limits help you determine the value of the contract. Every contract has a minimum and maximum price increment, also known as a *tick size*. Contracts move in ticks, which is the amount by which the futures contract increases or decreases with every transaction. Most stocks, for example, move in cents. In futures, most contracts move in larger dollar amounts, reflecting the size of the contract. In other words, one tick represents different values for different contracts.

For example, the *minimum tick size* of the ethanol futures contract on the CME is $29 per contract. This means every contract will move in increments of $29. On the other hand, the *maximum tick size* for ethanol on the CME is $8,700, meaning that if the tick size is greater than $8,700, trading will be halted. Exchanges step in to calm the markets when contracts are experiencing extreme volatility.

The exchanges establish minimum and maximum tick sizes based on the settlement price during the previous day's trading session. Determining the value of the tick allows you to quantify the price swings of the contract on any given trading session.

Trading months

Although you can trade futures contracts practically around the clock, certain commodities are available for delivery only during certain months.

For instance, frozen pork bellies on the CME are listed for the months of February, March, May, July, and August. This means that you can trade a July contract at any given point, but you can't trade a June contract — a contract that's deliverable in June — because that contract doesn't exist. On the other hand, crude oil on the CME is available all 12 months of the year.

Check the contract listing before you trade so you know for which delivery months you can trade the contracts.

The *front month* is simply the upcoming delivery month. For example, June is the front month during the May trading session.

In the world of futures, trading and delivery months have specific abbreviations attributed to each month. I list these abbreviations in Table 13-1.

TABLE 13-1 Monthly Abbreviation Codes

Month	Code	Month	Code
January	F	July	N
February	G	August	Q
March	H	September	U
April	J	October	V
May	K	November	X
June	M	December	Z

Traders use these abbreviations to quickly identify the months they're interested in trading. If you're placing an order with a futures broker (which I discuss in Chapter 14), knowing these abbreviations is helpful.

Delivery location

In case of actual delivery, exchanges designate areas where the physical exchange of commodities actually takes place. For instance, delivery of the CME's West Texas Intermediate (WTI) crude oil contract takes place in Cushing, Oklahoma, which is a major transportation hub for crude oil in the United States.

Last trading day

All futures contracts must expire at some point. The *last trading day* is the absolute latest time you have to trade that particular contract. Trading days change from exchange to exchange and from contract to contract. Be sure to check out the contract specifications at the different exchanges for information on the last trading day.

Trading hours

Before the days of electronic trading, contracts were traded through the open outcry system during specific time periods. Now, with the advent of electronic trading, you have more time to trade the contracts. Check the exchange websites (which I list in Chapter 14) for information on trading hours.

REMEMBER

Knowing at what times to place your trades has a direct impact on your bottom line because the number of market participants varies throughout the day. Ideally, you'd like to execute your orders when buyers and sellers are most plentiful because this increases your chances of getting the best price for your contracts.

Trading Futures on Margin

One of the unique characteristics of futures contracts is the ability to trade with margin. If you've ever traded stocks, you know that *margin* is the amount of borrowed money you use to pay for stock. Margin in the futures markets is slightly different from stock-market margin.

REMEMBER

In the futures markets, *margin* refers to the minimum amount of capital that must be available in your account for you to trade futures contracts. Think of margin as collateral that allows you to participate in the futures markets. *Initial margin* is the minimum amount of capital you need in your account to trade futures contracts. *Maintenance margin* is the subsequent amount of capital you must contribute to your account to maintain the minimum margin requirements.

TIP

Margin requirements are established for every type of contract by the exchange on which those contracts are traded. However, the futures broker you use to place your order may have different margin requirements. Make sure you find out what those requirements are before you start trading.

REMEMBER

In the stock market, capital gains and losses are calculated after you close out your position. In the futures market, capital gains and losses are calculated at the end of the trading day and credited to or debited from your account. If you experience a loss in your positions on any given day, you receive a *margin call*, which means that you have to replenish your account to meet the minimum margin requirements if you want to keep trading.

Trading on margin gives you a lot of leverage because you need to put up only relatively small amounts of capital as collateral to invest in significant dollar amounts of a commodity. For example, if you want to trade the soybean futures contracts on the CME, the initial margin requirement is $1,100. With this small amount, you can control a CME soybeans futures contract that has a value of approximately $359,200 (5,000 bushels at $71.84 per bushel)! This translates to a minimum margin requirement of less than 4 percent!

WARNING

Margin is a double-edged sword because both profits and losses are amplified to large degrees. If you're on the right side of a trade, you're going to make a lot of money. However, you're also in a position to lose a lot (much more than your initial investment) if things don't go your way. Knowing how to use margin properly is absolutely critical. I discuss in depth how to use leverage responsibly in Chapter 2.

Figuring Out Where the Futures Market Is Heading

You need to be familiar with a couple of technical terms related to movements in the futures markets if you want to successfully trade futures contracts. (Even by Wall Street standards, these terms are kind of out there.)

Contango

Futures markets, by definition, are predicated on the future price of a commodity. Analyzing where the future price of a commodity is heading is what futures trading is all about. Because futures contracts are available for different months throughout the year, the price of the contracts changes from month to month. When the front month trades higher than the current month, this market condition is known as *contango*. The market is also in contango when the price of the front month is higher than the spot market, and when late delivery months are higher than near delivery months. I include an example of the CME crude oil contract in contango in Table 13-2.

As the contract extends into the future, the price of the contract increases. Contango is, thus, a bullish indicator, showing that the market expects the price of the futures contract to increase steadily into the future.

TABLE 13-2 CME Crude Oil in Contango

Month	Settlement Price
December 2010	$82.68
January 2011	$83.40
February 2011	$83.98
March 2011	$84.45
April 2011	$84.94
May 2011	$85.00

Backwardation

Backwardation is the opposite of contango. When a market is experiencing backwardation, the contracts for future months are decreasing in value relative to the current and most recent months. The spot price is, thus, greater than the front month, which is greater than future delivery months. Table 13-3 shows the CME copper contract in backwardation.

TABLE 13-3 CME Copper in Backwardation

Month	Settlement Price
October 2022	$3.49
November 2022	$3.45
December 2022	$3.44

A market in backwardation is a bearish sign because traders expect prices over the long term to decrease.

Trading with Options

There's a big difference between futures and options. Often folks think of futures and options as being one and the same — that's understandable, because whenever you hear "futures," "options" is never too far behind. However, as I explain in the following sections, futures and options are different financial instruments with singular structures and uses. Realizing this difference right off the bat will help you understand these financial instruments better.

Futures give the *holder* (buyer) and *underwriter* (seller) both the right *and* the obligation to fulfill the contract's obligations. Options give the holder the right (or option) but not the obligation to exercise the contract. The underwriter of the option, on the other hand, is required to fulfill the contract's obligations if the holder chooses to exercise the contract.

When you're buying an option, you're essentially paying for the right to buy or sell an underlying security at a specific point in time at an agreed-upon price. The price you pay for the right to exercise that option is known as the *premium*.

REMEMBER

The technically correct way of thinking about options is as "options on futures contracts." In other words, the options contracts give you the option to buy futures contracts for commodities such as wheat and zinc. These options are different from stock options, which let you purchase stocks. In this section, I examine options on futures contracts because that's the focus of this chapter.

Following options in action

Understanding options can be challenging because they're, in fact, derivatives used to trade other derivatives (futures contracts). So, here's an example that applies the concept of options to a real-world situation.

You walk into a car dealership and see the car of your dreams. It's shiny and beautiful, and you know you'll look great in it. Unfortunately, it costs $100,000, and you can't spend that amount of money on a car right now. However, you're due for a large bonus at work — or you just made a killing trading commodities, take your pick! — and you'll be able to pay for it in two weeks. So, you approach the car dealer and ask them to hold the car for you for two weeks, at which point you can make full payment on it.

The dealer agrees but insists that they'll have to charge you $5,000 for the option to buy the car in two weeks for the set price of $100,000. You agree to the terms and pay the dealer a nonrefundable deposit of $5,000 (known as the *premium* in options-speak), which gives you the right, but not the obligation, to come back in two weeks and purchase the car of your dreams. The dealer, on the other hand, is obligated to sell you the car if you choose to exercise your option to do so. In this situation, you're the *holder* of the option, and the dealer is its *underwriter*.

Consider two different scenarios that could unfold during the two-week period:

>> In the first scenario, a few days after you purchase the option to buy the vehicle, the car manufacturer announces that it will stop making vehicles of this kind — the car is now a limited edition and becomes a collector's car. Congratulations! The value of the car has now doubled overnight! Because you and the dealer entered into an options agreement, the dealer is obligated to sell you the car at $100,000 even though the car now costs $200,000 — if you choose to exercise your rights as the option holder. You come back to see the dealer, and you buy the car at the agreed-upon price of $100,000. You can now either drive your new car or sell it at current market price for a cool $95,000 profit ($200,000 – $100,000 – $5,000 = $95,000)!

>> The second scenario isn't as rosy as the first. A few days after you sign the options agreement, the car manufacturer announces that there's a defect with the car's Bluetooth system. The car works fine, so the manufacturer doesn't need to recall it, but the Bluetooth player is defective and unusable. Because of this development, the value of the car drops to $80,000. (Drivers like listening to their music, after all.) As the holder of the option, you aren't obligated to purchase the car. Note that you have the right — but not the obligation — to follow through on the contractual agreements of the contract. If you choose not to purchase the car, you'll have incurred the $5,000 loss of the premium you paid for the option.

In a nutshell, that example is what trading options is all about. You can now apply this concept to profit in the capital markets in general and the commodities market in particular. For example, if you expect the price of the June copper futures contract on the CME to increase, you can buy an option on the CME that gives you the right to purchase the June copper futures contract for a specific price. You pay a premium for this option, and, if you don't exercise your option before the expiration date, the only thing you lose is the premium.

Understanding trader talk

REMEMBER

When talking about options, you need to know certain terms:

>> **Premium:** The price you actually pay for the option. If you don't exercise your option, the only money you lose is the premium you paid for the contract in the first place.

>> **Expiration date:** The date at which the option expires. After the expiration date, the contract is no longer valid.

>> **Strike price:** The predetermined price at which the underlying asset is purchased or sold.

>> **At-the-money:** When the strike price is equal to the market price, the option is known as being at-the-money.

>> **In-the-money:** In a call option, when the asset's market price is above the strike price, it's in-the-money. In the land of puts, an option is in-the-money when the market price is below the strike price.

>> **Out-of-the-money:** When the market price is below the strike price in a call option, that option is a money-loser: It's out-of-the-money. When the market price is greater than the strike price in a put option, it's out-of-the-money.

>> **Open interest:** The total number of options or futures contracts that are still open on any given trading session. Open interest is an important measure of market interest.

Selecting option traits

Every option has different characteristics, depending on how you want to exercise the option and what action you want to conduct when it's exercised. Put simply, you can use options that allow you to either buy or sell an underlying security. You can further specify at which point you want to exercise the options agreement. This section lays out these characteristics for you.

Call options: Calling all investors

If you expect rising prices, you can buy a *call option* that gives you the right — but not the obligation — to purchase a specific amount of a security at a specific price at a specific point in the future.

When you buy a call option, you're being bullish and expecting prices to increase. Call options are similar to having a long position. When you *sell* a call option, you expect prices to fall. If the prices fall and never reach the strike price, you get to keep the premium. If prices increase and the holder exercises their option, you're obligated to sell the holder the underlying asset at the agreed-upon price.

Put options: Putting everything on the line

A *put option* is the exact opposite of a call option because it gives you the right, but not the obligation, to *sell* a security at some point in the future for a predetermined price. When you think the price of a security is going down, you want to use a put option to try to take advantage of this price movement.

Buying a put option is one way of shorting a security. If prices do decrease, you can purchase the security at the agreed-upon (lower) price and then turn back and sell it on the open market, pocketing the difference. On the other hand, if prices increase, you can choose to let the option expire. In this case, you lose only the premium you paid for the option.

When you sell a put option, you believe that prices are going to increase. If you're correct and prices increase, the holder won't exercise the option, which means you get to collect the premium. So, when you sell a put option, you're actually being bullish.

TIP

Here are the possible combinations of buying and selling put and call options, accompanied by their corresponding market sentiment:

>> **Buying a call:** Bullish

>> **Selling a call:** Bearish

>> **Buying a put:** Bearish

>> **Selling a put:** Bullish

Looking at American options

When you buy an American option, you have the right to exercise that option at any time during the life of the option — from the start of the option until the expiration date. Most options traded in the United States are American options. You get a lot more flexibility out of them because you have the freedom to exercise them at any point.

Taking the European alternative

WARNING

The European option allows you to exercise the option only at expiration. This is fairly rigid. The only possible advantage of a European option over an American option is that you may be able to pay a smaller premium. However, because of its rigidity, I highly recommend using American options in your trading strategies.

Chapter **14**

Choosing a Professional and Trading Accounts

I f you're looking for ways to get involved in commodities, you have the option of hiring a trained professional to do the investing for you. Currently, plenty of money managers offer their services to help you invest in this market.

Of course, whenever you hand over your money to a manager, you want to make sure that you feel confident about this person's ability to invest your money wisely. In this chapter, I look at some vehicles you have at your disposal to invest in the commodities markets, and I offer you hands-on information to help you select the most suitable money manager for you.

In this chapter, I also give you an overview of commodity exchanges, those institutions that not only are responsible for setting global prices of all sorts of commodities, but also give investors a direct and transparent way to participate in the commodities markets.

Investing in Commodity Mutual Funds

A common way to invest in commodities is through a mutual fund. It may be the simplest way for you to get involved in the commodities markets because you're relying on a trained professional to do the investing on your behalf.

A *mutual fund* is a fund managed by an investment professional for the benefit of the fund investors. Mutual funds, by definition, can follow only a specific set of trading techniques. Mutual funds don't engage in sophisticated trading techniques such as arbitrage trades, special situations, long-short strategies, or distressed asset investing. These strategies are conducted primarily by *hedge funds*, which are similar to mutual funds except that they can engage in these sophisticated investment strategies. Most mutual funds follow *long-only strategies*, which are investment policies based on the *buy-and-hold principle*.

REMEMBER

Many different types of mutual funds have nothing to do with commodities. You can invest in stock funds, bond funds, currency funds, and even country-specific funds. But a number of mutual funds specialize in investing in only commodities or commodity-related products.

Plain-vanilla funds are your run-of-the-mill funds. If you've ever invested in a mutual fund, you should have no problem investing in these straightforward funds. How do you get started? You write your check, purchase shares of the mutual funds either through your broker or directly from the fund providers, and voilà! Of course, I recommend asking a number of questions before you write that check. You can find these qualifying questions in the following section.

Plain-vanilla funds are actively administered by a fund manager whose responsibility is to allocate capital across various subasset classes to maximize the fund's returns. Generally, these mutual funds invest in commodity-linked derivative instruments such as futures contracts and options on futures traded on the major commodity exchanges in New York, Chicago, and elsewhere. Other mutual funds may also invest in companies that process these raw materials, such as energy companies (see Chapter 6) and mining companies (see Chapter 9).

Asking the right questions

Before you invest in a mutual fund, you need to gather as much information as possible about the fund itself and the mechanics of investing in the fund. You can get answers to these questions directly from the fund manager or the fund's prospectus.

TIP

Call the mutual fund company directly and ask for a prospectus. A *prospectus* contains a wealth of information regarding management of the fund, the strategies the fund managers use, and details on fees and expenses. It's a great way to start gathering information on a prospective fund. Best of all, mutual funds send you their prospectus for free.

Some useful questions can help you zero in on the key points of mutual fund investing:

» **What's the fund's investment objective?** Different funds have radically different investment objectives. One may focus on *capital gains,* where the purpose is price appreciation, whereas another may specialize in *income investing* by buying assets, such as bonds, that generate an income stream. The fund's objective is one of the first pieces of information to look for.

» **What securities does the fund invest in?** This may seem like an obvious question when you're looking at commodities funds, but a number of funds claim that their main investment products are commodities, when in reality, only a small percentage of the fund is commodities related. I look at some of these funds in the later section "Seeing what's out there."

» **Who manages the fund?** You want to know as much as possible about the individuals who will be managing your hard-earned money. Most money managers in the United States have to be registered with the Financial Industry Regulatory Authority (FINRA). You can get information on a manager's personal background by checking the FINRA website at www.finra.org. Look for these key points:

  • **Experience:** How long has this person been a manager?

  • **Track record:** What kind of returns has the manager achieved for clients in the past?

- **Disciplinary actions:** Has this manager been disciplined for a past action? If so, find out more.

- **Registrations and certifications:** Does this manager have all the required registrations with the appropriate financial authorities to trade and invest on behalf of clients?

>> **What kind of strategy does the fund use?** A fund's strategy relies on a number of factors, including the investing style of the portfolio managers, the fund's objective, and the securities it chooses to invest in. Some funds follow low-risk, steady-income strategies, while others have a more aggressive strategy that uses a lot of leverage. Identifying the fund's strategy right away is critical.

>> **What's the profile of the typical investor in this fund?** The fund caters to the profile of its investors, which can be anywhere from highly conservative to extremely aggressive. You need to know what kind of individual is likely to invest in this fund and determine whether your risk tolerance squares with that of the other investors.

>> **What are the main risks of investing in this fund?** Whenever you invest, you take on a certain degree of risk: interest rate risk, credit risk, risk of loss of principal, liquidity risk, hedging risk, and geopolitical risk. For a detailed look at a number of different risks, see Chapter 2.

>> **What's the fund's track record?** Although past performance doesn't guarantee future results, it's always important to examine the fund's track record to get a sense of the kinds of returns the managers have achieved for their investors in the past. Most funds post their performance over a number of years; in particular, take a look at the key periods of the past three, five, and ten years.

WARNING

>> **What's the fund's after-tax performance?** Pay close attention to *after-tax* returns when looking at historical performance; they're a more accurate measure of the fund's performance and how much money you get to keep after you pay Uncle Sam. Many funds use big, bold charts to advertise their performance before taxes, but these can be misleading because a significant portion of these returns ends up in the government's coffers after taxes are taken out.

>> **What are the fund's fees and expenses?** Fees and expenses always cut into how much money you can get out of the fund. Look for funds that have lower expenses and fees. This information is available in the prospectus.

» What's the minimum capital an investor must commit?
A number of mutual funds require investing a minimum amount of money, ranging anywhere from $500 to $10,000 or more. The minimum requirement may also vary according to the type of investor. Someone investing in an individual retirement account (IRA), for example, may have to put up less money up front than someone investing through a brokerage account. Finally, many funds also require *minimum incremental amounts* after the initial investment amount. So, you may invest $1,000 up front but then be required to increase your investment by at least $100 each subsequent time you want to invest in the fund.

» Are there different classes of shares? Most mutual funds offer more than one class of shares to investors. The different classes are based on several factors, including sales charges, deferred sales charges, redemption fees, and investor availability. Examine each class of shares closely to determine which one is best for you.

» What are the tax implications of investing in this fund?
Talk to your accountant to determine the tax consequences of any investment you make.

As with almost everything else in finance, investing in commodity mutual funds requires mastering specific terminology. These technical terms can help you talk the talk:

» Expense ratio: The expense ratio is the percentage of the fund's total assets earmarked for general operational expenses. This is the amount used to run the fund, and it generally lowers total fund returns.

» Sales load: Some mutual funds sell their shares through brokerage houses and other financial intermediaries. A *sales load* is the commission the mutual fund pays to brokers who sell their shares to the general public. The investor pays the sales load. Some funds don't have a sales load; these are called *no-load funds*.

» Sales charge: A sales charge, sometimes referred to as a *deferred sales charge,* is a fee that the mutual fund investor pays when selling mutual fund shares. This charge is also known as a *back-end charge* because you pay a fee after you sell your shares.

> **Net asset value (NAV):** A fund's NAV is its total assets minus its total liabilities. Mutual funds calculate NAV on a per-share basis at the end of each trading day by dividing the difference between total assets and liabilities by the number of shares outstanding. A mutual fund's NAV is similar to a publicly traded company's stock price on a per-share basis.

Seeing what's out there

You can choose from two main commodity mutual funds: the PIMCO Commodity Real Return Strategy Fund and the Oppenheimer Real Asset Fund.

TIP

Although Oppenheimer and PIMCO offer the two most popular commodity funds, other firms are starting to offer similar products to satisfy the growing demand from investors for funds that have wide exposure to the commodities markets. To find out more about commodity mutual funds, you can use the Morningstar website (www.morningstar.com). This all-around excellent resource for investors includes lots of information related to commodity mutual funds, such as the latest news, updates, load charges, expense ratios, and other key data. It also uses a helpful five-star rating system to rate mutual funds.

The PIMCO Commodity Real Return Strategy Fund

With more than $30 billion in assets under management, the *PIMCO Commodity Real Return Strategy Fund* (PCRAX) is the largest commodity-oriented fund on the market. Although the fund is actively managed, it seeks to broadly mirror the performance of the Dow Jones–AIG Commodity Index (see Chapter 12 for the goods on this index). As such, the fund invests directly in commodity-linked instruments such as futures contracts, forward contracts, and options on futures. (For more on these instruments, flip to Chapter 13.)

Because these contracts are naturally leveraged, the fund also invests in bonds and other fixed-income securities to act as collateral to the commodity instruments. This fund offers two classes of shares: A and B. I encourage you to examine each class carefully to choose the best one for you.

- ▶ Class A shares have a minimum investment amount of $5,000, a front load of 5.5 percent, and an expense ratio of 1.24 percent.

- ▶ Class B shares require no front load, although they incur a deferred sales charge of 5 percent and an expense ratio of 1.99 percent.

The Oppenheimer Real Asset Fund

The *Oppenheimer Real Asset Fund* (QRAAX) is considerably smaller than the PIMCO fund. It tracks the performance of the Goldman Sachs Commodity Index, an index that tracks a broad basket of 24 commodities. (Turn to Chapter 12 for more info.)

With a $1,000 minimum investment requirement, Oppenheimer requires a little less capital up front than the PIMCO fund. It offers five classes of shares (A, B, C, N, and Y); Class A is the most popular among average individual investors. Class A shares have no deferred sales charge, although they have a front load of 5.75 percent and an expense ratio of 1.32 percent. So, even though you need less initial capital to invest in the Oppenheimer fund, it's slightly more expensive than the PIMCO fund because of the front-load charges and its expense ratio.

Mastering MLPs

If you're interested in investing in companies that are involved in the production, transformation, and distribution of commodities, one of the best ways to do so is to invest in a *master limited partnership* (MLP). MLPs are a great investment because of their tax advantage and high cash payouts.

The ABCs of MLPs

MLPs are public entities that trade on public exchanges. Just as a company issues stock on an exchange, an MLP issues shares that trade on an exchange. You can get involved in an MLP simply by purchasing its shares on an exchange. This is why an MLP is also called a *publicly traded partnership* (PTP).

TIP

Although most MLPs trade on the New York Stock Exchange (NYSE), a few MLPs also trade on the Nasdaq National Market (NASDAQ) and the American Stock and Options Exchange (AMEX). The later section "The nuts and bolts of MLP investing" lists a few MLPs and the exchanges they trade on.

The shares that an MLP issues are called *units,* and investors who own these units are known as *unit holders.* When you invest in an MLP, you're essentially investing in a public partnership. This partnership is run by a *general partner* for their benefit and, more important, for that of the *limited partners* (which you become when you buy MLP units).

The taxman rings once

One of the reasons I like MLPs so much for commodities investing is that, unlike regular corporations, they're taxed only once. Many publicly traded companies are subject to double taxation: They're taxed at the corporate level, as well as at the shareholder (individual) level. Not so with MLPs.

Because of congressional legislation, any MLP that derives 90 percent or more of its income from activities related to the production, distribution, and transformation of commodities qualifies for this tax-exempt status.

The income that an MLP uses to qualify for tax advantages is known as *qualifying income.* If an MLP can prove its qualifying income, it can "pass through" its income tax-free to its shareholders, who are then responsible for paying whatever taxes are appropriate for them. This is why MLPs are sometimes referred to as *pass-through entities.*

Curious to see how this tax advantage plays out in the real world? Suppose you're in the 35 percent tax bracket. You invest $1 in an MLP and $1 in a corporation. The corporation needs to generate $2.20 in income to distribute $1 of after-tax profits to you. The MLP, thanks to its favorable tax treatment, has to generate only $1.54 in income to give you back $1 of after-tax profits.

This tax status gives MLPs a competitive advantage over other publicly traded entities when they compete for assets. An MLP simply doesn't have to generate as much cash flow as a corporation to distribute similar levels of after-tax income to shareholders — and this fact has two possible implications. First, if it wants, the MLP can afford to overpay for an asset and still generate healthy cash flows for its investors. Alternatively, it can purchase an asset at a similar price from a competing corporation but generate more cash flow to investors because of its favorable tax treatment.

MLPs are required to distribute all available cash back to unit holders on a quarterly basis. When you own an MLP, you receive a K1 tax form, which is similar to the 1099 tax form you receive from a corporation.

TIP

Be sure to inform your accountant of your MLP investments in advance because most K1 forms aren't mailed out to shareholders until February. This gives you only a few weeks to account for the MLP income in your taxes.

Cash flow is king

The whole reason MLPs exist is to distribute all available cash back to the MLP unit holders, which has to be done on a quarterly basis. These factors determine how much cash is distributed to each investor:

>> How many units the investors hold

>> The incentive distribution rights (IDRs) created for the general partner (GP)

>> The difference between distributable and discretionary cash flow

The GP is responsible for distributing cash back to the limited partners (LPs) proportionally to their holdings. In other words, an investor who owns 1,000 units gets twice as much cash as an investor who owns 500 units in the same MLP. (But remember, this doesn't mean that the investor with the greater number of units gets to keep all that cash; the investor still has to pay taxes on this income, based on their tax profile.)

To promote the GP's efforts to increase cash flow for shareholders, many MLPs include incentives for the GP. Generally, the more cash flow the GP generates back to shareholders, the more cash the GP gets to keep. Although IDRs are different for each MLP, they're always based on a tier system. A typical IDR incentive structure for GPs increases the distribution rate to unit holders, as the following table shows.

Distribution Tier	Dollar Distribution	LP Payout	GP Participation
Tier 1	$0.50	98%	2%
Tier 2	$1.00	85%	15%
Tier 3	$1.50	75%	25%
Tier 4	$2.00	50%	50%

Using this tier distribution system, if the GP generates $1 of cash flow per unit (Tier 2), the LP gets 85¢ and the GP gets 15¢ of that dollar. However, a GP generating $2 of cash flow per unit (Tier 4) gets to keep 50 percent of that amount, or $1; the LP gets a smaller percentage (50 percent, down from 85 percent) but gets a higher cash payout ($1) than other tiers. The GP is, thus, encouraged to generate as much cash flow as possible because of the higher cut of the profits. This example shows the incentive behind this elegant and sophisticated tiered distribution system.

Therefore, it's in the best interest of the GP to maximize the cash flow to the investor. This point is important because the GP has a lot of discretion over how much of the available cash is actually redistributed to shareholders and how much will be used for operations related to the MLP — the difference between *distributable cash flow* and *discretionary cash flow*.

The nuts and bolts of MLP investing

So, how do you actually go about investing in an MLP? It's quite simple, really. Because MLPs are publicly traded, you can purchase any of them on the exchange on which it's traded by calling your broker to purchase MLP units or by buying them through an online trading account, if you have one. Either way, buying MLP units is as simple as buying stocks. Although most MLPs in the United States trade on the NYSE, a few trade on the NASDAQ and the AMEX.

TIP

Before you invest in an MLP, ask your broker the following:

>> What's the historical payout?

>> How much is cash flow?

>> What's the GP's IDR?

>> What are the operational activities?

>> How much assets are under management?

Heads up! Risk and MLPs

WARNING

Investing in MLPs comes with a number of risks. Here's a quick list of some of those risks so you don't come upon any surprises when you get your K-1 tax form in February:

>> **Management risk:** Because as an LP you have no say in the way the business is run, you're essentially handing over control to the GP to manage the MLP as they see fit. If you're not satisfied with the GP's performance, you can't do anything about it except withdraw your money from the MLP.

>> **Environmental risk:** Many MLPs operate sophisticated infrastructures such as pipelines and drilling rigs, which are often vulnerable to natural disasters such as hurricanes and earthquakes. Any of these may have a negative impact on your bottom line.

>> **Liquidity risk:** Because the MLP market is still fairly small compared to other assets such as stocks and bonds, you may face liquidity issues if you want to dispose of your units. Until liquidity increases in the MLP market, you risk not finding a buyer for your units.

>> **Terrorism risk:** MLPs' assets often include sensitive infrastructures that may be vulnerable to a terrorist attack.

Relying on a Commodity Trading Advisor

If you're interested in investing in commodities through the futures markets or on a commodity exchange, getting the help of a trained professional to guide you down this path is always a good idea. One option is to hire the services of a *commodity trading advisor* (CTA). The CTA is like a traditional stockbroker who specializes in the futures markets. This person can help you open a futures account, trade futures contracts, and develop an investment strategy based on your financial profile.

CTAs have to pass a rigorous financial, trading, and portfolio-management exam called the Series 3. Administered by the National Association of Securities Dealers (NASD), this exam tests the candidate's knowledge of the commodities markets inside and out. By virtue of passing this exam and working at a commodities firm, most CTAs have a fundamental understanding of the futures markets. CTAs are also licensed by the Commodity Futures Trading Commission (CFTC) and registered with the National Futures Association (NFA).

TIP

I've used these resources and found them helpful in finding the right CTAs:

>> **AutumnGold:** www.autumngold.com

>> **Barclays:** https://home.barclays

>> **IASG:** www.iasg.com

Each CTA has a unique investment approach and trading philosophy. Before you select a CTA, find out about each candidate's investment style to see whether it squares with your investment goals. You also have to decide how much of a role you want the CTA to play in your investment life. Do you want someone who will actively manage your funds or simply someone who will give you advice?

To answer these questions, you must first decide how involved you want to be in running your portfolio. If you're a hands-on kind of investor with free time to invest, you may consider investing on your own but keeping a CTA close by.

If you don't have a lot of time or in-depth knowledge of commodities and prefer to have the CTA manage your funds for you, consider these points when looking for a CTA:

>> **Track record:** Websites like www.autumngold.com and www.iasg.com rank CTAs by their historical track record. I recommend that you look at the longest historical track

record, which is the annualized return since the CTA began trading. However, it can also be useful to look at one-, three-, or six-month returns, as well as one-, three-, and five-year annualized returns.

>> **Disciplinary actions:** The NFA maintains a comprehensive database of all registered CTAs, including a record of any disciplinary action the CTA may have faced. Make sure that the CTA you may be doing business with has a clean record. The NFA database that tracks CTAs is called the *Background Affiliation Status Information Center* (BASIC), and you can access it through the NFA website at www.nfa.futures. org/basicnet. An additional resource is FINRA, which also maintains a comprehensive database of CTAs and other securities professionals. You can order a report on a CTA from FINRA by going to https://brokercheck.finra.org.

>> **Management fee:** Similar to most money managers, most CTAs charge a flat management fee. The industry average is 2 percent, although, depending on their track record, some CTAs charge higher management fees. These fees generally go toward operational expenses: paying employees, taking care of rent, mailing and printing marketing material, running a trading platform, maintaining a toll-free number, and so on.

>> **Performance fee:** Although a large portion of the management fee goes toward running the CTA's business, the performance fee provides an incentive for the CTA to generate the highest returns possible. This is the CTA's bread and butter. Again, performance fees differ among CTAs, although I've found that 20 percent seems to be a benchmark for most CTAs. Some CTAs with good track records may have higher performance fees, in which case you want to compare historical and actual returns among different CTAs to find the one with the highest distribution back to investors. However, a CTA who doesn't reach certain levels shouldn't get a performance fee. In other words, CTAs should be rewarded only for good performance; if they don't hit their numbers, they don't get to participate in the profits.

>> **Miscellaneous fees:** Watch out for these fees because they can add up really quickly — just like the miscellaneous fees you get on your cellphone bill. Ever opened your phone bill and found that miscellaneous fees increased your bill by 10 percent, 15 percent, or more? Your CTA may charge you

for such items as express mail deliveries, check and wiring fees, night desk charges (a fee you pay if the CTA trades your account after trading hours), and maintenance fees. For example, if you don't maintain a minimum amount in your account — such as $500 — you may be charged a fee.

>> **Margin requirements:** If you decide to open a margin account (as opposed to a cash account), you can borrow money from your CTA to purchase securities. Buying on margin gives you a lot of leverage (on both the upside and the downside), so knowing the details of the margin requirement is absolutely critical. (For more on using margin, take a look at Chapter 2.)

>> **Minimum investment requirement:** Many CTAs require that you invest a minimum amount of money with them. This can be as low as $1,000 and as high as $200,000. I recommend investing no more than 5 percent to 10 percent of your investing capital with a CTA. This way, you diversify your holding to include managed futures, but it won't come back to haunt you if the CTA performs badly.

Jumping into a Commodity Pool

Another way you can get access to the commodities futures markets is to join a *commodity pool*. As its name suggests, a commodity pool is a pool of funds that trades in the commodities futures markets. The commodity pool is managed and operated by a designated *commodity pool operator* (CPO), who is licensed with the NFA and registered with the CFTC. All investors share in the profits (and losses) of the commodity pool based on how much capital they've contributed to the pool.

Investing in a commodity pool has two main advantages over opening an individual trading account with a CTA. First, because you're joining a pool with a number of different investors, your purchasing power increases significantly. You get a lot more leverage and diversification if you're trading a $1 million account as opposed to a $10,000 account.

The second benefit, which may not seem obvious at first, is that commodity pools tend to be structured as limited partnerships. This means that, as an investor with a stake in the pool, the most you can lose is the principal you invested in the first place. Losing your entire principal may seem like a bad deal, but for the futures markets, it's pretty good.

Let me explain. With an individual account, you can purchase securities on margin. That is, you can borrow funds to buy futures contracts. What happens if the position you entered into with the borrowed funds does the opposite of what you expected it to? Now not only have you lost your principal, but you have to pay back your broker, who lent you the money to open the position. This means that you lose your principal and you still owe money, which is known as a *margin call*.

Now, because commodity pools are registered as limited partnerships, even if the fund uses leverage to buy securities and the fund gets a margin call, you're not responsible for that margin call. Hence, the only capital you risk is your principal. Of course, you want to perform due diligence on the CPO to keep the likelihood of the pool going bust as small as possible.

Ready, Set, Invest: Opening an Account and Placing Orders

When you're ready to start trading exchange-traded products, you have to choose the most suitable way to do so. Unless you're a member of an exchange or you have a seat on the exchange floor, you must open a trading account with a commodity broker who's licensed to conduct business on behalf of clients at the exchange.

REMEMBER

The technical term for a commodity broker is a *futures commission merchant* (FCM). The FCM is licensed to solicit and execute commodity orders and accept payments for this service. Another term for FCM is *introducing broker* (IB).

WARNING

Before choosing a commodity broker to handle your account, you have to perform a thorough and comprehensive analysis of the trading platform. You want to get as much information as possible about the firm and its activities. A few things to consider are firm history, clients, licensing information, trading platform, regulatory data, and employee information. You can find a detailed analysis of the criteria to use in selecting a broker earlier in this chapter.

Choosing the right account

After you select a commodity brokerage firm you're comfortable with, it's time to open an account and start trading. You can choose from a number of different brokerage accounts. Most firms will offer you at least two types of accounts, depending on the level of control you want to exercise over the account.

If you feel confident about your trading abilities, a *self-directed account*, in which you call the shots, is the most suitable account for you. On the other hand, if you prefer to have a professional make the trading decisions for you, a *managed account* is your best bet. In this section, I go through the pros and cons of self-directed and managed accounts so you can determine which one is best for you.

Self-directed account

If you feel comfortable with exchange-traded products and are ready to take direct control of your account, consider opening a self-directed account, also known as a *nondiscretionary individual account*. With this account, you take matters into your own hands and make all the trading decisions. If you have a good understanding of market fundamentals and want to get direct access to commodity exchange products, a self-directed account is for you.

TIP

Before you open a self-directed account, talk to a few commodity brokers. Each firm offers different account features. This is similar to buying a car — you want to test-drive as many cars as possible to get the biggest bang for your buck.

TIP

Specifically, ask about any minimum capital requirements the firm has. Some commodity brokers require that you invest a minimum amount of $10,000 or more. You also want to become familiar with account maintenance fees and the commission scale the firm uses. Knowing this information up front can save you a lot of heartache down the road. After you gather all the relevant information and open your account, you're finally ready to start trading and placing orders.

Managed account

In a managed account, you're essentially transferring the responsibility of making all buying and selling decisions to a trained professional.

Open a managed account in these cases:

>> You don't follow the markets on a daily basis but are interested in getting exposure to commodities.

>> You follow the markets daily but are unsure about which trading strategy will maximize your returns.

>> You don't have the time to manage a personal account.

>> You feel comfortable knowing that someone else is making trading decisions for you.

If these statements apply to you, you're ready to open a managed account. So, how do you get started? First, you need to determine your investment goals, time horizon, and risk tolerance. Then you need to find out about any minimum capital requirements, commissions, or management fees you may face. When you have this information, you can move on to choosing a CTA to manage the account.

REMEMBER

If you have mutual funds, the CTA is similar to a fund manager. The FCM, on the other hand, is more like a stock brokerage house. The FCM gives you a trading platform, whereas the CTA actually manages your accounts for you. Find out more about hiring a CTA earlier in this chapter.

If you perform due diligence and feel comfortable with your CTA, you're ready to turn over trading privileges. How do you do that? You have to sign a *power of attorney* document. After you sign that document, your CTA gets full trading discretion and complete control over the buying and selling of commodities in your account. The CTA then makes all the decisions, and you have to live with the good and sometimes bad decisions. If you trade stocks, this account is similar to having a discretionary individual stock account, in which your stockbroker makes trading decisions for you. The main benefit of the managed account is that you get a trained professional managing your investments. The drawback is that you can't blame anyone but yourself if you incur losses.

WARNING

A CTA is allowed by law to manage more than one account and have more than one client. However, a CTA must keep all managed accounts separate. Thus, there's no commingling of funds allowed and no transferring of profits or losses between accounts. A managed account differs from a *commodity pool*, in which your funds are "pooled" with those of other investors and you all share profits or losses. When you choose a managed account, make sure you get a CTA who will manage your account based on your personal risk profile.

Placing orders

Your trading account is your link to the commodity exchange. The broker's trading platform gives you access to the exchange's main products, such as futures contracts, options on futures, and other derivative products. Because the products traded on commodity exchanges are fairly sophisticated financial instruments, you need to specify a number of parameters to purchase the product you want.

The lifeblood of the exchange is the contract. As an investor, you can choose from a number of contracts, from plain-vanilla futures contracts to exotic swaps and spreads. (I discuss these products in depth in Chapter 13.) Whether you're buying a forward contract or engaging in a swap, you need to follow specific entry order procedures.

Here's a list of the parameters you need to indicate to place an order at the exchange:

>> **Action:** Indicate whether you're buying or selling.

>> **Quantity:** Specify the number of contracts you're interested in either buying or selling.

>> **Time:** By definition, commodity futures contracts represent an underlying commodity traded at a specific price for delivery at a specific point in the future. Futures contracts have delivery months, and you must specify the delivery month. Additionally, you need to specify the year because many contracts represent delivery points for periods of up to five years or more.

>> **Commodity:** This is the underlying commodity that the contract represents, such as crude oil, gold, or soybeans. Sometimes it's also helpful to indicate the exchange on which you want to place your order. This information is fairly significant because more of the same commodities are being offered on different exchanges. For example, the benchmark West Texas Intermediate (WTI) crude oil, which used to be traded only on the CME/NYMEX, is now available on both the CME/NYMEX floor and the ICE electronic exchange.

>> **Price:** This info may be the most important piece of the contract: the price at which you're willing to buy or sell the contract. Unless you're placing a market order (which is executed at current market prices), you need to indicate the price at which you want your order to be filled.

>> **Type of order:** A lot of different types of orders exist, from plain-vanilla market orders to more exotic ones such as *fill or kill* (FOK). See Table 14-1 for a list of the different order types. This info is an important piece of the order because you're indicating how you want to buy or sell the contract.

>> **Day or open order:** Market orders relate to price, and day or open orders relate to how long you want your order to remain open. In a *day order,* your order expires if it isn't filled by the end of the trading day. An *open order,* however, remains open unless you cancel it, it's filled, or the contract expires.

TABLE 14-1 **Defining Different Types of Orders**

Order Type	What It Means
Fill or kill (FOK)	Use this order if you want your order to be filled right away at a specific price. If a matching offer isn't found within three attempts, your order is canceled, or "killed."
Limit (LMT)	A limit order is placed when you want your order to be filled only at a specified price or better. If you're on the buy side of a transaction, you want your limit buy order placed at or below the market price. Conversely, if you're on the sell side, you want your limit sell order at or above market price.
Market (MKT)	A market order is perhaps the simplest type of order. When you choose a market order, you're saying you want your order filled at the current market price.
Market if touched (MIT)	A market if touched order sounds intimidating, but it's not. When you place an MIT, you specify the price at which you want to buy or sell a commodity. When that price is reached (or "touched"), your order is automatically filled at the current market price. A buy MIT order is placed below the market; a sell MIT order is placed above the market. In other words, you buy low and sell high.

(continued)

TABLE 14-1 *(continued)*

Order Type	What It Means
Market on close (MOC)	When you place a market on close order, you're selecting not a specific price, but a specific time to execute your order. Your order is executed at whatever price that particular commodity happens to close at the end of the trading session.
Stop (STP)	A stop order is a lot like a market if touched order because your order is placed when trading occurs at or through a specified price. However, unlike an MIT order, a buy stop order is placed above the market, and a sell stop order is placed below market levels.
Stop close only (SCO)	If you choose a stop close only order, your stop order is executed only at the closing of trading and only if the closing trading range is at or through your designated stop price.
Stop limit (STL)	A stop limit order combines both a stop order and a limit order. When the stop price is reached, the order becomes a limit order and the transaction is executed only if the specified price at which you want the order to go through has been reached.

5

The Part of Tens

Monitor market indicators and apply the data to improve your bottom line.

Count down the top ten investment vehicles for commodities, including futures markets, equities, and fund investing.

Chapter **15**

Ten Market Indicators You Should Monitor

The commodity waters can be perilous at times, and knowing how to navigate them is crucial. Keeping your eye on where the markets are heading — and where they've been — will help you develop a winning investment strategy.

One way to identify where the markets are heading is to watch certain market indicators. The ten key metrics highlighted in this chapter offer insight into what the markets are doing and help you design and calibrate an investment strategy based on the market fundamentals.

Consumer Price Index

The *Consumer Price Index* (CPI), compiled by the Bureau of Labor Statistics (BLS), is a statistically weighted average of a basket of goods and services purchased by consumers around the country. The CPI is the closest thing to a cost-of-living index and is sometimes used to gauge inflationary trends. If the CPI is rising, economists — especially the ones at the Federal Reserve — start worrying that inflation is creeping up. A rising CPI may then result in an increase in the federal funds rate (covered later in this chapter).

TIP

The CPI is sometimes broken down further into the *Core CPI,* which excludes items like food and energy. Comparing the CPI with the Core CPI can give you a good idea of how much consumers, who account for two-thirds of economic activity, are spending on commodities such as energy and agricultural products. Visit www. bls.gov/cpi for the latest data on the CPI.

EIA Inventory Reports

Energy traders are glued to their Bloomberg terminals every Wednesday morning (at 10:30 a.m. Eastern time, to be precise) waiting for the latest inventory reports. Those inventory reports come from the Energy Information Administration (EIA), which is the statistical branch of the Department of Energy (DOE), and they detail activity in the country's energy sector. They include a summary of weekly supply estimates, crude oil supply, and disposition rates (consumer consumption), as well as production, refinery utilization, and any movement in stock changes.

TIP

The EIA petroleum inventory reports may not get wide coverage in the press, but they have a direct impact on the price of crude oil and other energy products. Naturally, you'll want to monitor them regularly. You can find all the information about these reports by going to the EIA website at www.eia.gov.

Federal Funds Rate

Perhaps no other market indicator is as closely watched by investors as the *federal funds rate.* When the financial press talks about interest rates going up or down, they're almost always referring to the federal funds rate, which is established by the Federal Open Market Committee (FOMC). This is the short-term interest rate banks charge each other overnight for Federal Reserve balances. If the Fed wants to stimulate a sluggish economy, it tends to decrease this short-term rate. On the other hand, if the Fed believes that the economy is overheating — and, therefore, subject to inflation — it increases this rate, which makes borrowing money more expensive.

Gross Domestic Product

Gross domestic product (GDP) is one of the most closely watched economic indicators. GDP is essentially a measure of all the goods and services produced in a country by private consumers, the government, the business sector, and trade (exports/imports). GDP, especially *per-capita GDP* (which essentially measures purchasing power on an individual level), is a good indication of the likely demand for and activity in commodities. The higher the GDP growth, the more likely a country is to spend more money on purchasing crude oil, natural gas, and other natural resources. Of course, GDP gives you a big picture of the economic landscape and may not necessarily identify specific trends. That said, solid and growing GDP is a good measure of economic health and is a bullish indicator for commodities.

TIP

Theoretically, you can analyze the GDP of all countries, but I recommend looking closely at U.S. GDP, the largest economy on the planet, and the Chinese GDP, the fastest-growing economy in the world.

London Gold Fix

The Federal Reserve and other central banks hold gold bullion in vaults for monetary purposes, and economists sometimes use gold as a measure of inflation. Monitoring gold, both as a possible measure of inflation and for its monetary stability, is a good idea. Spot gold prices are fixed in London daily — in what is known as *London gold fixing* — by five leading members of the financial community. Precious metals dealers closely monitor the London gold fix and use it as a global benchmark for gold spot prices. You can also get an idea of where gold prices are heading by consulting the futures markets, specifically the COMEX gold futures prices provided by the Chicago Mercantile Exchange (CME/COMEX).

TIP Visit www.cmegroup.com for more on gold futures and www.bullionvault.com/gold-guide/gold-fix for the London gold fix.

Nonfarm Payrolls

As with the CPI, nonfarm payrolls are compiled by the BLS. Statistically, *nonfarm payrolls* include the number of individuals with paid salaries employed by businesses around the country. It doesn't include government employees, household employees (homemakers), individuals who work in the nonprofit sector, and workers involved in agriculture. Nonfarm payrolls include information on about 80 percent of the nation's total workforce, and this number is often used to determine unemployment levels.

TIP The nonfarm payroll report is released monthly, on the first Friday of the month, and doesn't include total employment; instead, it shows a change between the current employment levels and previous employment levels, as measured by the *new* number of jobs added. The higher the number, the stronger the economy and the more people hired by businesses — which all means that consumers have more money to spend. Although the link is indirect, higher nonfarm payroll numbers can be interpreted as a bullish sign for the commodities markets. Visit www.bls.gov/ces for more information on nonfarm payrolls.

Purchasing Managers Index

The *Purchasing Managers Index* (PMI), released by the Institute of Supply Management (ISM), is a composite index and a good indicator of total manufacturing activity, which, in turn, is an important barometer of overall economic activity. The manufacturing sector is a large consumer of commodities, such as crude oil and natural gas, and a strong PMI signals that manufacturers are doing well and are likely to spend additional dollars on commodities.

TIP The PMI is released at 10 a.m. Eastern time on the first business day of every month. You can view the reports at www.ismworld.org/supply-management-news-and-reports/reports/ism-report-on-business.

Reuters/Jefferies CRB Index

The *Reuters/Jefferies CRB Index* is the oldest commodity index and one of the most widely followed commodity benchmarks in the market. Although commodity indexes have their shortcomings — for example, they track only commodities on futures contracts, thereby ignoring important commodities such as steel — they're the best measure of where the commodities markets as a whole are heading. The Reuters/Jefferies CRB Index tracks 19 commodities — everything from crude oil and silver to corn and nickel. Turn to Chapter 12 for more on commodity indexes.

U.S. Dollar

Keeping your eye on what the U.S. dollar is doing is critical for a variety of reasons. U.S. dollars are the world's de facto currency, so most of the world's crucial commodities, from crude oil and gold to copper and coffee, are priced in them. Any shift in the dollar has an indirect impact on these important markets. For example, the integrated energy companies (the majors) have operations around the globe and often deal with the local currency in the area they're operating. Any shift in the local currency/U.S. dollar exchange rate has a direct impact on how the companies account for profits and expenses, as well as other metrics.

WTI Crude Oil

West Texas Intermediate (WTI) crude oil is one of the most widely followed benchmarks in the energy complex. It's a high-grade, low-sulfur, premium crude produced in West Texas. This light, sweet crude is traded on the NYMEX section of the Chicago Mercantile Exchange (CME/NYMEX) through a futures contract, which is widely quoted in the financial press and in analyst reports as a benchmark for global oil prices. More important, industry players use it as a benchmark for global oil prices.

Of course, because the price of the CME/NYMEX WTI refers only to light, sweet crudes, the price of heavy, sour crudes is going to be different. Currently, most heavy, sour crudes are priced relative to their lighter and sweeter counterparts. Turn to Chapter 3 for more on the different grades of crude oil.

An alternative global crude benchmark is the North Sea Brent, which is also a high-quality crude that's produced in the Norwegian/British North Sea. This contract trades on the Intercontinental Exchange (ICE).

Chapter **16**

Ten Investment Vehicles for Commodities

B ecause the commodities markets are so wide and deep, you have a number of investment vehicles to access these markets. A common misconception among investors is that you can trade commodities only by opening a futures account. The futures markets certainly provide an avenue into the commodities markets, but you have other tools at your disposal. I list the ten most important investment vehicles in this chapter.

Futures Commission Merchant

REMEMBER

Opening an account with a *futures commission merchant* (FCM) is the most direct way for you to invest in commodities through the futures markets. An FCM is registered with the National Futures Association (NFA), and its activities are monitored by the Commodity Futures Trading Commission (CFTC). When you open an account with an FCM, you can actually trade futures contracts, options, and other derivative products directly through the main commodity exchanges. Your orders are sometimes routed electronically or placed during the open outcry trading session.

However, you should only open an account with an FCM if you have a solid grasp of trading futures and options.

For more on futures contracts, check out Chapter 13; I discuss FCMs in depth in Chapter 14.

Commodity Trading Advisor

REMEMBER

A *commodity trading advisor* (CTA) is authorized by the CFTC and the NFA to trade on behalf of individual clients in the futures markets. A CTA is a registered investment professional who has a good grasp of the concepts of the futures markets. However, before you invest through a CTA, you should research their track record and investment philosophy. In Chapter 14, find out what you should be looking for when shopping for a CTA.

Commodity Pool Operator

Commodity pool operators (CPOs) are similar to CTAs in that they have the authority to invest on behalf of clients in the futures markets. The biggest difference is that CPOs are allowed to "pool" client accounts under one giant account and enter the markets en masse. The pooling of client funds offers two advantages: It increases the purchasing power of the fund, and it provides additional leverage.

REMEMBER

In addition, because a CPO is usually registered as a company, you can only lose your principal if things go wrong. In other words, you won't get any margin calls and owe the exchange money. Read Chapter 14 for more information on CPOs.

Integrated Commodity Companies

The equity markets offer a way for you to get exposure to commodities by investing in companies that process these natural resources. Some of these companies include large, integrated commodity-processing companies. In the energy space, these are companies like ExxonMobil (NYSE: XOM) and Total (NYSE: TOT) that have exposure to crude oil and natural gas in both the exploration and the distribution phase of the supply chain. I examine the integrated energy companies in Chapter 3.

In the metals complex, companies like Rio Tinto (NYSE: TRP) and BHP Billiton (NYSE: BHP) mine minerals and metals as varied as palladium and nickel. These integrated mining companies have operations throughout the globe. I cover them in Chapter 9.

Specialized Commodity Companies

TIP

If you want to get exposure to a specific commodity through the equity markets, you can always invest in *specialized* commodity companies. These companies focus either on one commodity or on one aspect of the supply chain. For example, oil tanker operators focus on transporting crude oil from point A to point B; that's the extent of their activities, which I uncover in Chapter 6. Other such companies include Starbucks (Nasdaq: SBUX; see Chapter 10), which focuses strictly on selling and marketing coffee-related products. These are good companies to invest in if you want exposure to a specific commodity through the equity markets.

Master Limited Partnerships

REMEMBER

Master limited partnerships (MLPs) are hybrid investment vehicles that invest in energy infrastructure. They are, in fact, private partnerships that trade on public exchanges, just like stocks. This unique combination has several advantages.

>> Because the MLP is a partnership, it has tremendous tax advantages because it doesn't pay taxes on the corporate level, only on the individual level. It's not subject to the double taxation that many corporations are subject to.

>> The MLP's mandate is to distribute practically all its cash flow directly to shareholders. It's not uncommon to have an MLP return $3 or $4 per unit owned.

Check out MLPs in Chapter 14.

Exchange-Traded Funds

Since they first emerged on the scene, the popularity of *exchange-traded funds* (ETFs) has soared. And for good reason. They're privately run funds that trade on a public exchange, just like stocks. This ease of use has directly contributed to their popularity among investors. In recent years, a number of ETFs have been introduced that track the performance of commodity-related assets, such as gold, silver, and crude oil.

But it's not just individual commodities that are now tracked by ETFs. Commodity indexes, such as the Deutsche Bank Liquid Commodity Index (AMEX: DBC), also has an ETF that tracks its performance. Turn to Chapter 12 for a complete listing of ETFs on the market.

Commodity Mutual Funds

Investors who are used to investing in mutual funds will enjoy knowing that a number of mutual funds invest directly in commodities. Two of the biggest such mutual funds are the PIMCO commodity fund and the Oppenheimer fund, both covered in Chapter 12.

Some funds seek to mirror the performance of various commodity benchmarks, while others invest in companies that process commodities.

Commodity Indexes

A commodity index acts a lot like a stock index: It tracks a group of securities for benchmarking and investing purposes. Commodity indexes are constructed and offered by different financial institutions, such as Goldman Sachs and Standard & Poor's, and they follow different construction methodologies. As such, the performance of the indexes — there are currently five — is different across the board. Most of these indexes can be tracked either through the futures markets or through ETFs. I devote Chapter 12 to these indexes.

Emerging-Market Funds

Due to geographical happenstance, commodities are scattered across the globe. No single country dominates all commodities across the board. However, a few countries do dominate specific commodities. South Africa, for instance, has the largest reserves of gold in the world, Saudi Arabia has the largest oil reserves, and Russia has the biggest palladium reserves. As the demand for commodities has increased, the economies of these emerging markets have been soaring. One way to play the commodities boom is by opening up your portfolio to emerging-market funds.

Index

A

Abu Dhabi, 55
Abu Dhabi Investment Authority (ADIA), 55
Abu Dhabi Investment Council (ADIC), 55
Aframax, 100
after-tax performance, 228
agricultural commodity, 17–18. *See also specific commodities*
airline/aircraft industry, 130, 211
Alcoa (AA), 131, 147–148
Allegheny Energy (AYE), 66
Alliant Energy (LNT), 66
alternative energy, 69–75, 164. *See also energy commodity*
aluminum, 15, 125, 130, 131–132, 147–148, 213
Aluminum Association, 130
Aluminum Corporation of China (ACH), 132, 148
American Clean Power Association, 74
American depository receipt (ADR), 144–145
American Gas Association, 67
American option, 223–224
American Petroleum Institute (API), 50
American Soybean Association, 163
American Stock and Options Exchange (AMEX), 189
Anglo Platinum Group, 137
Anglo-American PLC (AAUK), 124, 144–145
AngloGold Ashanti Ltd. (AU), 115–116
anthracite, 77
anthracite coal, 80
Arabica coffee, 153
arbitrage, 10
ArcelorMittal (MT), 129, 148–149
Arch Coal (ACI), 81
Argentina, 119, 160

Asia, urbanization in, 22. *See also specific countries*
assets, 176–177, 180
Association for Iron & Steel Technology, 127
at-the-money, 222
Australia, 77, 78, 119, 139, 140
automobile industry, 17, 62–63, 164
AutumnGold, 236
average freight rate assessment, 100

B

back-end charge, 229
Background Affiliation Status Information Center (BASIC), 237
backwardation, 219
Baker Hughes, Inc. (BHI), 93–94
Barclays, 236
Barrick Gold Corporation (ABX), 116
Better Business Bureau, 114
Beyond Petroleum (BP), 53
BHP Billiton, 142–143
big oil company, 52–54
biodiesel, 164
biomass energy, 74–75
bituminous coal, 79
BNY Mellon, 145
Bolivia, 119, 121
BP Statistical Review of World Energy, 45
Brazil
    biomass industry within, 74
    cocoa in, 155
    coffee in, 152, 153
    corn in, 160
    crude oil in, 44, 47, 91–92
    ethanol in, 75
    industrialization in, 24

Brazil *(continued)*
  nickel in, 140
  orange juice in, 158
  soybeans in, 163
  steel in, 127, 129
  sugar in, 156, 157
Bretton Woods Agreement, 108
BRIC countries, industrialization in, 23.
    See also specific countries
British thermal unit (Btu), 59–60, 77
Bureau of Labor Statistics (BLS), 61, 247,
    248, 250
business cycle, 28–29, 143, 175
butane, 60
buy-and-hold principle, 226

C

call option, 222–223
Cameco Corporation (CCJ), 83
Cameroon, 155
Canada
  crude oil in, 42, 43, 44, 47, 48
  gold maple leaf coin of, 114
  uranium in, 83
  wheat in, 161
capital gains and losses, 217, 227
cash flow, in master limited partnership
    (MLP), 233
catalytic converters, platinum use for, 122
cattle, 18, 166–168
CBOT Mini-Silver (YI), 121
cement, 23
Central Appalachian coal (CAPP), 80
Chevron, 53
Chicago Mercantile Exchange (CME)
  coal and, 80
  corn futures contract of, 159–160
  crude oil futures contract of, 46, 212
  feeder cattle futures contract of, 167–168
  frozen pork bellies futures contract of,
    169–170
  futures market and, 10

lean hogs futures contract of, 168
live cattle futures contract of, 166
natural gas and, 65, 66
soybean futures contract of, 164
soybean meal futures contract of, 165
soybean oil futures contract of, 164–165
S&P Goldman Sachs Commodity Index
    (S&P GSCI) and, 197
TRAKRS of, 201
website for, 66, 80, 84, 86, 167, 250
wheat futures market of, 162
Chile, 119
China
  aluminum production within, 148
  coal in, 77, 78
  corn in, 160
  crude oil in, 44, 47, 49
  gold holdings of, 110
  industrialization in, 23–24
  orange juice in, 158
  silver in, 119
  solar energy in, 71
  steel in, 127, 128
  sugar in, 157
  wheat in, 161
Churchill, Winston, 76
CME Feeder Cattle Index, 167
CME/CBOT E-Micro Gold (MGC), 117
CME/CBOT Mini-Gold (YG), 117
CME/COMEX Copper (HG), 133–134
CME/COMEX Gold (GC), 117
coal, 15, 76–81
cocoa, 17, 155–156
coffee, 17, 152–154
Colombia, 152, 153, 155
COMEX Silver (SI), 121
Commitment of Traders report, 33
commodities. *See also specific commodities*
  as asset class, 1, 19
  benefits of, 1
  defined, 8, 207
  deliverability of, 9

fundamentals regarding, 36–37
growth of, 1
history of, 9
inelasticity of, 25–26
liquidity of, 10
long term focus of, 27
questions regarding, 37
risks regarding, 30–33
as safe haven, 26
seasons for, 28
statistics regarding, 7, 20
tradability of, 8–9
in the 21st century, 20–24
uniqueness of, 25–28
uses for, 8
commodity company
due diligence regarding, 34–35
master limited partnership (MLP), 13, 64, 185–186, 231–235, 255
overview of, 185
publicly traded, 12–13, 185
commodity fund, 183–184
Commodity Futures Trading Commission (CFTC), 118
commodity index. *See also specific indexes*
anatomy of, 194–195
as benchmark, 192
benefits of, 187–188, 192–193
choosing, 205
components of, 194
defined, 192
deliverability of, 195
exchange-traded fund (ETF) and, 193
futures contract and, 193
as indicator, 193
liquid investing instrument, 187–188
as liquid investment vehicle, 193
liquidity of, 195
making money using, 193
overview of, 11, 182, 192, 256
rebalancing features of, 194
rolling methodology of, 194

third-party manager and, 193
tradability of, 195
weightings of, 194
commodity mutual fund, 184, 226–231, 256
commodity mutual fund manager, 35
commodity pool, 238–239
commodity pool operator (CPO)
DBC ETF as, 189
defined, 11, 35
overview of, 183, 238–239, 254
Commodity Research Bureau Index (CRB) (Reuters/Jefferies), 197–199, 205, 251
commodity trading advisor (CTA), 11, 35, 182–183, 235–238, 241–242, 254
component weighting, 194
compressed natural gas (CNG), 62–63
Consol Energy (CNX), 81
Consolidated Edison (ED), 86, 87
construction, aluminum usage within, 130
Consumer Price Index (CPI), 247–248
contango, 218–219
copper, 16–17, 125, 132–135, 146–147, 219
Copper Development Association, 133
Core CPI, 248
corn, 18, 159–161
Corn Refiners Association, 161
corporate governance risk, 33
CPFL Energia (CPFL), 75
crude oil
classification of, 50
consumption statistics of, 47
deliverability of, 9
demand figures of, 46–47
density of, 50
drill ship for, 91
drilling barge for, 90
dry land drilling of, 92–93
earnings from, 51–55
exploration of, 90–94
exports of, 47–49
financial crisis and, 51
formation of, 49

crude oil *(continued)*

futures contract of, 212, 213, 214, 218–219, 251–252

global reserve of, 43–45, 46

grades of, 51

imports of, 47–49

jack-up rig for, 90–91

measurement of, 59

misinformation regarding, 42–43

offshore drilling of, 90–92

offshore oil platform for, 91

oil fields for, 93–94

oil import dependency and, 98

as online, 27

overseas, 54–55

overview of, 15, 41–42

Persian Gulf War and, 9

production of, 45–46, 90–94

products from, 95

profiting from, 90–94

realities regarding, 42–49

refineries investment for, 95–97

Russia-Ukraine War and, 31, 45

semisubmersible rig for, 91

shipping of, 97–103

statistics regarding, 41, 50, 76, 97

submersible rig for, 91

sulfur content of, 50

transportation and, 63

Cuba, 140

currency, 133, 139

current account, 54

cycles, business, 28–29, 143, 175

D

day order, 243

dead weight ton (DWT), 100

deferred sales charge, 229

demand destruction, 82

density, of crude oil, 50

dentistry, gold usage for, 109

derivatives, 207

Deutsche Bank Commodity Index Tracking Fund (DBC), 184, 189

Deutsche Bank Liquid Commodity Index (DBLCI), 189, 203–204

Diamond Offshore Drilling (DO), 91–92

diversification, 37–38

diversified mining company, 12

dividend, 86, 102–103

Dominican Republic, 155

Dominion Resources (D), 86

Dow Jones Commodity Index (DJCI), 199–201

drill ship, 91

drilling barge, 90

due diligence, risk and, 33–37

Duke Energy Corp. (DUK), 86, 87

E

economy, 28–29, 31, 51, 103, 175

Ecuador, 155

elasticity, 25

electric utility company, 12

electric vehicle (EV), 103–104

electricity

coal and, 77

current affairs and, 84–85

investing in, 85–86

measurement of, 85

natural gas and, 62

nuclear energy for, 82–84

off-peak/on-peak, 85–86

overview of, 15

solar energy for, 70, 71–73

steam and, 85

trading, 84–87

wind energy for, 73–74

electronics, gold usage for, 109

emerging-market fund, 257

energy commodity, 8–9, 15–16, 69–70, 196. *See also* renewable energy; specific commodities

Energy Efficiency & Renewable Energy
  (EERE), 71
Energy Information Administration (EIA)
  figures of, 44, 45
  inventory reports of, 248
  prediction of, 75
  website of, 45, 46, 62, 84, 97, 98, 248
Energy Select Sector SPDR (XLE), 53–54
Entergy Corp. (ETR), 86
Environmental Protection Agency (EPA), 135
environmental risk, of master limited
  partnership (MLP), 235. See also risk
equity market, 12–13
ethane, 60
ethanol, 15, 75, 213, 215
Ethiopia, 153
European option, 224
Evergreen Emerging Markets Growth
  (EMGYX), 55
exchange-traded fund (ETF). See also specific
  funds
  accessing commodity markets through,
    190–192
  benefits of, 188
  commodity index and, 193
  examples of, 190–191
  gold, 114–115
  oil company, 53–54
  overview of, 13, 184, 187–190, 256
  purchase of, 189
  silver, 120
  uranium, 83–84
expense ratio, 229
expiration date, 222
export, 47–49, 64
ExxonMobil, 32, 53, 96

F

federal funds rate, 248–249
feeder cattle, 18, 167–168. See also cattle
fees, of commodity trading advisor (CTA),
  237–238

ferrous metal, 138. See also metals
fill or kill (FOK) order, 243
finances, 174–180
financial futures, 207
Financial Industry Regulatory Authority
  (FINRA), 227
fineness, of gold, 112
FINRA, 237
First Solar, Inc. (FSLR), 72
forwards, 209
fossil fuel, 49, 76
France, 110, 157, 162
Freeport-McMoRan, Inc. (FCX), 134, 146–147
front month, 215
Frontline Ltd. (FRO), 101, 102
front-month contract, 194
frozen concentrated orange juice-type A
  and B (FCOJ-A and B), 17–18, 158.
  See also orange juice
frozen pork bellies, 18, 169–170, 213, 215
frybrids, 164
fully integrated company, 66
futures, 207, 208
futures account, 193
futures commission merchant (FCM), 11,
  182, 239, 241, 253–254
futures contract
  of aluminum, 131
  buy side of, 210
  of cocoa, 156
  of coffee, 153–154
  conditions of, 209
  of copper, 133–134, 219
  of corn, 159–160
  of crude oil, 212, 213, 214, 218–219,
    251–252
  defined, 208–209
  delivery location for, 216
  of ethanol, 213, 215
  of feeder cattle, 167–168
  front month for, 215
  of frozen pork bellies, 169–170, 213, 215
  hedgers for, 210–211

futures contract *(continued)*
  holder of, 213, 220
  last trading day of, 216
  of lean hogs, 168
  of live cattle, 166
  monthly abbreviation codes for, 216
  of natural gas, 65–66
  of orange juice, 158–159
  overview of, 208–209
  persons trading, 210–212
  placing orders on, 242–244
  of platinum, 123
  premium of, 220
  price limits of, 214–215
  price quote of, 214
  product grade of, 214
  risk size of, 214–215
  sell side of, 210
  of silver, 121
  size of, 213–214
  of soybean meal, 165
  of soybean oil, 164–165
  of soybeans, 164, 217–218
  speculators for, 211–212
  standardization of, 212
  of sugar, 156
  trading hours of, 216
  trading months of, 215–216
  trading unit of, 213–214
  underlying asset of, 213
  underlying quantity of, 213
  underwriter of, 213, 220
  of wheat, 162
  writer of, 213, 220
futures market
  backwardation, 219
  contango, 218–219
  direction of, 218–219
  due diligence regarding, 36
  exposure to, 181–183
  keeping track of, 212–217
  margin in, 217–218

  options within, 219–224
  overview of, 10–11, 208–209
  purpose of, 209
  structure of, 209
Futures Trading Commission (CFTC), 11

G

galvanization, 17, 138
gasoline, 25, 57, 62–63, 214
General Electric (GE), 73
General Maritime Corp. (GMR), 101
general partner (GP), 232, 233–234
geopolitical risk, 31–32
Gerdau (GGB), 129
Germany
  coal in, 77, 78
  crude oil in, 47, 49
  gold holdings of, 110
  steel in, 127
  wheat in, 162
Ghana, 155
global population, capitalizing on, 21
global production weighting, 195
Global X Uranium ETF (URA), 83–84
gold
  applications of, 108
  contracts, 117–118
  demand for, 26
  discovery of, 9
  ductility of, 110
  exchange-traded fund (EFT), 114–115
  forms of, 112–114
  Krugerrand, 114
  liquidity of, 117–118
  malleability of, 110
  measurement of, 111–112
  overview of, 16, 108–109
  physical investment in, 112–114
  price of, 108
  purchase of, 14
  purity of, 111–112

quasi-indestructibility of, 111
rarity of, 111
stocks in, 115–117
uses of, 109
Goldman Sachs Natural Resources Sector index, 54
gravity, of crude oil, 50
Great Plains Energy (GXP), 86
Greenspan, Alan, 32
gross domestic product (GDP), 23, 249
Gulf Cooperation Council (GCC), 54

H

Halliburton Co. (HAL), 94
heavy crude, 50
hedge fund, 226
hedger, 210–211
high-grade number 2 and number 3 yellow corn, 159. *See also* corn
hogs, lean, 18, 168–169
holder, 213, 220
Honduras, 153
Hurricane Katrina, 45
Hydrocarbon Age, 9
hyperinflation, 174

I

IASG, 236
import, of crude oil, 47–49
income investing, 227
income tax, 179
index. *See* commodity index
India
coal in, 77, 78
coffee in, 153
corn in, 160
crude oil in, 47, 49
gold holdings of, 110
solar energy in, 71
steel in, 127
sugar in, 157

wheat in, 161
Indonesia
coal in, 77, 78
cocoa in, 155
coffee in, 152, 153
copper in, 147
corn in, 160
nickel in, 140
Industrial Revolution, 76
industrialization, 22–24, 58–61, 118, 123
The Industry Catalogue of Gold Bars Worldwide, 113
inelastic goods, 25–26
inflation, 26–27, 31–32, 174–175
initial margin, 217
integrated commodity company, 254–255. *See also specific companies*
integrated energy company, 13
Intercontinental Exchange (ICE), 10, 46, 154, 156
Intergovernmental Panel on Climate Change (IPCC), 71
Internal Revenue Service (IRS), 178
International Aluminum Institute, 130
International Cocoa Organization, 155
International Coffee Organization, 152
International Energy Agency (IEA), 44, 45
International Maritime Organization, 98
International Monetary Fund, 110
International Petroleum Investment Corporation (IPIC), 55
International Platinum Association, 123
in-the-money, 222
introducing broker (IB), 239
investment objective, 227
investment vehicle, 10–11, 12–14, 184. *See also specific vehicles*
investor profile, 228
Iowa Soybean Association, 163
Iran, 43, 44, 48
Iraq, 43, 44, 48
Iron Age, 126
Iron and Steel Statistics Bureau, 127

iShares COMEX Gold Trust (IAU), 115, 184

iShares Goldman Sachs Natural Resources Sector (IGE), 54

iShares Silver Trust (SLV), 120, 184, 191

iShares S&P Global Energy Sector (IXC), 54

Italy, 49, 110

Ivory Coast, 155

J

jack-up rig, 90–91

Japan, 47, 49, 78, 110, 127

jewelry, 109, 111, 118, 123

K

karat, 111

Kazakhstan, 48, 77, 78, 162–163

Kitco, 114

Knightsbridge Tankers (NVLCCF), 102

Kuwait, 9, 43, 44, 48

L

lean hogs, 18, 168–169

leverage, pitfalls of, 29–30

liabilities, calculating value of, 177

Libya, 43

light crude, 50

lignite coal, 79

limit (LMT) order, 243

limited partner, 232

liquefied natural gas (LNG), 59, 63–64

liquid investing instrument, 187–188, 193

liquidity, of commodities, 10, 117–118, 212

liquidity risk, of master limited partnership (MLP), 235. See also risk

live cattle, 18, 166–167. See also cattle

livestock, 18, 152, 166–169

LME Copper (CAD), 134

London gold fixing, 249–250

London Metal Exchange (LME), 131

long-only strategy, 226

Lucid Group, Inc. (LCID), 104

M

maintenance margin, 217

managed account, 240–242

managed fund, 13–14, 35–36, 227–228

management fee, of commodity trading advisor (CTA), 237

management risk, of master limited partnership (MLP), 235. See also risk

manager, choosing, 35–36

Marathon, 53

margin, 29–30, 217–218, 238

margin cell, 30

market if touch (MIT) order, 243

market on close (MOC) order, 244

market (MKT) order, 243

master limited partnership (MLP), 13, 64, 185–186, 231–235, 255

mergers and acquisitions (M&A), 148–150

metals. See also specific metals
  ferrous, 138
  overview of, 16–17, 107–108, 125–126
  purchase of, 14
  as safe haven, 26
  tracking, 141
  urbanization and, 22

methane, 60

metric ton (MT), 126

Mexico, 119, 121, 153, 157, 158, 160

million metric ton (MMT), 126

minimum capital requirement, 240

minimum incremental amount, 229

minimum investment requirement, 238

mining companies, 141–150. See also specific companies

molybdenum, 147

money, gold usage for, 109

money manager, selecting, 14

Morningstar, 230

Morocco, 71, 73

Musk, Elon, 104

mutual fund, 13–14, 184, 226–231, 256

N

Nabors Industries (NBR), 92
National Association of Wheat Growers, 163
National Coffee Association of the U.S.A., 152
National Corn Growers Association, 161
National Futures Association (NFA), 236, 237
National Oilseed Processors Association, 165
natural gas
  applications of, 58–63
  chemical composition of, 60
  commercial uses for, 62
  companies of, 66–67
  compressed (CNG), 62–63
  demand for, 60
  electricity and, 62
  futures, 65–66
  home uses for, 61
  industrial uses of, 58–61
  investing in, 64–67
  liquefied (LNG), 59, 63–64
  measurement of, 59–60
  overview of, 15, 57–58
  reserves of, 64–65
  Russia-Ukraine War and, 31
  saving money on, 61
  statistics regarding, 64
  transportation uses for, 62–63
  transporting, 63–64
natural gas vehicle (NGV), 62
net asset value (NAV), 188, 230
net worth, 176–178
Netherlands, 49, 110
New Gold, Inc. (NGD), 116
New York Board of Trade (NYBOT), 208
New York Stock Exchange (NYSE), 75, 132
Newmont Mining Corporation (NEM), 116, 145–146
nickel, 17, 133, 138–140, 139
Nicor, Inc. (GAS), 66

Nigeria, 48, 155
Noble Corporation (NE), 92
no-load fund, 229
nonfarm payroll, 250
nonrewable fossil, 57. *See also specific commodities*
Noor, 73
Nordic American Tankers (NAT), 102
Norilsk Nickel, 137, 139
North American Palladium (PAL), 137
Norway, 48
Nuclear Age, 9
nuclear energy, 15, 82–84
Nucor Corp. (NUE), 129

O

off-peak electricity, 85–86
offshore drilling, for crude oil, 90–92
offshore oil platform, 91
oil
  classification of, 50
  consumption statistics of, 47
  deliverability of, 9
  demand figures of, 46–47
  density of, 50
  drill ship for, 91
  drilling barge for, 90
  dry land drilling of, 92–93
  earnings from, 51–55
  exploration of, 90–94
  exports of, 47–49
  financial crisis and, 51
  formation of, 49
  futures contract of, 212, 213, 214, 218–219, 251–252
  global reserve of, 43–45, 46
  grades of, 51
  imports of, 47–49
  jack-up rig for, 90–91
  measurement of, 59
  misinformation regarding, 42–43

oil *(continued)*
  offshore drilling of, 90–92
  offshore oil platform for, 91
  oil fields for, 93–94
  oil import dependency and, 98
  as online, 27
  overseas, 54–55
  overview of, 15, 41–42
  Persian Gulf War and, 9
  production of, 45–46, 90–94
  products from, 95
  profiting from, 90–94
  realities regarding, 42–49
  refineries investment for, 95–97
  Russia-Ukraine War and, 31, 45
  semisubmersible rig for, 91
  shipping of, 97–103
  statistics regarding, 41, 50, 76, 97
  submersible rig for, 91
  sulfur content of, 50
  transportation and, 63
oil company, 52–54
Oil & Gas Journal, 43, 44, 45
oil import dependency, 98
on-peak electricity, 85–86
open interest, 222
open order, 243
Oppenheimer Real Asset Fund (QRAAX),
    197, 230, 231
options, 207, 208, 219–224
orange juice, 17–18, 157–159
Organization for Economic Co-operation
    and Development (OECD), 79, 109
out-of-the-money, 222
Overseas Shipholding Group, Inc.
    (OSG), 101
over-the-counter (OTC) market, 208, 209

P

Pacific Ethanol (PEIX), 75
Pakistan, 157, 162
palladium, 17, 135–136, 137–138

Pan American Silver Corporation
    (PAAS), 121
Panamax, 100
pass-through entity, 232. *See also* master
    limited partnership (MLP)
Patterson-UTI Energy Inc. (PTEN), 93
Peabody Energy (BTU), 81
per-capita GDP, 249
performance fee, of commodity trading
    advisor (CTA), 237
Persian Gulf War, 9
Perth Mint Certificate Program (PMCP), 113
Peru, 119, 121, 153, 155
Petrobras, 92
petroleum, 49, 100–103. *See also* crude oil
Phelps Dodge Corporation (PD), 134,
    146–147, 149
Philippines, 140
physical commodity, 9, 14. *See also specific
    commodities*
PIMCO Commodity Real Return Strategy
    Fund (PCRAX), 230–231
Pizarro, Francisco, 9
PJM Interconnection, 85
plain-vanilla fund, 226
platinum, 14, 16, 121–123, 124
  facts and figures of, 122–123
  futures contract for, 123
  industrial uses for, 123
  jewelry uses for, 123
  mining companies for, 124
  overview of, 16, 121–122
  purchase of, 14
  uses for, 122–123
platinum group of metals (PGM), 126
poison pill strategy, 148–149
Poland, 77, 78, 119
population, global, capitalizing on, 21
pork bellies, frozen, 18, 169–170, 213, 215
portfolio, making room for commodities
    within, 181
power industry, 85–86. *See also* electricity
power of attorney document, 241
premium, 220, 222

Producer Price Index (PPI), 60–61
production-weighted methodology, 194
propane, 60
prospectus, 227
publicly traded company, 12–13, 185
publicly traded partnership (PTP), 13, 64, 185–186, 231–235, 255
Purchasing Managers Index (PMI), 250
put option, 223

Q

Qatar, 67
qualifying income, 232

R

raw materials, for biomass energy, 74–75
recession, 175
refineries, 95–97. *See also* crude oil
regional transmission organization (RTO), 85
regular hexahedron, 59
renewable energy, 69–75, 164. *See also* energy commodity; specific commodities
Reuters/Jefferies Commodity Research Bureau Index (CRB), 197–199, 205, 251
Rio Tinto, 143–144
risk
    appetite for, 179–180
    corporate governance, 33
    environmental, 235
    geopolitical, 31–32
    liquidity, 235
    management, 33–38, 235
    of master limited partnership (MLP), 235
    of mutual funds, 228
    of oil-shipping industry, 103
    overview of, 30–33
    size, 214–215
    sovereign government, 30–31

speculative, 32–33
terrorism, 235
Rivian Automotive, Inc. (RIVN), 104
Robusta coffee, 153
Rogers International Commodities Index (RICI), 201–203
roll yield, 194
Romania, 160
Russia
    biomass industry within, 74
    coal in, 77, 78
    coal reserves within, 78
    crude oil in, 43, 44, 47, 48
    nickel in, 139, 140
    Norilsk Nickel, 137, 139
    palladium in, 136
    platinum in, 122
    silver in, 119
    steel in, 127
    sugar in, 157
    wheat in, 161
Russia-Ukraine War, 31–32, 45, 175

S

sales charge, 229
sales load, 229
sanctions, 31
Sau Paulo Stock Exchange (BOVESPA), 75
Saudi Arabia, 43, 44, 47, 48, 71
Schlumberger Ltd. (SLB), 94
seasonality, 151
securities, 227
Securities and Exchange Commission (SEC), 11
self-directed account, 240
semisubmersible rig, 91
Series 3 exam, 236
Shell, 53
shipping, of crude oil, 97–103
short ton, 77

silver
    exchange-traded fund (EFT), 120
    futures contracts for, 121
    investing in, 119–121
    mining companies of, 120–121
    overview of, 16, 118
    physical investment in, 120
    purchase of, 14
    uses for, 118, 120
    Wheaton Precious Metals Corp. (WPM),
        121, 146
silver halide, 118
soft commodity, 151
solar energy, 15, 70, 71–73
solar photovoltaic energy, 72
solar thermal energy, 72
South Africa
    Anglo Platinum Group, 137
    Anglo-American PLC (AAUK), 144–145
    Boer Wars within, 9
    coal production of, 78
    gold Krugerrand coin of, 114
    palladium production within, 136
    platinum production in, 122
South Korea, 47, 49, 127
Southwest Airlines (LUV), 211
sovereign government risk, 30–31
sovereign wealth fund (SWF), 54
soybean meal, 18, 165
Soybean Meal Info Center, 165
soybean oil, 18, 164–165
soybeans, 18, 29–30, 163–164, 217–218
S&P Goldman Sachs Commodity Index
    (S&P GSCI), 195–197
Spain, 49
SPDR Gold Shares (GLD), 191
specialized commodity company, 255.
    See also specific companies
speculative risk, 32–33
speculator, 211–212
spiders, 53–54
spot market, 208

stainless steel, 139
Standard & Poor's Depository Receipts
    (SPDR), 53–54
standardization, 212
Starbucks (SBUX), 154
steam, electricity generation through, 85
steel
    ArcelorMittal (MT), 129, 148–149
    facts regarding, 126–127
    investing in, 128–129
    measurement of, 126
    nickel and, 17
    overview of, 16, 126
    statistics regarding, 125
    top production companies of, 128
sterling silver, 120. See also silver
Stillwater Mining Company (SWC), 124, 137
stocks, 29–30, 115–117, 217
stop close only (SCO) order, 244
stop limit (STL) order, 244
stop (STP) order, 244
Strathmore Corporation (STM), 83
Street Tracks Gold Shares (GLD), 115, 184
strike price, 222
sub-bituminous coal, 79
submersible rig, 91
Suezmax, 99, 100
sugar, 17, 156–157
sulfur content, of crude oil, 50
Sunoco, Inc. (SUN), 96
Suntech Power Holdings (STP), 72–73
Switzerland, 110

T

Taiwan, 49
tanker spot rate, 98
taxation, 178–179, 232
Teekay Tankers (TNK), 101–102
terrorism risk, of master limited
    partnership (MLP), 235. See also risk
Tesla Motors (TSLA), 104

Tesoro Corp. (TSO), 96
Thailand, 157
therms, 60
tiered methodology, 198
track record, 228, 236–237
tradability, of commodities, 8–9
trader, 212
TRAKRS, 201
Transocean, Inc. (RIG), 92
transportation, 62–63, 75, 97–104, 130, 135–136
tropical commodity, 151
troy ounce, 111
Turkey, 127, 162

U

UEX Corporation (UEX), 83
Uganda, 153
Ukraine, 77, 160, 162
ultra-large crude carrier (ULCC), 99, 100
underlying asset, 213
underwriter, 213, 220
United Arab Emirates, 43, 44, 48, 71
United States
   coal in, 77, 78, 79
   corn in, 160
   crude oil in, 23, 42, 43, 44, 45, 46–47, 49
   electricity usage within, 62
   gold eagle coin of, 114
   gold holdings of, 110
   natural gas use within, 61, 63–64
   orange juice in, 158
   silver in, 119
   soybeans in, 163
   steel in, 126–127
   sugar in, 157
   wheat in, 161
United States Oil Fund (USO), 191
uranium, 8–9, 15, 82, 83, 84
uranium ETF URA (URA), 188–189
urbanization, 21–22

U.S. Department of Agriculture, 167
U.S. dollar, 251
U.S. Oil Fund (USO), 184
U.S. Steel (X), 129
U.S. Wheat Associates, 163
utilities company, 12, 86
UxC, 84

V

Valero Energy Corporation (VLO), 96
vegetable oil, 18
Venezuela, 43, 44
very large crude carrier (VLCC), 99, 100
Vietnam, 152, 153

W

waste, biomass energy and, 74–75
wealth, building, 174–175
websites
   Aluminum Association, 130
   American Clean Power Association, 74
   American Gas Association, 67
   American Soybean Association, 163
   Association for Iron & Steel Technology, 127
   AutumnGold, 236
   Barclays, 236
   Better Business Bureau, 114
   BNY Mellon, 145
   BP Statistical Review of World Energy, 45
   BullionVault, 250
   Bureau of Labor Statistics (BLS), 61, 248, 250
   Chicago Mercantile Exchange (CME), 66, 80, 84, 86, 167, 250
   Commitment of Traders report, 33
   Commodity Futures Trading Commission (CFTC), 118
   Copper Development Association, 133
   Corn Refiners Association, 161
   Energy Efficiency & Renewable Energy (EERE), 71

websites *(continued)*

Energy Information Administration (EIA), 45, 46, 62, 84, 97, 98, 248

Financial Industry Regulatory Authority (FINRA), 227

FINRA, 237

Global X Uranium ETF (URA), 84

IASG, 236

The Industry Catalogue of Gold Bars Worldwide, 113

Intergovernmental Panel on Climate Change (IPCC), 71

Internal Revenue Service (IRS), 178

International Aluminum Institute, 130

International Cocoa Organization, 155

International Coffee Organization, 152

International Energy Agency (IEA), 45

International Maritime Organization, 98

International Platinum Association, 123

Iowa Soybean Association, 163

Iron and Steel Statistics Bureau, 127

Kitco, 114

Morningstar, 230

National Association of Wheat Growers, 163

National Coffee Association of the U.S.A., 152

National Corn Growers Association, 161

National Futures Association (NFA), 237

National Oilseed Processors Association, 165

Oil & Gas Journal, 45

Producer Price Index (PPI), 61

Purchasing Managers Index (PMI), 250

Rigzone, 92

Soybean Meal Info Center, 165

U.S. Department of Agriculture, 167

U.S. Wheat Associates, 163

UxC, 84

Wheat Foods Council, 163

World Coal Association, 81

World Cocoa Foundation, 155

World Steel Association, 127

Yahoo! Finance, 94, 103

West Texas Intermediate (WTI), 46, 204, 216, 251–252

wheat, 9, 18, 31, 161–163

Wheat Foods Council, 163

Wheaton Precious Metals Corp. (WPM), 121, 146

white knight strategy, 148

wind energy, 15, 73–74

wind farm, 73

World Coal Association, 81

World Cocoa Foundation, 155

World Steel Association, 127

writer, 213, 220

Z

Zimbabwe, 136

zinc, 17, 133, 138

About the Author

Amine Bouchentouf is a partner at Commodities Investors, LLC (CI), an international financial advisory firm headquartered in New York City that provides long-term strategic advice to individuals, institutions, and governments around the world. CI also invests directly on behalf of clients in a wide range of industries relating to natural resources, from crude oil and gold to natural gas and steel.

Amine holds a degree in economics from Middlebury College. In his spare time, he enjoys playing golf, traveling, and socializing with friends.

Dedication

This book is dedicated to my most steadfast supporters — my family, especially my wonderful wife, Keily. You have always been there for me when I needed you and have always supported me in every endeavor I've decided to undertake. I would not have been able to accomplish half the things I've done without your tremendous support, and for that I am deeply grateful.

Author's Acknowledgments

I'd like to acknowledge the first-rate editorial team at Wiley for their input and assistance through every stage of this process. A writer hopes for nothing more than to have a team of editors who will support their general creative vision, and I was extremely fortunate to be able to follow through on my vision for the book with the guidance of a knowledgeable group of editors.

Publisher's Acknowledgments

Senior Acquisitions Editor:
Tracy Boggier

Senior Managing Editor:
Kristie Pyles

Compilation Editor:
Georgette Beatty

Editor: Elizabeth Kuball

Production Editor:
Saikarthick Kumarasamy

Cover Images:
Frame: © aleksandarvelasevic/
Getty Images
Paper texture: © Dmitr1ch/
Getty Images
Inset: © 13ree_design/
Adobe Stock